YGIS
OF
INDIA

YOGIS
OF
INDIA

Timeless Stories of their
Lives and Wisdom

SIVARUPA

wisdom
tree

© Sanjeev Shukla, 2012

First published 2012
Reprinted 2012, 2013

ISBN: 978-81-8328-255-0

Published by
Wisdom Tree
4779/23, Ansari Road
Darya Ganj, New Delhi-110002
Ph.: 23247966/67/68
wisdomtreebooks@gmail.com

Printed in India

Contents

This book is dedicated to my Guru,

'The Untainted One',

the *janmasiddha* yogi — Paramhansa

Swami Niranjanananda Saraswati — who,

I pray, will someday make me a disciple.

Introduction

My journey from atheism to a state of theistic or spiritual belief began in the mid-1980s, and was both painful and pleasurable. During this period, I read about the lives of many Indian mystics and felt that their lives reflected a completeness of elements that inspired in me—love, compassion, dispassion, struggle, penance, transformation and miracle.

There are two aspects to the spiritual romance central to the life of mysticism—one, between the Lord and the devotee, and the other between the guide and the aspirant. Some consider both to be the same, while others reject the latter. I belong to the controversial school of thought that holds that without a guru or a guide, the spiritual romance of the aspirant will be incomplete. But, even for those aspirants who reject this view, the life of a mystic will always hold great relevance, as the mystic has demonstrated the capability to transcend the boundaries of mundane existence. And, this is what inspires me to share some tales of transformational lives across a series of volumes.

This is the first volume, and it contains accounts of some exceptional saints who are closest to my heart. With a few exceptions, the first few volumes will focus on saints who lived in recent times—within the last 200 years. Later volumes will document lives of saints from earlier periods, or from different religions or faiths.

Indian saints and mystics are addressed by different titles – sadhus, *tapasvis, brahmacharis, yatis, bhaktas,* swamis, *paramhansas, avadhuts,* sants, tantrics, sufis, *arihants, tirthankars, siddha purusas,* dervishes, *mayis/ matas,* babas, *goswamis, pirs, auliyas, murshids, aghoris* or gurus – but in essence, all of them are yogis – those who have attained the objective of the path of yoga. But, the eternal travellers I write about are part of a rare creed – those who have already attained liberation, yet take birth time and again to guide others on sacred paths.

Among my foremost inspirations are my *paramgurus,* Swami Sivananda Saraswati and Paramhansa Satyananda, but I have documented only the former's brief biography in this volume, as the latter has only recently taken *mahasamadhi.*

Among other saints who are closest to my heart is my family guru, Paramhansa Ram Mangal Das. Ramakrishna Paramhansa, Sai Baba of Shirdi, Mahayogi Gambhirnath, Tailanga Swami, Baba Lokenath Brahmachari and Chaitanya Mahaprabhu are also very dear to me. There are others such as Seshadri Swamigal and Ramana Maharshi of Tiruvannamalai, too, who I cannot forget. Then there is Swami Nityananda of Ganeshpuri, the guru of Swami Muktananda and Lahiri Mahashay – the teacher of Kriya Yoga – and Ramdas Kathia Baba, the Vaishnava yogi par excellence. The sufis of the Chisti Silsila, who represent love and the eclectic spirit of Islam, are some true marvels of God. I could go on, but I would rather let readers be touched themselves by the beauty of their lives across the chapters of my books.

Once, Sant Nabhadas – the medieval author of *Bhaktamala* was asked by his guru to document the biographies of saints. He protested saying, 'It is possible, though difficult, for one to narrate the glories of God, but the glory of saints is impossible to narrate,' and so I will not attempt the impossible. One may fall short of words to describe a saint, and a chapter is as inadequate to capture the essence of his life as a book, which itself is insufficient as a volume devoted solely to any of these saints. I can attempt only to capture some events in their lives and sketch brief outlines.

On Frauds, Cheats and Charlatans

The world of saints is crowded with fakes, frauds, cheats and incomplete aspirants. And, I believe, it will always be so. William Shakespeare wrote in one of his masterpieces, 'Some men are born great, some achieve greatness, and some have greatness thrust upon them.' Similarly, many pretenders were born fakes, many grew up into fakes and many had fakeness thrust upon them.

Seldom we come across a true saint in life — a genuinely elevating experience, and more so, to recognise a saint as a true one. Constant devotion to a saint is even rarer, but the rarest of all is to dedicate oneself to such souls and follow their directions. And, if all of these do happen, liberation is assured. If creation is the cosmic principle and liberation is an exception to the rule, the path to liberation will be difficult, as the exception cannot become the rule. It is probably for this reason that true saints generally remain hidden in remote locations, and if and when they live and move within the world, they are invisible among the vast numbers of charlatans and frauds. It is for this reason that I feel the role of a charlatan is intrinsic to the cosmic principle of creation and the higher principles of liberation and, therefore, I respect his presence.

The saint Goswami Tulsidas wrote in the *Ramacharitamanasa* (*Balkanda*):

> *Bandau sant asajjan charanā,*
> *Dukhaprada ubhaya bīcha kachhu barnā*
> *Bichhurat ek prāna hari lehī,*
> *Milat ek dukha dārun dehi*
> I bow to the feet of both the saint and the unholy,
> For both give us pain, though with a difference,
> One the pain of separation,
> And the other pain at meeting.

While miracles happen for various reasons in the presence of a mystic, the mystic is not in essence a miracle monger trying to impress seekers. A true miracle lies in the transformation of the soul. A genuine seeker will, therefore, not seek miracle mongers, but those who transform. And, let us not be in a hurry, for patience — searching and yearning — will eventually bring us to the saint who will set us on our path of spiritual romance, and rest all our questions with his presence, in the process setting us free. Hurrying this process may bring us to an incomplete soul, a charlatan or maybe even a great soul but not one destined to take us onto the path to liberation.

Communion with Truth

Goswami Tulsidas has written about the glory of communion with the truth:

Shath sudharahi satsangatī pāyi,
Pāras parasi kudhātu suhāyī
The wretched become pure in communion with truth,
Just as the sorcerer's stone converts to gold any base metal that
it touches.

The company of saints is a form of communion with truth and a biographical account of saints, how-so-ever brief, replicates the physical company of saints, at least to a degree.

Caveat Emptor

Though I have written articles before, they were mostly technical in nature. More importantly, I have never written a book before in my life and am consequently ill-equipped to churn out large volumes of quality literature. I am also not as well read as most contemporary biographers are. So, at the start itself, I must apologise for the inadequacies of my writings, or 'ramblings', as a friend put it. To make up for my inadequacies, however, I invoke the grace of the saints and mystics to touch the hearts of the readers. I request the readers to ignore the lack of research or erudition and to meditate on the lives of these truly life-transforming giants and feel the presence of the saints instead of merely reading this as a story. Each saint is unique and can be compared only to him or herself.

Readers would also need to excuse my style of writing, since in some places I have taken the liberty of recounting a few instances from the perspective of those who had experienced them. In the process, I have imagined and written their thoughts. These may not be part of the sources I have referred to, but they serve to make these stories come alive more rather than be mere sections of dry biographical research.

Readers should also be warned that I have no spiritual qualification to write these biographical sketches. However, I sincerely hope this book, and others in the series that follow, give them a glimpse of these immortals who are no more with us in a physical body.

I end this introduction with a couplet from Nabhadas:

Bhakti-bhakta-bhagwanta-guru,

Chaturnāma vapu ek

Inké pad vandan kiyé,

Nasey vighan aneka

(Great) devotion, (perfect) devotees, God and the guru,

These four may appear different, but are the same;

On bowing before any of these,

Many obstacles (on the path of liberation) are destroyed.

I thank everyone for making this book happen.

RAMAKRISHNA PARAMHANSA
(1836-86)

Hridi kandar tāmas bhāskar he,
Tum vishnu prajāpati shankar hey
Parabrahma parātpar ved bhane,
Gurudeva dayā kara dīna jane

O Lord, you are like the Sun, bringing light to the
dark recesses of the heart,
You are verily Vishnu, Brahma and Shankar,
You are the ultimate form of God,
Whose glories have been sung in the Vedas,
O great guru, shower mercy and compassion on
The humble souls who have sought refuge in you.

Ramakrishna: The Paramhansa of Dakshineshwar

L allu Baldev was deeply agitated. Some months ago, he had
renounced the world in search of a spiritual guru. He had roamed
the length and breadth of India, desperately seeking a true saint
but could not find anyone who could satisfy his heart and intellect.
It appeared to him that salvation was beyond reach, and that he would
end up wasting his life in the rut of materialism, a thought that filled
him with despair. He wandered into a desolate spot on the outskirts of
Vrindavan, one of the sacred cities of India and resolved to end his life
by jumping into the Yamuna River. Just when he was about to do so,
a bearded man miraculously appeared by his side and held his hand.
Lallu was so upset that he did not pause to wonder how someone could
appear from nowhere and that too at an isolated spot. The man asked
Lallu why he was committing suicide, to which the young man replied
tearfully, describing his plight, often repeating that he no longer wished
to continue a Godless existence.

The man could associate with Lallu's discomfort. He blessed him
with a gentle touch, which calmed him immensely. It was as though
his whole being was dissolved and elevated to a plane of bliss, where

he experienced pure spiritual existence. He did not know how long he remained in that condition but after some time, the man, once again, touched him and brought him back to the normal plane. Lallu had finally found his guru, a saint who could 'dispel the darkness' with a mere touch.

This saint hailed from Bengal and was then travelling across north India, visiting various holy cities. He was camping at Vrindavan. He took Lallu back to where he was putting up with his fellow travellers. Lallu stayed with him for a few days, learning techniques of meditation, developing new insights into spiritual life and stabilising his experiences. After a while, the saint gave Lallu the spiritual name, Ananda Sharan[1], and advised him to return home. Ananda Sharan returned to Dhaulpur, his hometown in Rajasthan, but he dedicated his life to assimilating and spreading the teachings of that saint. The guru's touch had changed him and though he didn't meet him again in the physical plane, Ananda Sharan lived in close identification with his guru.

The saint returned to Dakshineshwar in Bengal. In course of time, he became very well-known and after he left his mortal frame, he was made even more popular by his band of disciples led by the dynamic Swami Vivekananda. The saint was Ramakrishna Paramhansa, known to some as the 'mad priest of the Dakshineshwar Kali temple'.

Who was this saint who could transform the consciousness of spiritual aspirants with a mere touch, a look or a thought?

Background to the Birth

Khudiram Chattopadhyaya, a resident of Kamarpukur village in Bengal, was a simple-hearted devotee of Lord Rama. Khudiram's wife, Chandramani (Chandra Devi), was also a pure-hearted soul who used to have many spiritual experiences. They had two sons, Ramkumar and Rameshwar, and a daughter, Katyayani. Khudiram often had visions of the Lord in his dreams. Once, before moving to Kamarpukur, Khudiram was sleeping in a field. The Lord appeared in his dream and told him that he was pleased with Khudiram's devotion and had decided to come to his home in the shape of an idol. The Lord also indicated its location, which incidentally was at a nearby spot in the same field. Khudiram woke up and went to the spot and found Lord Rama's idol there. He took it home and the family began to worship it as their presiding deity. The family was not very prosperous, but they were happy to spend their life in devotion to the Lord.

Many years later, he went to Gaya, where Hindus offer prayers in memory of their ancestors. It is also the place where the feet of Lord Vishnu (in the form of Gadadhar[2]) are enshrined in the famous Gadadhar temple. One night, when Khudiram was sleeping in Gaya, he dreamt that he was entering the Vishnu temple and his ancestors were also present there. He saw Lord Vishnu ahead of him. The Lord told Khudiram that he was happy with his devotion and promised to come to his house in the form of a child. Khudiram protested, explaining he was extremely poor and would not be able to serve the Lord properly. However, the Lord mentioned that he would be satisfied with his devotee's meagre resources. Khudiram woke up in a state of bliss but was also slightly unhappy – he wasn't sure whether he would be able to raise a divine child. Moreover, Khudiram was over sixty years old – he was curious to see how a child would be conceived at that age.

When Khudiram returned home, his wife acquainted him with her dream. She had dreamt that a divine soul was in the room and even when she woke up, she had the same perception. She lit a lamp and checked the doors, but found them locked from inside. So, nobody could have possibly entered the house. Another day, during his absence, she had seen a light emerge from a Siva temple and enter her womb. Khudiram then narrated his dream to her, and they both agreed that, according to the signs, they would soon have a child who would have divine qualities. They also decided that if the Lord had decided to take birth in their house, he would make arrangements for his own upbringing. During the pregnancy, Chandramani had many spiritual visions, which further convinced her of the divinity of the child to come.

Nine months later, Chandramani gave birth to a baby boy. It was 17 February 1836, a time that was considered extremely auspicious, astrologically, for the birth of an exceptional divine being. The couple named the boy Gadadhar, as they considered him to be an embodiment of Lord Vishnu.

Growing Up

As a child, Gadadhar was loved by everyone for his pleasing appearance. Being the youngest, he received a lot of love from his elder siblings — Ramkumar, who was already in his thirties when Gadadhar was born, and Rameshwar, who was ten years old. The parents, however, experienced many incidents that made them concerned for the welfare of their son — Chandramani, once, saw a grown-up man sleeping on the bed instead of the child. She raised a hue and cry but when everyone gathered, they only saw the little Gadadhar on the bed. Though the couple knew that their son was no ordinary one, they could not transcend the bonds of parenthood and would always consider him a helpless child.

Gadadhar grew up in the loving atmosphere of the village. Villagers enjoyed his company and would ask him to sing devotional songs. But, Gadadhar did not always stay that way. Unfortunately, at the tender age of seven, Gadadhar lost his father. The event had a profound impact on the boy, and his behaviour became very gentle towards his mother.

Gadadhar would, sometimes, spontaneously experience a blissful state of self-absorption, where he would completely lose external consciousness. On one such occasion, he was asked to enact the role of Lord Siva in a play. He was wearing a wig of long, matted locks and had a leopard skin wrapped around his body. He became deeply contemplative, associating himself completely with Lord Siva and completely lost touch with the external world. Many people tried hard to awaken him but nobody could get him out of this peculiar condition. There were many such incidents in which he lost his external consciousness, but the elders neither understood nor attached much importance to these states.

In the meantime, Ramkumar had set up a school in Calcutta (now Kolkata), where he taught Sanskrit. He also performed priestly functions at various homes. As work increased, Ramkumar asked Gadadhar to join him so that the latter could work as a priest, while he could concentrate on his teaching.

Advent in Dakshineshwar

The Kali Temple

Rani Rasomani — a devout, wealthy and noble lady — had built a grand temple dedicated to Goddess Bhavatarini Kali in Dakshineshwar on the outskirts of Calcutta. Its construction was planned after she had received a vision in which the Goddess had asked her to do so. When she expressed her desire to inaugurate it, she faced opposition from the priests. Due to caste considerations, the orthodox priests refused to participate in the worship and inauguration of the temple, as she belonged to what was then considered a low caste. Rasomani, meanwhile, had visions of the Goddess asking her not to delay the proceedings. She finally found a learned priest, none other than Ramkumar, who agreed to perform the inauguration ceremony of the temple. Ramkumar inaugurated the temple in a grand event that reportedly cost ₹2,00,000, an unheard of sum in those days.

Rani Rasomani was satisfied that her wish had come true. She was also impressed by Ramkumar's pure temperament. She offered him the position of the priest in the temple. Ramkumar agreed and moved to Dakshineshwar in 1855. A short while later, Gadadhar also joined his brother. In the temple complex, there were two smaller temples, one dedicated to Lord Krishna and the other to the twelve forms of Lord Siva. Ramkumar convinced Gadadhar to accept the role of the priest at the Krishna temple.

Meanwhile, a profound change was occurring in Gadadhar's life, something that had begun with his father's untimely demise. He would spend more and more time in solitude, praying and meditating. Although this caused discomfort within Ramkumar, he did not take the matter seriously. However, after a few months, his health deteriorated. He began to coach Gadadhar to take over the responsibilities as the priest of the Kali temple. In this connection, Gadadhar was required to receive initiation into the mantras of the Goddess. He received this initiation from Kenaram Bhattacharya, a spiritually advanced devotee of Goddess Kali, the Divine Mother. Gadadhar went into a state of spiritual ecstasy at the time of initiation. Later, he began to worship the Divine Mother in the Kali temple.

Soon, Ramkumar passed away and Gadadhar found himself as the permanent priest of the temple. He was deeply shocked at the sudden demise of his brother, who was thirty-one years older than him. Ramkumar had treated Gadadhar almost as a son since their father's death. Gadadhar now experienced the sorrow-filled transient nature of the universe and felt a deep distaste for material life.

The Call for Grace

A new chapter began in Gadadhar's life. He began meditating like a man possessed and would call out to the Divine Mother for a manifestation. Gadadhar had heard that, in the past, the Divine Mother had appeared to great sages—Ramprasad and Chandidasa. He would repeatedly ask Her why She was not appearing before him. He would also get deeply absorbed in the rituals he performed in the temple and would spend hours in the service of the Divine Mother. During late evenings, he would disappear in the forest adjoining the temple and, in that solitude, would meditate throughout the night.

Despite his best efforts, Gadadhar could not keep his sadhana a secret. His nephew Hriday – son of his cousin, Hemangini – found out about his meditative activities in the forest and tried to dissuade him from continuing those. Hriday was worried that as his uncle was not getting adequate sleep, it would harm his health. He decided to keep an eye on Gadadhar and would follow him deep into the forest. Once, Hriday tried to scare his uncle by throwing stones around him while the latter was meditating, but Gadadhar continued undisturbed. He was totally absorbed in his meditation. Hriday finally gave up the idea of stopping his uncle and decided to let him continue with his spiritual endeavours.

Gadadhar later recounted that during this period of his life, he would feel an unseen force locking him up in the meditative pose, and he would then experience perfect stillness. The same force would unlock him from his pose after his meditation was over.

Gadadhar prayed fervently to receive a vision of the Divine Mother. However, for many days, he achieved no success and each passing day appeared to be a torture. One night, he became so disturbed that he imagined his wish would never be fulfilled. At that point, he was all alone in the temple. He began to cry in despair and called out to Her continuously. He felt that there was no point in continuing his life if it did not contain glimpses of divinity. He picked up a sword that was lying at the feet of Kali's idol. Just when he was about to bring it down on his neck, the Divine Mother revealed her transcendental form to him.

For a long, long time, Gadadhar was lost in a blissful state. He felt the temple and the adjoining environment disappear completely. This was not an ordinary vision. In those moments, he had achieved the object of his meditation.

Intense Sadhana

For how long Gadadhar remained in that state is not known. But now that he had witnessed divinity, he was even more motivated to continue his meditation – the object was complete grace and reaching the state of unhindered experience. He would spend hours on end calling out to the Divine Mother and meditating. For him, separation from the Divine Mother was unbearable. He would often roll on the ground in agony and rub his forehead on the floor, while crying out to Her – unmindful of onlookers. Service of the deity in the Kali temple now became a living ritual for him. He would go on for long stretches of time absorbed in the rituals. He would speak to the Divine Mother, laugh and joke with Her and feed Her as he would to a living being. He would, sometimes, offer prasad to the deity and would then eat it himself.

Sometimes, he would treat an animal as the Divine Mother. Gradually, Gadadhar began to have more and more visions of the Divine Mother. He would speak to Her and She in turn would guide him and explain philosophical truths. Gadadhar would, sometimes, also see a sannyasi emerge from within his body, and the sannyasi would instruct him on the path of meditation.

Casual observers found Gadadhar's behaviour extremely strange and rumours spread that he had gone mad. This also worried the temple administrators who, later, complained to Mathura Babu, Rani Rasomani's son-in-law. Mathura Babu was a practical man who managed the Rani's estate. The temple officials were certain that once Mathura Babu would see Gadadhar's strange behaviour, he would dismiss the latter from the post of the temple priest. But, Mathura Babu had his own way of dealing with situations. One day, he came unannounced to the temple and quietly observed Gadadhar. He was deeply impressed with the latter's devotion and strictly instructed the temple staff not to interfere with the devotee and his worship.

Those days, Gadadhar would experience two deep emotional states – if they could at all be called that. One was the state of unimaginable devotion and the other of experiencing the agony of separation, moving continuously through these states led to a variety of afflictions in his body. All the time he felt his body burning and would endure unbearable physical pain and heaviness. He sensed the reason, but was unable to withdraw himself from the state of intense longing. Sometimes, he wanted to call out to the Divine Mother to relieve his physical suffering, but the minute he focussed his thoughts on Her, his consciousness was transformed. He would lose all desires and again immerse himself in devotional practices.

Tantric Sadhana

In 1863, Bhairavi Brahmani, a yogini arrived in Dakshineshwar. She had practised many austerities and had perfected the sadhanas under the tantric system of worship. She had seen Gadadhar in a vision and received a mandate from the Divine Mother to guide him on the path of tantric sadhana.

Gadadhar, who had never met the yogini, also had an intuition about her arrival. Shortly after she had reached Dakshinehwar, he requested Hriday to escort her to the temple. Hriday was unsure as to how would he recognise her. He was caught in a dilemma; he couldn't say no to his uncle and didn't know how to proceed further. Meanwhile, Gadadhar could sense his nephew's confusion; he gave Hriday the yogini's description and also told him where he could find her. Hriday wondered how Gadadhar knew so much about the yogini but, by now, he had also realised the futility in trying to understand his uncle's actions and words. So, without much ado, he went looking for her. Hriday found a lady exactly where he had been directed to, and she also fitted his uncle's descriptions. Soon, he brought her to the Kali temple. The minute she saw Gadadhar, she recognised him[3]. The recognition was mutual between the guru and the disciple.

The yogini asked Gadadhar if he would like to practise tantric and yogic sadhanas under her direction, to which he readily agreed. That day, when the yogini sat down in prayer, she had some revelations and unprecedented transcendental experiences. She realised that Gadadhar was no ordinary disciple.

The yogini had maternal feelings for Gadadhar. He, too, behaved like a child with her. He described the various ailments that had afflicted him in the last four years of sadhana and repeatedly asked her if he was indeed mad as many people thought. The yogini quoted many instances from spiritual texts (the tantras and bhakti texts), to illustrate that Gadadhar's condition was that of a highly elevated soul and that some of the greatest of saints in the past had undergone a similar experience.

Then commenced Gadadhar's phase of tantric sadhana. The yogini would arrange the requisites and, then, initiate Gadadhar into the sadhana. He would perfect it within a few hours, or at the most a few days. Practices that took spiritual aspirants years to become adept at were mastered by him in very brief periods. In a short while, to the yogini's surprise, he had perfected all the important sadhanas embodied in the sixty-four principal tantric scriptures. Bhairavi Brahmani was initially amazed at Gadadhar's elevated state, and she gradually began to look upon him as divine incarnation of the Lord.

After much deliberation, the yogini called a meeting of learned saints to show them Gadadhar's potential and discuss his spiritual accomplishments and also his physical problems. Her objective was to seek the views of the wise men on the surmise that Gadadhar was indeed a divine incarnation. Some of them, including Vaishnav Charan and Pandit Gauri, concluded that Gadadhar was an exceptional saint and an avatar. They also quoted from the shastras, confirming that he was not sick. They opined that his physical problems were due to a peculiar state of *Mahabhava*[4]. Once, Bhairavi Brahmani remarked, 'Nimai and Nitai have both taken birth in this body this time[5].'

The yogini had also begun to experience a sense of pride in being the guide to such a great disciple and tried to dominate Gadadhar's life. It was strange to see such a great yogini becoming jealous of the other perceived attachments in his life. However, after a few months, she blessed him and moved on from Dakshineshwar. She spent the rest of her life in contemplation, having herself spiritually benefitted from Gadadhar's company.

Raja Yoga Sadhana

At this point, Totapuri, an adept of Raja Yoga, arrived in Dakshineshwar. He was a proficient yogi, had transcended all fetters of material existence and had achieved the state of Nirvikalpa Samadhi. Though he was the guru of an ashram in northern India, where he had over 700 disciples, he roamed around naked from place to place, spending his time meditating in different parts of the country. He had the ability to recognise the spiritual capability of aspirants. When he saw Gadadhar, he was astounded at the concentration of spiritual power within him. He immediately offered to initiate Gadadhar into the path of yoga.

Gadadhar, as in all spiritual matters, asked the Divine Mother whether he should follow Totapuri. The Divine Mother gave Her assent and explained that She Herself had brought the yogi to Dakshineshwar. Gadadhar was delighted to hear this and, subsequently, requested Totapuri to initiate him.

Totapuri took Gadadhar to a hut and asked him to meditate on the space between the eyebrows. For quite some time Gadadhar was unable to meditate, since he kept getting lost in the vision of the Divine Mother. Finally, Totapuri lost his patience and pressed a crystal hard into the spot and then told Gadadhar to try and concentrate once again. Gadadhar instantly lost himself in deep meditation. Totapuri locked his disciple in the hut and went away. When he returned after two days, he was anxious to know about his disciple's progress. He unlocked the door to find Gadadhar lost in the state of Nirvikalpa Samadhi. In those two days, Gadadhar had achieved the state of a Paramhansa! Totapuri had taken forty years to achieve that state, and was astounded by his pupil's accomplishment. He tested his student's body for breathing and heartbeat and was surprised to see no signs of life, confirming that the samadhi was indeed genuine.

Totapuri considered himself blessed to have a disciple of that calibre. After guiding him for a few more days, Totapuri left Dakshineshwar. He continued with his wanderings and was never heard of again. Some say he finally settled in an ashram on the outskirts of the holy city of Jagannath Puri.

Gadadhar, now a Paramhansa, immersed himself in the state of samadhi. He would later recount to his disciples that he stayed in an unbroken state of Nirvikalpa Samadhi for six months, whereas an ordinary man would have left his body after being in such a state for merely twenty-one days. During this period, a sadhu appeared from nowhere, and served him religiously. He would clean, bathe and forcibly feed the Paramhansa. After six months, the Divine Mother appeared before the Paramhansa and advised him now to stay instead in a state of devotional ecstasy and use his body as an instrument to guide other spiritual seekers.

Other Sadhanas

While Gadadhar had already attained the ultimate objective of spiritual life, he continued to practise other sadhanas. This was probably because he had an intuition that many devotees with diverse backgrounds and orientation would flock to him for guidance.

The Paramhansa received initiation into the Rama Tarak Mantra from Jatadhari, a wandering monk who was an adept in Bhakti Yoga. Jatadhari was very advanced spiritually and would carry a small idol of the Lord, Rama Lalla, the child Rama, with him. Apparently, Rama Lalla would interact with Jatadhari in a human form and would speak and play with him, but Jatadhari did not reveal this secret to anyone. After he met the Paramhansa, Rama Lalla began to reveal himself to the Paramhansa. Eventually, Jatadhari gave the idol to him, saying the Lord wished to stay on with the Paramhansa.

One day, the Paramhansa decided to practise devotional practices in accordance with Islam. Later, he met a Sufi saint, Govind Sahib, and sought the latter's guidance in practising them. Govind Sahib instructed the Paramhansa on the message of the *Koran* and taught him some devotional practices. While absorbed in these practices, the Paramhansa would not even visit the Kali temple[6]. Finally, he received a vision indicating the fact that he had achieved the culmination of the Islamic faith.

The Christian thought also influenced the Paramhansa. A painting depicting the Virgin Mary with the infant Jesus in her arms used to hang in his room. Once, when he was discussing the life of Jesus Christ with some well-read devotees, he was completely absorbed in the subject. Later, he felt that the painting in his room became lifelike. He also had a vision of Christian priests praying to Lord Jesus. For three days, he was absorbed in contemplation of the vision and these subjects. He felt his traditional and cultural Hindu thought patterns getting dissolved. On the third day, while walking in the temple garden, he saw a divine person – in a human form – approaching him. He heard a voice proclaiming, 'This is Jesus Christ, the great yogi.' The divine form came close to him and entered his body.

After reaching the ultimate destination according to various spiritual paths, the Paramhansa concluded that the ultimate reality was indeed one. It has been said in the Hindu scriptures:

Ékam sat viprā bahudhā vadanti

Truth is One, the wise men describe it in many different ways.

The Paramhansa had realised this truth, not from an intellectual standpoint, but from an experiential one.

His fame had spread. Now he came to be known as Ramakrishna Paramhansa. But despite his high attainment, some people still considered him to be a madman, given his unpredictable behaviour and childlike mannerisms.

Marriage

Meanwhile, Chandramani, the Paramhansa's mother, was worried at the news she would hear about her son and thought it would be appropriate to marry him off. She hoped marriage would bring some change in his behaviour and began to look for a bride. Unfortunately, every attempt to find a suitable girl failed. Finally, one day, the Paramhansa, in an elevated spiritual state, described to his mother a house in the village of Jayrambati, close to Kamarpukur, where she would find his bride-to-be. She immediately despatched a Brahmin matchmaker, who found all details tallying with the Paramhansa's description. The marriage was fixed and the mother, happily, went about making the arrangements.

The Paramhansa was married in May 1859 to Saradamani Devi, the daughter of Ramchandra Mukhopadhyaya. Shortly after, Saradamani, then merely five years old, went back to her parental home and, a little later, the Paramhansa returned to Dakshineshwar.

Many years later, Saradamani Devi (called Sri Sarada Devi by devotees) came to stay with the Paramhansa in the Dakshineshwar temple.

The Paramhansa had, however, transcended bodily attachments and his relationship with Sri Sarada Devi was, sometimes that of a teacher and a guide, sometimes that of a child needing care, sometimes of a devotee, but never of a man in need of physical companionship.

Ramakrishna *Leela*

The Touch of Money

The Paramhansa often mentioned that he could not bear to touch money. He had undergone so many rigorous spiritual disciplines based on the belief of the impermanence of material objects that his constitution could not bear contact with such articles anymore.

In the early days of his interaction with the Paramhansa, his disciple Swami Vivekananda wished to test him. He, therefore, placed a coin under the Paramhansa's bedspread when he was not in the room. The Paramhansa came to the room in a short while but the minute he sat on the bed, he cried out in pain, 'Aah! My whole body is burning!'

Swami Vivekananda immediately removed the coin and apologised, explaining his motive. The Paramhansa, instead of being angry was quite pleased. He approved of his disciple's conduct. He added that one must test the guru and be satisfied before accepting him.

The Divine Mother in All

The Paramhansa saw all women as avatars of Goddess Kali, the deity he considered the Divine Mother of the universe. He was a *brahmachari* and had supreme control over his sexual desires. Since he exhibited many characteristics of madmen and also suffered extremely poor health due to various causes, some thought that his rigid control over carnal desires was probably creating a nervous disability. Once, an individual thought of a plan—he decided to rope in some prostitutes to seduce the saint. The Paramhansa was led into their room, but when he saw the prostitutes taking off their clothes, he could only see them as divine forms of the Goddess and went into a transcendental state. The women realised he was a holy man and left the room, aborting all their plans of seducing him.

The master often visited the house of a devotee, Balaram Basu, and would affectionately interact with the women of his household. Once, in their presence, he saw a prostitute who was also his devotee. He called out to her with similar affection. The ladies of the family were scandalised, but did not say anything. Later that day, the Paramhansa took them to the temple of the Divine Mother. He bowed and prayed out aloud, 'Mother! You have verily become both the chaste woman and the prostitute.' That was when the women realised their folly and experienced the pure non-discriminating nature of the Paramhansa.

Once, Haldhari, the saint's cousin, commented that the Paramhansa was worshipping a form of God that was tamasic in nature, a reference to Goddess Kali. The Paramhansa was deeply hurt and ran to the temple and asked the Goddess if She was indeed tamasic. The Goddess replied that She was above all—sattvic (pure), rajasic (material) and tamasic (evil). She explained the philosophical basis of Her divinity. Ramakrishna Paramhansa was elated and ran to his cousin's hut, kicked open the door and jumped on him. He pinned his cousin down and began to repeat what the Divine Mother had said, while rocking back and forth on his shoulders. Haldhari had a vision of the Divine Mother in the Paramhansa's body. He apologised to him and worshipped him with flowers.

The Sadguru or the Lord?

Mathura Babu, once, came to the Dakshineshwar Kali temple to meet the saint. He was directed to the latter's room where he saw the Paramhansa pacing up and down the room. He was amazed to see his form change to that of the Goddess Kali when he walked in one direction, and then to Lord Siva when he walked in the other direction. Mathura Babu rubbed his eyes in disbelief but the vision persisted. His eyes swelled with tears in an outpouring of devotion and, with great difficulty, the Paramhansa managed to quieten him.

The Saviour

Mathura Babu's wife, Jagdamba Dasi, was very ill and was on her deathbed. The worried husband beseeched the Paramhansa to save her life, saying he would not be able to continue to serve the master if she died, as she was his link to the temple property and administration. The Paramhansa blessed Mathura Babu, and his wife recovered. He had taken her illness upon himself and suffered intense stomach pain for the next six months.

State of Unity

The master Paramhansa would often experience the non-dualistic state. Once, he saw two boatmen fighting, and the stronger of the two gave the weaker a hard blow on his back. The Paramhansa cried out in pain and, to his nephew, Hriday's surprise, the saint's back was swollen at the very same spot where the boatman was hit. Hriday realised that the Paramhansa had experienced complete identification with the boatman who was attacked.

Detachment

It is a common belief that with success, people tend to become proud and selfish. Hriday often exerted control over the Paramhansa, since he had served him during the latter's sadhana phase. Despite warnings, he, once, even hurt Sri Sarada Devi with his words. But, the Paramhansa continued to tolerate Hriday's arrogant and insolent behaviour, as he was indebted to him for the loving care with which he had served him for many years. However, once, Hriday got into a quarrel with the Dakshineshwar temple management, and they asked him to leave the premises immediately and permanently.

Hriday straight away went to see the saint and acquainted him with the management's decision. The Paramhansa began to walk out of the temple premises with his nephew. He was lost in his devotional mood and moved as though he was an unattached child. Nobody could guess that he was leaving forever the place, he had stayed in for so long, and where he had performed various spiritual practices and received so many visions. However, the temple management saw him going and begged him to stay, clarifying they had asked only Hriday to leave due to his misdemeanours. On hearing this, the Paramhansa turned back as if he had nothing to do with the entire episode.

The Devotee's Offering

The Paramhansa was always keen to partake of a pure devotee's offering. Gopaler Ma, an extremely poor devotee, once bought some inexpensive sweets for the saint. When she reached the Kali temple, she saw many rich devotees carrying lots of expensive sweetmeats for him. She felt ashamed of her offering. The master, however, sought her out and asked her, 'What have you brought for me?' Gopaler Ma was compelled to offer those sweets to him. He ate them with relish.

Supernatural Powers

The Paramhansa had acquired various powers during his period of tantric sadhana. When asked what he thought of them, he pointed at a pile of dirt and said that he equated occult powers with it. But, often his devotees experienced spontaneous activation of his occult powers.

Swami Vivekananda was once lying in his bed at night in his house in Calcutta. He suddenly felt his inner (subtle) body being withdrawn from his physical body and pulled to Dakshineshwar. There, the Paramhansa gave him some spiritual guidance and united the subtle body with his physical body.

A renowned saint and contemporary, Sri Vijaykrishna Goswami, was once in Dhaka, a city far away from Dakshineshwar, when the Paramhansa appeared in his room. The saint bowed down and touched him to verify if the manifestation was in flesh and blood. He was surprised to see that it was indeed so.

Omniscience

There are numerous instances that illustrate the power of omniscience in Ramakrishna Paramhansa.

Once, when he was a young priest in the Kali temple, he was conducting a ritual and a crowd of devotees had gathered around in the sanctum sanctorum. Rani Rasomani also joined in along with her guards.

She was sitting with eyes closed, apparently in a state of devotion, when the Paramhansa slapped her hard, saying, 'Even in this place you are thinking about material things and comforts?' The crowd was stunned and the lady's guards caught hold of the young priest. Rasomani, however, asked them to release him. She had been contemplating on some material affairs and was surprised as to how the priest knew what was going on in her mind.

On another occasion, Surendra Nath Mitra, a householder disciple, was conducting Navaratri worship of the Divine Mother in his house. He had organised the puja against stiff opposition from his relatives. The objections were based on some superstitions, but Surendra insisted on performing it as he had the blessings of the Paramhansa. Unfortunately, the Paramhansa himself could not attend the ritual as he was unwell. However, at the most auspicious moment, the point between the eighth and the ninth night, Surendra was overcome by emotion and began to cry out to the Divine Mother, with tears streaming down his cheeks. The master described the scene that was taking place in Surendra's house, far away in Calcutta, to his disciples in Shyampukur. He then sent Swami Vivekananda and other disciples to comfort Surendra. When they reached Surendra's house, they found that the Paramhansa's description of the scene was uncannily accurate.

The Transfer of Power

There are many, many instances of the Paramhansa transmitting spiritual power and states to his devotees and disciples. Hriday, once, beseeched him to grant him a mystic experience. Soon after, he began to receive mystic visions, but he could not handle the experiences. Once, he followed the Paramhansa into Panchavati at night and saw visions of his own past lives and those of the master. He began to scream loudly and the Paramhansa touched him, beseeching the Divine Mother to withdraw Hriday's visions. The visions immediately ceased, but the saint assured Hriday that the visions would reoccur when it was time.

Mathura Babu too underwent something similar. He, once, requested the Paramhansa to give him the state of Bhava Samadhi, or the samadhi of devotional ecstasy. The Paramhansa granted him the boon, but after four days, Mathura Babu sent for the saint. The devotee appealed to him to withdraw the experience, as he could not stand it any longer. He claimed he had not slept for three nights, as the devotional state was unmanageable. The Paramhansa complied with the devotee's wishes.

A very important incident related to this power of the Paramhansa occurred in the last days of his life. Towards the end, the saint developed throat cancer and was shifted to Cossipore (now Kashipur) garden house in Calcutta in mid-1885. His disciples and devotees had taken the accommodation on rent, as the doctors had advised them that the best-possible treatment could be rendered only in the city. It was 1 January 1886 when the Paramhansa was taking a stroll in the garden, accompanied by Girish Chandra Ghosh — a disciple — when he suddenly posed a question, 'Girish, I believe you are spreading the word that I am an incarnation of God? What do you see in me that makes you say these things?' Girish bowed before him, then fell to his knees and said, 'Even the great, gifted historian biographers like Veda Vyasa and Valmiki could not adequately describe the glories of the Lord with their writings. How can I describe your greatness[7]?'

The Paramhansa suddenly went into an exalted state of consciousness and began to bless the disciples with spiritual visions[8]. For some reason, he informed some individuals that they would achieve success in their endeavours later in their lives[9]. Others, meanwhile, felt ecstatic, experienced transcendental spiritual states or received mystic visions. These experiences were not temporary in nature but ones that caused permanent transformation in the recipients.

Distributing the Fruits

The Beginning

When the Paramhansa had completed various sadhanas, it was time for passing on the knowledge and guiding various aspirants along the yogic paths that he had perfected. Many people flocked to see him, while some wished to hear him, others came merely to see the 'madman'. Many came to the master to seek direction or to share their sorrows and hopes with him. However, the Paramhansa, who was completely immersed in the sea of spirituality, was disappointed to hear so much material talk from the seekers who visited him. He longed to hear words of pure, unadulterated devotion. He prayed to the Divine Mother to send him genuine seekers. The Divine Mother, in return, assured him that She would send him disciples of the calibre he was looking for and gave him visions of the key disciples who would come to him. The Paramhansa would be satisfied with the Divine Mother's assurance, but his impatience would again get the better of him after some time.

He would, sometimes, climb up to the roof of the temple and cry out loudly, 'Where are you? When will you come?'

And then, gradually, the gems that the Divine Mother had promised him began to trickle in. Many of his disciples went on to become great yogis. The Paramhansa's wife, Sri Sarada Devi, was herself a spiritual giant. Among others, six of his key disciples – Naren, Yogen, Baburam, Rakhal, Niranjan and Purno – were considered to be those who were eternally free yogis from their past lives itself, classified by the Paramhansa as *Isvarakotis*, or those who belonged to the category of God. This acknowledgment of the disciples' elevated spiritual state also came to the Paramhansa in the form of a vision in which the Divine Mother showed him these six as the eternally free yogis. Of these disciples, Yogen lived close to the temple and had been spotted by the Paramhansa in his younger years. The others appeared on the scene from 1878 onwards. Rakhal was the first of the six to arrive and Purno the last (Purno in Bengali means completion). With Purno's arrival, the Paramhansa realised that all his key disciples had arrived.

Sometimes, the Paramhansa would mention to people that 'a devotee belonging to this place is coming today[10]'. He would even mention where the devotee was coming from. This usually implied that the devotee had a spiritual connection with the Paramhansa from a previous life. The Paramhansa also felt emotionally attached to his disciples. Baburam, once, recounted how the master would cry when some beloved pupil of his would leave Dakshineshwar.

The Paramhansa had utmost regard for pure souls. When he came across such a person, he would spend hours talking to him, guiding him on spiritual topics and even feeding him – just like a parent would treat a child. On the other hand, if an impure soul came close to him or touched him during samadhi, he would experience unimaginable pain. He, therefore, allowed very few people to perform personal service to him.

Be a Devotee, Not a Fool

The Paramhansa would encourage devotees to immerse themselves in their chosen sadhana, but maintain a state of material consciousness or awareness in their day-to-day dealings. His disciple, Yogen, remained absorbed in meditation all day – ignorant of happenings around him. Once, Ramakrishna Paramhansa sent Yogen to the market to buy an article. When Yogen returned, the Paramhansa found that he had not bargained well. He scolded him, saying, 'I thought you were a devotee, but you behave like a fool.' This incident illustrated his philosophy of maintaining material consciousness that many saints overlook in training their disciples.

A Unique Path to Each

As a guru, the Paramhansa would spend hours guiding his disciples on the path chosen for them. For each seeker, the path was unique. For those attached to the formless aspect of God, he would guide along a particular path. For others, who were attached to a divine form, he would align his teachings to their inclination. Each would achieve progress or receive visions in accordance with the path they adopted.

Even in their day-to-day behaviour, the Paramhansa's instructions were tuned to the different temperaments of his disciples. For instance, once, Niranjan was travelling in a boat when he heard some people criticising his guru as a fake god-man. Niranjan was a fearless soul.

He loved the Paramhansa with all his heart. He was so enraged that he began to rock the boat violently, almost causing it to capsize. He calmed down only when others apologised and beseeched him to stop. The Paramhansa chastised him for this act, and cautioned him against uncontrolled anger. He asked him whether public criticism would make any difference to the quality of his (the Paramhansa's) spiritual attainment. On another occasion, Yogen, a very gentle soul, told his guru that he had heard some people speaking ill of him but had remained unmoved, ignoring them. This time, the Paramhansa scolded Yogen for silently listening to vain public gossip about the guru.

However, the Paramhansa did not want his disciples to become dry monks, solely engaged in philosophical discussion. He would encourage them to play games such as *golakdham*[11]. He was full of jokes, would often poke fun at them or others. Once, the Paramhansa shared an interesting bit about Sri Vijaykrishna Goswamiji with his disciples. Although Goswamiji was bulky, he used to dance to the rhythm of music during kirtans, lost in the divine bliss. The Paramhansa appreciated such deep involvement on part of the saint, but would also worry that Goswamiji may end up bringing down the entire building.

Testing the Disciples

Though attached to his disciples, the Paramhansa was known to test them at various levels. He would look for signs of spirituality on their bodies. He even knew how to judge the inner quality of disciples based on their biological activities. He had gathered an exceptional amount of knowledge in divining spirituality through physical appearance and activities – this is part of a subject called *Samudrik Shastra*, but his knowledge was not bookish. For instance, he would check the weight of the disciple's hands and arms, and gauge some elements of his spiritual attainment. Once, the Paramhansa confided in one of his disciples about a test to see whether the aspirant was a renunciate by nature or a materialistically oriented person. He mentioned that, usually, disciples whose urine flowed out on the left side would be materialistic in nature, and those whose urine flowed to the right would be renunciates. His tests would also examine the mental make-up of an individual and his attitude towards wealth and the opposite sex. The Paramhansa would also test, from time to time, the growth in the individual's devotion.

The Guru Forever

It is said that the guru, the divine guide, remains the guide of the disciple across infinite lives if necessary, until the disciple attains the goal of existence. The Paramhansa, as a guru, would continuously strive to improve the spiritual nature of his disciples. Where the disciple strayed, the guru would step in to bring him back on course.

Yogen, the Paramhansa's disciple, bowed to family pressure and married much against his own wishes. For some time, he felt the doors to spiritual advancement were closed to him. He stopped visiting his guru, ignoring even the repeated messages from the latter. Yogen was a dear disciple of the Paramhansa and the saint yearned for contact with him. One day, when he heard that Yogen had delayed in repaying some money he owed to another man, the Paramhansa devised a way of drawing Yogen to himself. He sent a message to his disciple, criticising him for not returning the money and indirectly calling him a cheat. Yogen was hurt and decided he would definitely visit the Paramhansa and clarify the truth, but swore that it would also be his last meeting with him. However, when he saw the Paramhansa, he realised that the saint had only used the barb as a way of meeting him. That day, the Paramhansa showered a lot of affection on Yogen and assured him that his spiritual progress would continue despite his marriage. The disciple was left speechless and overwhelmed with the Paramhansa's loving grace.

Some Key Disciples

When a great soul takes human birth, it is believed that he is accompanied by many other divine souls who support him in his mission. Of the many associates and disciples of the Paramhansa, many were considered such divine souls. Sri Sarada Devi was considered an incarnation of the Divine Mother, while Lakshmi Devi (the Paramhansa's niece) was considered an incarnation of an aspect of the Divine Mother. Nistarini Ghosh, one of his devotees, was also considered a partial incarnation of one of the ten forms of the Divine Mother. His six divine disciples led inspiring lives. Five of them became monks in their later lives, while one of them (Purno), remained a householder. The following section contains glimpses of the lives of the five *Isvarakoti* monastic disciples. I have also included the life of Pratap Chandra Hazra, a cousin of the Paramhansa, who was miraculously transformed from a small-minded materialist to a saint, purely as a result of an unwilling blessing from the master.

Swami Vivekananda

No discussion on Ramakrishna Paramhansa is complete without at least a mention of Narendranath Dutta, or Naren as he was called. Naren was born in January 1863 in Calcutta, to Vishwanath Dutta and Bhuvaneshwari Devi. Prior to his birth, his mother had a dream, in which Lord Siva had blessed her and agreed to be born as her son. Incidentally, the boy also closely resembled his grandfather, a devout individual, who had renounced the world for a life of spirituality, and hence, many thought that Naren was a reincarnation of his grandfather.

The boy was brought up in a rational yet devout environment. Even as a young child, Naren would lose himself in contemplation and meditation. Once, when he was meditating, a snake crawled close to him. Other children playing in that area ran away, but Naren continued with his contemplation, undisturbed. Naren was later questioned why he did not react to the snake. He responded, 'I knew nothing of the snake or of anything else. I was feeling inexpressible bliss.' This was before he was even six!

He was an exceptionally gifted yogi from birth itself. He, once, described to the Paramhansa that, since childhood, whenever he slept, he would see a light between his eyebrows and would fix his eyes on it.

He would lose himself watching the light change form and eventually, would drift into sleep when the light burst into millions of lights and enveloped him. Until the Paramhansa could explain the significance of such an event, Naren had naively assumed that that was how everyone fell asleep!

Naren would approach many saints and devotees and ask them whether they had seen God. Most people avoided the question, or gave dry philosophical answers. When Naren met the Paramhansa for the first time, he similarly questioned him whether he had seen God. 'Yes, I have seen God, and I see God clearer than I see you,' replied the Paramhansa emphatically. This left a great impression on Naren. Naren was then a young man of eighteen.

Naren considered Ramakrishna Paramhansa a great saint, but also thought he was a little mad. In their first meeting the Paramhansa had babbled something about Naren's previous birth, which he could not understand. On his second visit, the Paramhansa touched Naren and the latter lost all consciousness. Naren found himself in a transcendental state beyond comprehension. He began to scream and, after some time, the Paramhansa touched him again and brought him back to a normal state. During the third visit, the Paramhansa again touched Naren, but this time to send him into a trance, in which the saint asked him various questions about his previous lives. Naren became more and more attached to the Paramhansa and progressed in his sadhana under the master's direction.

When the Paramhansa was shifted to Calcutta for treatment, a young group of devotees, including Naren, left their homes to serve the saint. Naren assumed leadership of this group. Day and night, the group looked after their beloved master. A few days before the Paramhansa's departure, he passed on all his spiritual and supernatural attainments to Naren and requested him to take care of his band of disciples. Naren went into a trance, and when he emerged, he saw the Paramhansa crying. The master told Naren, 'I have given you everything

I had and have now become a pauper.' When the Paramhansa passed away, Naren and the others decided to dedicate their lives to fulfilling their guru's vision. They took monastic vows and assumed monastic names. Naren initially took the name Swami Vividhishananda, but later changed it to Swami Vivekananda on the request of the Raja of Khetri.

In 1893, Swami Vivekananda travelled to Chicago to address the World Parliament of Religions, where he achieved great fame. This wouldn't have been possible had the Paramhansa not appeared in a vibrant vision before the disciple, when he was nervously standing at the podium before a mammoth crowd. Swamiji lost external consciousness. He could not recollect what he spoke. When he emerged from his trance-like state, he saw the crowds clapping and cheering and learned that he had just delivered a historic speech. From that day onwards, Swamiji became famous in the West and many people became his disciples.

Under the leadership of Swami Vivekananda, Ramakrishna Mission was established in 1897, when he returned from the West with his new disciples. Later, he laid the foundations of a monastery, Ramakrishna Math, in the fond memory of his guru. The first monastery came up in Baranagore (now Baranagar), in a dilapidated house on the outskirts of Calcutta, where the young monastic disciples had shifted to shortly after the master's *mahasamadhi*. Subsequently, in 1892, the monastery was moved to Alambazar, and then in 1897, to Belur, across the River Ganga from Dakshineshwar. It was close to this spot in Belur that a grand ashram was built in 1899, and which became the mission's headquarters. An ashram was also set up in Mayavati in the foothills of the Himalayas. These institutions progressed substantially under Swami Vivekananda's guidance. Ramakrishna Mission dedicated itself to service of humanity and directly and indirectly espoused social and humanitarian causes. The mission did extensive work for education, freedom from dogma, emancipation of women, poor and the needy.

Spiritual aspirants of these institutions worked tirelessly to bring relief during natural disasters as well. In these monasteries, extensive training was given to young men for carrying out the objectives of the mission. They were also prepared mentally and physically for the life of *sannyasa*.

While Swamiji worked tirelessly for Ramakrishna Mission, the core of the mission remained spiritual. Many young men dedicated their lives to serve the humanity and achieve the pinnacle of attainment in spiritual endeavours. The disciples were in awe of Swami Vivekananda's spiritual stature.

An episode from Swamiji's life underlines his spiritual achievements. Once, Sarat Chandra — a devotee of Nag Mahashay, who was a renowned saint and Swamiji's contemporary — requested his guru to initiate him with a mantra. Nag Mahashay was a great devotee of the Paramhansa, but he did not wish to initiate disciples. He, therefore, refused to fulfil Sarat's request but assured the pupil that one day, he would receive initiation from Lord Siva himself. Later in his life, Sarat began to interact with the *Isvarakoti* disciples of the Paramhansa. Once, Sarat happened to spend time with Swami Vivekananda in the Alambazar monastery. Swamiji was fast asleep on the cot when Sarat suddenly saw Lord Siva's form in place of the renowned saint. He shook himself repeatedly, but the vision of Lord Siva persisted. Later, Sarat did indeed receive the initiation from Swami Vivekananda. He realised that Swami Vivekananda was no different from Lord Siva and concluded that the words of Nag Mahashay were indeed prophetic.

As it happened with his guru, Swamiji also had an intuition that his end was near. He had declared that he would not live to be forty. Ramakrishna Paramhansa had told his disciples that Naren would not live long, once he recognised who he really was. It was rumoured that Swami Vivekananda realised his true self during a visit to the Amarnath shrine. Shortly afterwards, he studied a calendar and secretly fixed a date for his final departure, probably based on an auspicious date as per astrology.

On 4 July 1902, the nominated day, when everybody was busy in the evening prayers at Belur Math, Swamiji quietly went to his room and spent an hour in meditation and *japam*. He then called an attendant to open the windows and fan him as he lay on his bed. For an hour, the attendant fanned Swamiji, who appeared to be sleeping or meditating. He then merged his consciousness with God and voluntarily cast off his body. The signs on his body revealed that he had taken the final samadhi as per the description in the yogic scriptures.

Swami Brahmananda

Rakhal Chandra Ghosh was born in Calcutta in January 1863 to Ananda Mohan and Kailashkamini Ghosh. Rakhal's purity of the soul was attested to by the fact that Ramakrishna Paramhansa, whose body was so pure that he could not bear the touch of ordinary people, allowed Rakhal to serve him.

The Paramhansa considered Rakhal as his spiritual son, based on a vision the Divine Mother had shown him. Even as an adult, Rakhal would behave like a small child in the presence of the Paramhansa. Once, Rakhal told him that he was hungry. As there was no food ready at that time, the Paramhansa walked to the River Ganga and began calling out, apparently to nobody in particular, saying, 'Gaurdasi! Bring some food. Rakhal is hungry.' Surprisingly, soon afterwards, a boat came in and Gauri Ma (the Paramhansa's devotee who he called Gaurdasi) stepped out and gave them some sweetmeats she had prepared. The Paramahansa gave these to Rakhal to eat.

As said earlier, the Paramhansa encouraged and guided the aspirants according to their spiritual inclinations. Rakhal believed in a personal God, and did not endorse the concept of the formless aspect of the Divine. The Paramhansa guided Rakhal in meditation. As a result, Rakhal experienced various elevated states, but meditation was not always easy. Once, when Rakhal was despairing at the lack of transformation within his consciousness, the Paramhansa wrote a mantra on the disciple's tongue. The impact was so great that Rakhal experienced inexpressible joy[12].

The Paramhansa showed Rakhal the benefit of serving a holy man. Once, the Paramhansa coaxed Rakhal into massaging his legs. While Rakhal massaged his master's legs, he had a vision of the Divine Mother, and realised the value of his words. Over the years, with the Paramhansa's grace, Rakhal had many divine visions and experienced a deep spiritual transformation.

After the death of the Paramhansa, Rakhal left his home and joined Naren and the band of disciples who had dedicated themselves to the master's mission. Rakhal embraced *sannyasa* and assumed the name of Swami Brahmananda. He became the head of the Ramakrishna Mission after Swami Vivekananda passed away.

Brahmananda belonged to the category of saints who so completely identify themselves with the guru that they virtually become the guru themselves. Once, a disciple was lamenting in front of Brahmananda that, in his lifetime, he had not seen the Paramhansa. Brahmananda spoke in a peculiar voice assuring the disciple that indeed he had. The disciple looked up and saw Ramakrishna Paramhansa sitting before him in place of Brahmananda. The next moment, it was Brahmananda again.

Brahmananda initiated many disciples in his life. He could use his spiritual force to charge aspirants during initiation and infuse the spirit of detachment in them. Once, a conflict broke out between the sadhus of the Ramakrishna Advaita Ashram and the Home of Service in Kashi (both parts of the larger Ramakrishna Mission). All attempts to reconcile the differences failed. In desperation, the head of the ashram wrote to Swami Brahmananda, urging the latter to intervene to sort out the difficult situation. Brahmananda wrote back saying he would settle the matter during his forthcoming trip to Kashi. When he reached there, Brahmananda spent time with the monks in meditation and prayer. He then initiated them into *sannyasa*, and took them all to such a high spiritual plane that the differences automatically subsided. He left without saying a word about reconciling differences, but the spiritual force that he infused them with automatically achieved the objective. Brahmananda's level of spiritual attainment can be gauged from his remark, 'Spiritual life begins with Nirvikalpa Samadhi[13]'.

Even after he became the head of the Ramakrishna Mission, his innocent childlike behaviour continued. He loved to play pranks on people. Once, a spiritual aspirant, who was new to the Ramakrishna Math, came looking for Brahmananda and met him. The aspirant asked him who Brahmananda was. Brahmananda pointed to Swami Sivananda, a friend, who was visiting the monastery at that time, and the aspirant approached Sivananda. When Sivananda sent the aspirant back to Brahmananda, he again sent the aspirant back to Sivananda. Finally, seeing the aspirant's plight, he admitted he was Brahmananda and chatted with him for a while.

Another time, some devotees came to meet him, they found him jumping around and playing with children, whereas they had expected to see a grave and grand, old saint instead.

The Paramhansa had described Brahmananda's previous life to some of his disciples and had mentioned that if and when Brahmananda has a vision of his past life, he would not retain his body for long. Towards the end of his life, Brahmananda indeed had visions of his previous births. He withdrew himself from life mentally, and in a few months, in April 1922, gave up his mortal body.

Swami Premananda

Baburam Ghosh was born in December 1861 to an aristocratic family of Antpur, close to Calcutta. His mother, Matangini Devi, was a devout soul who would often lock herself in her room and meditate for the entire day. His sister, Krishnabhavini, was married to Balaram Basu, a great devotee of the Paramhansa, who went on to introduce his entire clan to the renowned yogi, many of whom became his devotees.

The seeds of divinity were apparent in Baburam from the early years. As a child, he would often imagine meditating in a hut on the banks of the holy Ganga with another monk. Right from childhood, he was on a lookout for a guru who would guide and help him find answers to his questions, the most important being, how to meet God. His dreams of finding a guru were fulfilled when he joined the Metropolitan School in Shyambazar in Calcutta. The headmaster there was Mahendranath Gupta (popularly known as M., the author of *Gospel of Ramakrishna*), and one of his classmates was Rakhal. It was Rakhal who took Baburam to meet the Paramhansa.

The first time Baburam set his eyes on the Paramhansa, the latter was in a state of divine intoxication and needed help to walk back to his room in the Kali temple.

The Paramhansa's state left an impression on Baburam. When Baburam met the saint again, the latter examined his appearance and concluded that Baburam was a pure soul. Balaram Basu, who witnessed these events, was also deeply impressed by the words of the Paramhansa. The Paramhansa, later, requested Baburam's mother to give him Baburam, who could take care of him, as her son was a pure soul. The mother duly obliged the master and Baburam shifted to Dakshineshwar Kali temple. The Paramhansa kept a close watch on the spiritual progress of Baburam, who quickly learnt a lot while serving the master. This is evident from an anecdote when Baburam went against the rules of the Paramhansa. One day, Baburam had uttered a lie while engaged in a discussion with friends, and when he later met the Paramhansa, the master told him for so me reason he was unable to touch him. Baburam then realised his mistake and understood the importance of remaining pure at heart in order to achieve spiritual success and also for being able to serve the Paramhansa.

After the master died, Baburam joined Rakhal and Naren to spread the teachings of the Paramhansa in the country. He assumed the name of Swami Premananda and permanently shifted to the monastery at Baranagore. He also joined the other disciples in their travels across India, visiting holy sites. They would immerse themselves in meditation and spiritual practices and would return to the monastery from time to time.

When Belur Math was established, Premananda was a key pillar of the monastery. After Swami Vivekananda's death, Premananda became the administrator of the monastery. He was a strict disciplinarian and often scolded the inmates, though he loved them deeply, and was often called 'mother of the Math.' He himself was seemingly inexhaustible as he would work tirelessly in the monastery and guide initiates by example.

Premananda was one of the central pillars of the Ramakrishna Mission, but in 1918, his health began to fail. To recuperate, he moved for a few days to Deoghar, now in Jharkhand. Here, he met the great yogi Balananda Brahmachari. Balananda was a realised master. He perceived that Premananda had no attachment to his own body, and prophesied that the latter would not live for long.

A few months later — on 30 July 1918 — Premananda left his body, reverentially looking at an oil painting of the Paramhansa that read, 'Grace, grace, grace.'

Swami Niranjanananda

The exact date and place of the birth of Nitya Niranjan Ghosh (Niranjan) are not known, but it is believed he was born in August 1862 at Rajarhat-Vishnupur, close to Calcutta.

He was a healthy and handsome lad of eighteen when he first met the Paramhansa. Niranjan was then living with his uncle. At that time, influenced by his uncle, he was involved in various occult pursuits, such as psychic healing and communicating with spirits. The meeting with the Paramhansa was also related to an abortive psychic experiment. The Paramhansa counselled Niranjan to avoid such pursuits, cautioning the latter that he would become a ghost if he kept contemplating on ghosts. Instead, he asked Niranjan to contemplate on the Lord and his life would become divine. At the end of this meeting, the Paramhansa asked Niranjan to stay with him in Dakshineshwar.

The Paramhansa left a great impression upon him and Niranjan accepted the offer readily. Niranjan had recently used his psychic powers to heal a deeply suffering wealthy man and the episode had left a strong impact on his mind, firmly establishing the futility of wealth and material pursuits. It had created an aversion for material life and a longing for a genuinely spiritual life. This further prompted him to obey the Paramhansa.

The Paramhansa guided Niranjan in meditation and also initiated him with a mantra. One day, the Paramhansa touched Niranjan and, for three days and nights, Niranjan was absorbed in a 'continuous vision of a mysterious light'. He could not stop chanting the Lord's name.

Niranjan was part of a small band of disciples who the Paramhansa saw as complete renunciates, with no other master but God. He was, therefore, extremely unhappy to learn that Niranjan had taken up a job in an indigo plantation, but was relieved to hear the reason behind this action. Niranjan had accepted the job offer only to support his aged mother and not with a motivation to lead a materialistic life[14.]

Eventually, Niranjan left his job—the Paramhansa was delighted. And when Niranjan came to visit him, the latter described his visions of Niranjan in the indigo plantation. Niranjan realised that the Paramhansa had divine insight and always kept a watch over his disciples. He, once, told the master, 'Formerly, I loved you...but now, it is impossible to live without you.' Such love for the guru does not spring in the heart of an impure devotee.

During the last days of his life, when the Paramhansa was unwell, Niranjan finally left his home and shifted in to serve the master. After the master's *mahasamadhi*, Niranjan took *sannyasa* and Swami Vivekananda named him Swami Niranjanananda. He shifted in with the other disciples when they established a monastery in Baranagore.

He also spent many days travelling the country, performing austerities in various parts. The severe austerities also had an impact on his health; he developed persistent dysentery. He then decided to move to the holy city of Haridwar—now in the state of Uttarakhand—where the climate would aid rejuvenation. He bid a tearful goodbye to Sri Sarada Devi, which gave an insight to other disciples that he probably had a premonition that he would never return.

He continued his difficult sadhanas despite his failing health. On 9 May 1904, he breathed his last in the state of samadhi.

Swami Yogananda

Jogindra Nath Roychoudhary (Yogen) was born in March 1861. He belonged to the village of Dakshineshwar. His father was a devout soul who had no interest in leading a material life; he had given up everything for being close to the Lord.

Thus, Yogen was brought up in a spiritual environment; his father became his first guru. His childhood was very different from that of the other children. An introvert, he used to often lose interest in games and would withdraw into a contemplative state, where he repeatedly felt he belonged to a different world.

The Paramhansa would, sometimes, visit their house to listen to the readings of the *Bhagvata* and other scriptures. Yogen was, however, never interested in meeting the 'mad brahmin', as the Paramhansa was referred to.

One day, however, he went to meet the Paramhansa, after reading an article on his life in *Sulabh Samachar*, a journal promoted by the Brahmo Samaj branch led by Keshab Chandra Sen. He heard the master speaking on God and was mesmerised by his words. After the crowd dispersed, the Paramhansa sought out Yogen. He spoke highly about Yogen's father and asked the young man to come again.

Yogen started visiting the Paramahansa and soon began to advance spiritually. Sometime around 1884, he began to spend long hours in prayer and meditation, which alarmed his family. The family decided to get him married. Yogen was unwilling but he relented before his mother's tearful pleading.

Yogen was not destined for a married life and, on the very first night, he began to loudly chant the Lord's name. He never slept on the same bed as his wife. He felt he had ruined his spiritual life because of one instance of weakness. He also felt he could not face the master and avoided him for many days, but the master eventually met him and reassured him that nothing will be able to stop him in his spiritual endeavours. 'Even a hundred thousand marriages will be powerless to affect you!' promised the Paramhansa. At Yogen's request, the Paramhansa also blessed his wife. Yogen's spirit of renunciation kept increasing. He began to spend many days in the Dakshineshwar temple with the Paramhansa. The master guided Yogen into spiritual practices, and also on matters regarding elements of diet and the lifestyle suitable for a spiritual life.

After the master passed away, the spirit of renunciation only deepened. He travelled to Deoghar and Vrindavan with Sri Sarada Devi, who initiated Yogen with a mantra in Vrindavan. After spending a year there, he travelled to various holy cities in India and returned to the Baranagore monastery. Here, he was initiated into *sannyasa* and was given the name Swami Yogananda.

Of all the disciples of the Paramhansa, Yogen was the extremist. Throwing caution to the winds, he would not care for meals, or other bodily comforts and would meditate like a man possessed. This ultimately harmed his body, but Yogen persisted in his spiritual pursuits.

He was deeply respected by his fellow disciples. Once, in his last days, Swami Vivekananda told him, 'Yogen, you get well; let me die instead.' Shortly before Yogen left his body, Sri Sarada Devi had a vision that the Paramhansa had come to take Yogen. Before he breathed his last, another fellow disciple, Swami Shivananda (Tarak), asked him if he remembered the master. Yogen replied with certainty, 'Yes, I remember the master more — even more, much more.' He died on 28 March 1899.

Pratap Chandra Hazra

Pratap Chandra Hazra, a cousin of the Paramhansa, had supposedly renounced his home for a spiritual life. Hazra lived in Dakshineshwar and would spend the whole day in prayer and chanting. He was also well read in the philosophical texts, but had no experience of the spiritual world. Moreover, he practised austerities for psychic powers and material gain. The Paramhansa knew Hazra's nature well and would warn his disciples against spending too much time with him. Naren, who was fond of discussing philosophy and metaphysics, found Hazra good company for his discussions. He must have realised Hazra's shortcomings, but despite the Paramhansa's cautioning, he continued to interact with him. Though Hazra never accepted the Paramhansa as his guru, his behaviour and exchanges with the saint and his disciples offer a wonderful insight into the life of the Paramhansa.

Hazra was envious of the Paramhansa's fame and would often misguide seekers who came looking for the master. Once, some spiritual seekers came to meet the Paramhansa for the first time. They approached Hazra and asked him if they knew where the master was. He lied and told them that the master was away to Calcutta and that he would guide them instead. Hearing this, Ramakrishna Paramhansa came out and called out to the visitors and took them into his room.

Once, Hazra criticised the Paramhansa for being too attached to his disciples. A saint, he opined, should be above all attachments, including that for his disciples. Hearing this, the Paramhansa became grave and went into a state of samadhi. The state was so deep and powerful that the hair on his head and in his beard stood on its end and his body became hard. There was an electric atmosphere in the room. Seeing this, his disciple, Ramlal, began to beseech his master to return to his normal form. After a short while, the Paramhansa left his meditative state. It was then that the disciples realised that it was only for their spiritual benefit that he continued his interactions and even his existence in the normal plane, but could, at any time, merge himself into the Absolute.

Another time, the Paramhansa gave a discourse on the univ
of God to Naren. The Paramhansa explained the doctrine
scriptures, which considered everything as God and nothing but ﹏od.
Soon after this interaction with the guru on the omnipresent nature of
the Lord, Naren had an urge to share his thoughts with Hazra. The two
were laughing away at the matter, when Ramakrishna Paramhansa
entered their room. He was aware of the discussion, yet was smiling
as always, in a blissful state. Then he touched Naren. The disciple went
into a transcendental state and experienced the truth of the doctrine — he
saw God everywhere in everything. The experience lasted a few days
and transformed his consciousness.

But before taking *mahasamadhi*, the Paramhansa did bless his cousin;
Naren played a crucial role in this. He personally took Hazra to meet
the master. Initially, the master was reluctant but his arguments could
not put a stop to Naren's persistent requests. Finally, he relented.
The Paramhansa assured Naren that Hazra would experience a
transformation in the last years of his life.

Though many people viewed Hazra in a poor light all his life, true
to the words of the Paramhansa, a miraculous transformation did occur
in him towards the end. He even announced that he was about to leave
his body and told the people around that the Paramhansa had come to
take him. Hazra's transformation was a beautiful tale and reflected how
even the unwilling blessings of a saint can lead to a change in anyone's
mindset, no matter how corrupt.

Casting off the Body

The Paramhansa would, sometimes, point to the north-west, saying he
would be reborn in that direction for the benefit of mankind, and would
work for the salvation of many, many spiritual aspirants.

Many years earlier, the Paramhansa had explained to Sri Sarada
Devi the events that would precede his death. He told her that when
he would begin spending nights in Calcutta and eating from plates
that others had eaten in, she should understand that his time was near.

Once, these circumstances began to manifest themselves, Sri Sarada Devi realised with a feeling of dread, that the end was near.

When a minor ailment of sore throat became throat cancer, the Divine Mother, once, appeared before the Paramhansa. She explained that this was bound to happen as he had come into contact with the sins of many; his body had assumed their sins.

Devotees moved the Paramhansa to places where the climate was conducive to recovery and also where they could serve him and nurse him back to health. Dr Mahendralal Sarkar, a famous medical practitioner, began to treat the Paramhansa but his condition continued to deteriorate. On 16 August 1886, the Paramhansa cast off his body. His face was a picture of purity and ecstasy, and his eyes were focussed on his eyebrow centre.

The illness and the service rendered by the disciples appeared to be a game for the Paramhansa — to bind them into a sense of common purpose. He continued to guide his disciples along the path of their sadhanas.

A New Beginning

The Paramhansa did leave his body, but he remained in spirit. He could and did appear in flesh and blood or in visions before his devotees to guide them and assist them in times of trouble.

Shortly after the Paramhansa cast off his body, a monk arrived from the holy city of Ayodhya. He had seen a vision that indicated that a great yogi — an avatar of God — was living in Bengal. He had set off to meet the saint and had identified him as Ramakrishna Paramhansa, but had reached too late. He was so disappointed that he gave up food and sat in a deserted spot, bemoaning his fate. But a few days later, Ramlal, Paramhansa's cousin, found the man radiant and happy. Curious to know what had happened, Ramlal asked him how he had gotten over his grief. The monk explained that while he had been refusing to eat, the Paramhansa had appeared before him and had given him some food in an earthen pot. The Paramhansa then vanished, leaving the monk with the earthen vessel.

Another similar incident occurred when his *Isvarakoti* disciples were trying to adjust to the life of monkhood, particularly in the exercise of begging for food. However, they fell on hard times, as all of them hailed from good families and had never undergone such an experience. Seeing his beloved disciples in such a hapless condition, the Paramhansa appeared before an affluent devotee, Surendra, and advised him to contribute money to help feed these disciples. Surendra immediately agreed and sought out the disciples and assisted them.

In India, there is a tradition for Hindu widows to wear simple, white clothing and discard jewellery completely. As the Paramhansa's body was no more, Sri Sarada Devi was taking off her bangles when her husband appeared before her and asked her not to do so. He asked her, 'Where have I gone? I have just gone from one state to the other.' After this episode, she did not wear clothes traditionally meant for a widow. But, the guilt that she was perhaps behaving in contravention to society did not completely subside in her, until one day, the Paramhansa appeared before her and asked her to feed him khichri. Another time, when she was travelling to Vrindavan, the Paramhansa appeared outside the window of the train, and advised her to keep her jewellery bag carefully.

Once, Swami Vivekananda met Pawahari Baba in Gazipur close to Kashi and was impressed by the latter's state of renunciation and yogic attainment. Swamiji requested the latter to teach him Nirvikalpa Samadhi. Pawahari Baba told Swami Vivekananda to come to him at night. When Swamiji was leaving his hut at night he had a vibrant vision of the Paramhansa and the latter had tears in his closed eyes. Every night, when Swamiji would want to go to Pawahari Baba, he received this vision. This affected Swamiji so much that after several unsuccessful attempts, he gave up the idea of learning samadhi from Pawahari Baba altogether!

Swami Premananda was a strict vegetarian. Some of the kitchen staff, though, was not careful about separation of food at Belur Math and

Swamiji being unhappy, would often voice his displeasure. One night, after he had spoken unpleasant words to the cook about the matter, he had a vision of the master who asked him, 'So, do you think I loved you because of your vegetarianism?' The master then vanished, leaving Swami Premananda chastened. Another time, Swami Premananda had an argument with Swami Brahmananda. The heated discussion took an ugly turn and Swami Brahmananda ended up scolding Swami Premananda and the latter decided to leave Belur Math. As he reached the gate, he felt someone tugging at his clothes and turned to see the master, who asked him, 'Where are you going, my child?' Premananda immediately returned repentant to the monastery.

The master, his disciples realised, was truly eternal.

ॐ

Endnotes

1. Ananda Sharan literally means 'Refuge of Bliss'. I have met Amba Sharan, the foremost disciple of Ananda Sharan. Amba Sharan, himself a great yogi and guru, describes this episode in the introduction to his book on Swara Yoga.
2. Gadadhar literally means 'Wielder of the Mace' and refers to the form of Lord Vishnu where he holds a mace, a popular weapon in Hindu mythology.
3. The yogini explained that the Divine Mother had shown her the faces of three chosen disciples, two of whom she had already met and initiated; the Divine Mother had indicated that the yogini would find the third (Gadadhar) on the banks of the River Ganga.
4. Many individuals have attained very high states of devotion, but rarely have they experienced a state of *Mahabhava*. Mythologically—Radhika, the *gopi*-consort of Krishna—and historically, Chaitanya Mahaprabhu, have been known to have undergone this experience.
5. Nimai (Chaitanya Mahaprabhu) and Nitai (Swami Nityananda), two great saints of the Vaishnava Bhakti school of the fifteenth and sixteenth centuries, were considered divine incarnations. Both of them hailed from Bengal. Brahmani considered the Paramhansa a joint incarnation of these saints when she interpreted a vision that he had described to her.
6. The Paramhansa did not visit the temple as Islam prohibits idol worship.
7. Veda Vyasa is the author of the Puranas and the *Mahabharata*, while Valmiki is the author of the *Ramayana*. Both these saints extolled the glories of the Lord in their works.
8. Known as Kalpataru day, as the Paramhansa virtually became a Kalpataru, or a wish-fulfilling tree, according to Hindu mythology.
9. One of them was Akshay Kumar Sen, who later in his life experienced a great transformation and went on to write poetic compositions and biographical works based on the life and teachings of the Paramhansa, including *Sri Sri Ramakrishna Punthi, Padye Sri Sri Ramakrishna Paramahamsa Dever Upadesh* and *Sri Sri Ramakrishna Mahima*. He was also responsible for spreading the message of his master to a large number of devotees in the rural parts of Bengal.
10. The Paramhansa often referred to himself in the third person. He would, sometimes, refer to himself as 'this place,' symbolising a detached attitude to his own body.
11. Like the popular, Snakes and Ladders, this game used to take the player up to Heaven, and any mistake would bring him down to Hell.
12. The tantric tradition includes writing of mantras on the tongue of the aspirant. Traditionally, many Indians write mantras on the tongues of children, often with the stick of the pomegranate plant dipped in honey. This is a powerful practice, especially if done when the person writing the mantra has perfected it after the prescribed number of *japams* (called *purscharana*). The Paramhansa often transmitted spiritual power by writing mantras on the tongues of the aspirants with his fingers.
13. Many consider Nirvikalpa Samadhi as the most advanced stage, and the goal of spiritual life, but Brahmananda considered it the beginning.
14. He did not normally discourage devotees from leading the lives of householders, but it was not the case with the disciples he considered *Isvarakotis*. He believed they were not born to lead materialistic lives.

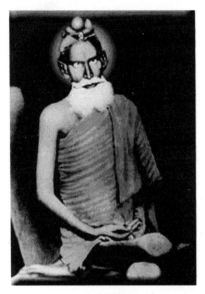

BABA LOKENATH BRAHMACHARI
(1730-1890)

Hey Vishwanāth Shivashankar Devadeva,
Gangādharam Pramathanāyak Nandikesha
Bāneshwarandhakaripô Hara Lokenath,
Sansāradukha Gahanājjagadisha Raksha

O Lord of the universe, O Siva, O Shankar! Lord of the Gods!
O Carrier of Ganga! O Chief of Pramathas! O Lord of Nandi,
O Enemy of Baneswara and Andhakasura,
O Siva! O Lord of the Universe!
Please save me from the deep sorrow of life.

Lokenath Baba: The Brahmachari of Baradi

Dengu Karmakar's despair increased as he thought of the impending court session. An ironmonger by profession, Dengu was a poor man and recent developments had aggravated his state of poverty. He belonged to a village called Baradi, now in Bangladesh, and used to visit Daud Kandi village — in the present-day state of Tripura — for business. Some time ago, he had been dragged into a criminal case, where he was sure he would be pronounced guilty and, probably, even sentenced to death, though he was innocent. Dengu's lawyers had extracted so much money out of him that he was deep in debt. He was desperately seeking more loans but was unsuccessful. And worse, the threat of imprisonment, or even death, loomed large over him.

While he walked to the courthouse, deep in these worrisome thoughts, he saw what initially appeared to be a naked madman lying on the ground. But, there was something uncanny about this man — possibly the tallest man Dengu had ever seen, his large eyes remained unblinking and lost to this world, his matted locks resembling the crown of a king; his entire demeanour reflecting compassion. Dengu was reminded of royalty despite the apparent egolessness of this 'madman'. Suddenly, he felt a sense of peace and serenity as one feels in the company of a saint. He bowed before the man and began to weep, describing his problems to him.

The naked sadhu reassured Dengu, telling him not to seek loans and that the court judgment would be in his favour. The sadhu said he had 'written the judgment through the hands of the judge'. Startled by these words, Dengu had a feeling flooding through his mind, that nothing in the courtroom could hurt him any longer. He paid his respects to the saint and hurried towards the courtroom, each step again rekindling the doubt and despair he had lived with in the past months.

He need not have worried; the judge pronounced the verdict in favour of Dengu. His first feeling was one of relief and, almost immediately after, of love and faith towards the saint. He rushed back to the spot where he had first seen the sadhu. The saint was sitting there, exactly where he had left him, though he was apparently lost in a state of samadhi. Tears of joy flowed from Dengu's eyes as he lay prostrate at the saint's feet. After some time, the saint came out of his state of samadhi and affectionately patted Dengu's head. Dengu instantly decided that this man was his saviour and that he would take him home to stay and would care for him. Faced with Dengu's insistence, the saint reluctantly agreed and accompanied him to his home.

Living with Dengu

Unfortunately, Dengu's family did not approve of his decision to bring the naked man home, and they would insult the sadhu. In addition, the children of the locality would trouble the sadhu, who appeared lost to the world. Children would often stone the saint and chase him into thorny bushes. Dengu would drive them away and tearfully bathe the saint's wounds, but the latter would reassure him that nothing affected him. Once, the saint elaborated on the results of regular Hatha Yoga practices—his body and his blood had changed its form and the children's stones rarely hurt him. And, when they did, healing was rapid.

Despite the harassment by the neighbourhood children and almost hostile behaviour of Dengu's family, the saint stayed on in the house, purely on account of the love and devotion Dengu had for him. And the saint's presence had brought good fortune to the family. However, shortly after Dengu's death, the saint left the house and moved on. His linkage with Dengu was apparently not of this life alone[1].

Fortunately, by now, the saint had become very popular among the masses and was considered a great yogi. This was the result of an incident when he had scolded a group of pandits and had demonstrated the power of the Gayatri Mantra[2] in unravelling the knots of the sacred thread.

When the people in Baradi began to recognise Baba as a saint, the Nag family (the local landlords), were also influenced by his fame. The landlords were powerful people and most of the agricultural land in the vicinity of Baradi belonged to them. It was this family that contributed the land for Baba's ashram. The villagers constructed a simple ashram on this land. The saint donned a simple cloth and began to live there and, from there, his fame spread across to many parts of the world.

The saint's name was Lokenath and he was popularly known as Lokenath Baba or Baba Lokenath. Lokenath in Sanskrit means 'Lord of the World'. Baba is a title commonly used for addressing saints in India, though it also refers to father, grandfather, elderly soul or also a loved one. Since he was a *brahmachari*, he was also referred to as Baba Lokenath Brahmachari. Sometimes, he was called *Baradi ke brahmachari*, or the *brahmachari* living in Baradi.

Birth, Childhood and Growing Up

Lokenath was born in 1730[3] in Chourasi Chakla, a village north of Calcutta. He was the fourth child of his parents, both of whom were deeply religious by nature. His father, Ram Narayan Ghoshal, and mother, Kamla Devi, were simple and pious souls. There is a tradition in India that holds that the act of willingly adopting *sannyasa* results in the salvation of the sannyasi's ancestors' souls. On account of this tradition, Lokenath's father wanted his first child to lead a life of sannyasi, but the mother's love did not allow it to happen. Then came the second child and then the third, yet the mother refused to give in to the father's wishes. Ram Narayan, meanwhile, kept praying he would eventually have one child who could be a sannyasi.

Finally, his prayers bore fruit. When Kamla Devi was expecting their fourth child, she finally gave her consent to Ram Narayan's wishes. After the baby was born, she confessed to her husband that she also felt the same desire to dedicate the child to a life of *sannyasa*. The new born had a radiant appearance and captivating eyes. He was named Lokenath. Since Lokenath's parents had identified him for the life of a sannyasi, they did not put him through any formal education. Instead, they encouraged him to absorb as much as he could of the Hindu scriptures and to keep the company of elders who were well versed in spiritual knowledge.

The parents did not have to try too hard to infuse spirituality into the boy. Lokenath was different from other children. He would spend time alone and would lapse into a deep meditative state and stay like that for hours. His eyes would freeze and his body would become stiff like stone. One of his friends was a girl called Sumitra. She would, at times, sweep and clean the area around Lokenath's meditation spot. Other children would not understand what was happening to the boy. They would often report anxiously to his parents that Lokenath was neither speaking nor opening his eyes even when they pushed him. While the mother would be concerned, Ram Narayan Ghoshal realised at such times that his son had the signs of a great yogi and was well suited for the life of a sannyasi, which he was destined for.

Even as a child, Lokenath would, sometimes, question blind superstitions and beliefs. He, once, encouraged the discriminated castes to participate in worship at the village temple. This created a furore, but Lokenath stuck to his beliefs and argued with his father in support of his views.

The Guru

When Lokenath came of age, his father approached a scholar, Guru Bhagwan Ganguly, and invited him to conduct his son's *yagnapavita samskara* – the sacred thread ceremony[4] – and take charge of the child's spiritual life. Guru Bhagwan Ganguly was a *grihastha*[5] saint, well versed in Vedic, yogic and tantric scriptures. Ram Narayan explained to the saint that he and his wife were keen to see Lokenath as a sannyasi. After hearing Ram Narayan, the yogi probably had an intuition of the child's wisdom and ability. He readily agreed to the proposal[6].

It was the year 1742, and Lokenath was merely twelve years old. Guru Bhagwan conducted the sacred thread ceremony for Lokenath as well as Beni Madhav, a close friend of Lokenath. Traditionally, after the ceremony, the Hindu child puts up a pretence of leaving the house to adopt the life of a sannyasi and is persuaded to return home. However, in this case, the participant in the ceremony, Lokenath, was actually adopting the life of a monk and leaving his home – never to return.

Beni Madhav insisted that he too would accompany Lokenath and renounce material life. While Lokenath's parents had reconciled to their child's eventual parting several years ago, Beni Madhav's insistence came as quite a shock to his parents. However, after much persistence, Beni Madhav's parents' opposition gave way to blessings.

Many people of the village had gathered to witness the ceremony. They had heard the news that the two youngsters were leaving home and adopting *sannyasa*. Some questioned the parents' wisdom in allowing their children to go away and lead such a hard life, while others looked on in awe and reverence at the event as something they would perhaps never witness in their lifetime again.

After the ceremony was over, the monks left the village and set off under the guidance of their teacher, begging for alms on the way. Guru Bhagwan and the two children first travelled towards Calcutta and visited the holy shrine of the Divine Mother at Kalighat[7].

For some days, the three travellers spent their time in Kalighat. Here the young boys found many sadhus with grave expressions and long, matted hair. This was a source of entertainment to the children, and they would trouble these yogis by pulling their locks and beards and running away. When the saints complained to Guru Bhagwan, he told them that he himself was just a householder and that the boys were merely in his custody. He further explained that the boys had adopted a monk's life and, therefore, belonged to the clan of the sadhus themselves. He had no right to intervene in an 'internal' matter. However, he later cautioned the boys against troubling the sadhus. Lokenath replied that he found these sadhus very strange, moving around without cutting their hair, wearing only a loincloth in public and begging for alms. Lokenath and Beni Madhav were still wearing the new dhotis given to them during the thread ceremony. Guru Bhagwan wondered whether the boys had truly understood the gravity of the step they had taken in adopting *sannyasa*. He explained to them that they would also one day be like the sadhus – with loincloths, matted hair and a begging bowl.

Lokenath was quick to understand the guru's words. He realised that he and Beni Madhav had not yet completely severed their ties with their homes, as their parents still sent money for their upkeep in Kalighat. He immediately insisted that they all leave Kalighat, lest their renunciation be affected in any way.

Guru Bhagwan was very pleased with his pupil's sensitivity and decision. The three of them left Kalighat and began to wander around the countryside like itinerant monks. Lokenath would never question his master; his devotion was unqualified and absolute.

Intensification of Sadhana

Lokenath and Beni Madhav now began their spiritual practices under the guidance of Guru Bhagwan. They undertook severe fasts for the purification of the body and the mind. These fasts were combined with Hatha Yoga practices that enabled them to stay without food for long periods. They initially perfected day-long fasts, then progressed gradually to two-day fasts, then three-day fasts, then a week-long fast, and then a fortnight-long fast. Finally, they attempted a month-long fast. Lokenath twice completed such a long fast successfully, while Beni Madhav completed it once.

Serving the Disciples

Guru Bhagwan was an exceptional mentor in terms of providing spiritual guidance to his disciples. He wanted Lokenath and Beni Madhav to single-mindedly devote themselves to their meditations. While the two disciples meditated for long periods, the guru on the other hand completely devoted himself to serving his disciples and ensuring nothing disturbed them.

He would go out to neighbouring villages to beg for alms for the disciples. He would then return and cook for all of them. There were times during the intense fasting and meditations when Guru Bhagwan would prohibit the disciples from moving – even to pass urine or defecate. When they needed to, he would physically move them and clean them. He would also clean the spot where the disciples had relieved themselves while they remained deeply absorbed in their meditation. In the annals of history, such service of disciples has not been recorded elsewhere.

Returning to the Village

There is a practice among monks in India in which sannyasis return to their home after twelve years of observing *sannyasa*. Guru Bhagwan also brought the two young *brahmacharis* to their native village. As the village folk heard of the arrival of Guru Bhagwan and his two disciples, they gathered around and welcomed them. Many came forward to serve the three travellers, one of them was a young widow, Sumitra, who had also been a childhood friend of Lokenath. She began to sincerely serve Lokenath and gradually their friendship was revived, and they spent long hours talking. In a short while, Lokenath began to find it difficult to meditate steadfastly, as his mind would drift to his friend. Her memories would play in his mind. When he realised that this was the play of maya, he began to pester his master to leave, but his guru his master kept postponing the departure. One day, despite Lokenath's passionate plea to leave, the master refused, claiming to be unwell. Lokenath lost his patience with his teacher and chased the latter with a stick, insisting they leave. Guru Bhagwan then relented and the three travellers, once again, resumed their travels. The master subsequently revealed that the period had been a test for Lokenath, who had succeeded in escaping the tentacles of maya.

Facets of the Training

The two pupils had to undergo strict training. Lokenath would, sometimes, complain of ants biting him and disturbing his meditation. One day, he saw his guru putting sugar around his asana. Lokenath then realised that this was an integral part of his training to increase his meditative stability amid noise, insect bites and other such disturbances.

Guru Bhagwan would instruct the disciples according to his amassed knowledge. However, he restrained them from reading any scriptures themselves. Lokenath, once, asked his guru why he did not allow them to read the scriptures, when saints needed to be well versed in them.

Guru Bhagwan told Lokenath that they need not rely on 'borrowed knowledge' from books and that the spiritual practices the two disciples were undergoing would lead them to a state of supreme spontaneous knowledge from within.

After a period of over thirty years of practising Hatha Yoga, Lokenath expressed his desire to learn Raja Yoga, the yoga of advanced meditation. Guru Bhagwan had trained Lokenath in the science of Hatha Yoga – to prepare him physically, mentally and psychically for higher spiritual practices. However, it is believed, he tested Lokenath's proficiency in Hatha Yoga by making the latter cook rice on his thighs. After Lokenath successfully performed this task, Guru Bhagwan began training him in Raja Yoga.

One day, during his meditations, Lokenath saw visions about his previous birth. He recalled his life as Sitanath, a householder yogi who had never married. He described his life and the village to his guru. Guru Bhagwan took the two disciples to the village and verified Lokenath's descriptions – they found everything as described by Lokenath.

Liberation

Lokenath immersed himself in higher meditation practices with single-minded concentration. Guru Bhagwan Ganguly would take care of his disciples, ensuring that nothing would come between them and the object of their meditation. One day, when he was returning from a nearby river, the guru saw light emanating from the cave where Lokenath was meditating. He rushed inside, where he saw the entire cave bathed in holy light. Baba Lokenath had attained liberation, the ultimate aim of the yogi, the most-difficult attainment in all of God's creation. This was the moment that the guru had lived for and had dedicated his life to. Tears of joy streamed down his eyes.

When Lokenath looked around him, it was the gaze of one who had gained complete knowledge. He looked up at his guru, the man who had given him the most precious gift in Creation, with reverence. He realised that he had gone beyond his guru's own achievement, who in this life would never attain the Absolute. It was as if his entire life with the guru flashed before him, as he realised that he had – from the very beginning – always sacrificed his own spiritual progress for the progress of Lokenath, ensuring that he reached the divine summit. The sacrifice was probably because Guru Bhagwan Ganguly had recognised the potential greatness in Lokenath's soul, but such an act of sacrifice is incomparable. The master was now almost 150 years old and his body was approaching its end. Lokenath felt intense pity for his guru for he had yet to attain complete salvation. A stream of tears now flowed down as a mixture of love, reverence and pity.

What a sight it must have been – the master crying in happiness for the disciple's attainment and the disciple crying in pity at the great master's incompleteness. Finally, the master broke the silence and said, 'Lokenath, when I give up this body, I will immediately take birth again, and I will come to you for liberation. You will have to then guide me to it.'

Lokenath nodded while still weeping – for him to conceive separation from the guru was itself difficult; he lay prostrate in devotion at the master's feet. This was probably the only time that the roles of spiritual teacher and student were sought to be consciously reversed.

However, the guru is eternally the guru and the disciple eternally the disciple. Lokenath said, 'I am yours and I shall remain yours. You will work out your own liberation through this body of your disciple. I will be too happy to serve you (in this way).'

Soon after this event, the guru and his disciples went to Kashi. Here, the master gave up his body at Manikarnika ghat, one of the prominent spots on the banks of the holy Ganga. Before doing so, Guru Bhagwan handed over charge of his two disciples to Tailang Swami, a perfect yogi, who was known in Kashi as the 'Living Siva'.

It remained a matter of speculation as to which one of Lokenath Baba's disciples was the reincarnation of Guru Bhagwan Ganguly. Most disciples who pondered over the question considered Rajnikant Brahmachari, Brahmananda Bharati and Ramkumar Chakraborty to be the possible individuals.

Moving On

After Guru Bhagwan's passing away, Lokenath and Beni Madhav continued their travels along with Tailang Swami. The three yogis travelled across Afghanistan, Persia, the Arabian Peninsula and Israel/Palestine, before returning to India and moving to the Himalayas.

Lokenath and Beni Madhav decided to move to the higher altitude of the Himalayas. They spent a few years in Badrikashram, preparing their bodies for the cold, snowy environment in the upper reaches of the Himalayas. Tailang Swami, who also wanted to accompany them in their journey, joined them. They then waited another year, until Tailang Swami was ready, and all of them finally crossed over to Tibet and went on to Siberia, before returning to India via China.

Tailang Swami advised Lokenath Baba to return to the plains and begin the mission he had come to perform in the world. After travelling together for many months, Beni Madhav decided to move on to Assam to visit the holy shrine of Ma Kamakhya[8]. Lokenath Baba and Beni Madhav then parted ways, but Baba promised to bless his friend in his *sookshma deha*[9] whenever the latter invoked his presence. Baba finally moved on to Baradi, where he eventually settled in his ashram.

The Nag Family

Once, a dispute arose between the Nag family – the landlords of Baradi – and the farmers who cultivated their land, as they refused to pay the contractual portion of the produce. This was a major cause of concern for the family. Soon, the elders in the family decided to seek Baba's advice in this matter, but one of the younger landlords adamantly asked, 'Why should we ask Baba? The land rights are ours.' However, the elders prevailed and the Nags went to meet Baba. To their surprise, the yogi's initial reaction was, 'Why should you ask me? The land rights are yours.' They realised that Baba was omniscient and knew of their conversation. They pleaded with him to sort out the issue. Baba told them not to take a violent stand. He also said they could take their dues from his Baradi ashram if they so desired. The landlords, unfortunately, took a decision against his advice. They hired thugs and used force against the farmers, leaving one seriously injured. Things went against the landlords, and criminal proceedings were initiated against them.

Now, the landlords felt they had got into trouble by ignoring the advice of a realised saint, so they approached Baba again. This time, he was reluctant to advise them, as they had ignored it initially, but relented in the face of their pleas. He scolded them for their violent activities. He told them they must not appoint a lawyer and must take care of the grievously injured farmer. Once again, the landlords rejected his advice, since they felt that they would get into deeper trouble if they did not hire a lawyer. Events took a turn for the worse when, a few days later, the injured farmer died and murder charges were now levelled against the landlords.

Now the landlords had no option but to again seek the saint's advice. They begged him to forgive their wrongs and save them. He was livid to hear about the incidents but agreed to have them rescued. This time, he asked each member of the family to contribute a certain amount to compensate the victim's family. He asked them to return to him on the day of the verdict. On that day, when they came to meet him, he assured them that they wouldn't face the hardships, as he had written the verdict in their favour. The landlords could not believe his words but, in a short while, the news of their acquittal reached them. This episode increased their faith and devotion towards the saint.

On another occasion, a member of the Nag family was returning to his village in a boat. It was night and a violent storm broke out. The boat began to rock dangerously and the landlord was certain that he would die. He began to fervently pray to God and, in a short while, he saw the form of Baba in the boat. Soon thereafter, he felt a strong supernatural power controlling the storm. He reached home safe and sound.

Over time, the family became committed devotees of Baba.

Lokenath's *Leelas*

For over half a century that Baba stayed in Baradi, he guided innumerable seekers, distributing the wealth he had earned over many years of austerities. Baba lovingly nurtured devotees and sculpted the consciousness of disciples. Some incidents relating to his life as a guru are captured in the following paragraphs.

The Youths and the Lion

Baba lived in a time of great socio-religious renaissance in India, and many organisations were working towards ridding the society of mindless rituals and superstitions. Members of such groups used to aggressively voice their opinion on certain established Hindu customs in public. Some young members of such organisations took to attacking sadhus, since they believed that most of them were frauds. They also planned an attack on Lokenath Baba and, one night, they sneaked into the ashram with sticks and other weapons and hid outside Baba's room. They were waiting for Baba to come out to attack him.

In those days, the ashram was situated in a densely forested area, and many wild animals would also stray into it. To the horror of the youths, they saw a lion quite close to where they were walking in their direction. They ran into a room to take refuge. They then saw Lokenath Baba walking out of his room in the direction of the lion. They thought the lion would complete the work they had come for. To their amazement, when Baba approached it, it lay prostrate on the ground, as if in reverence, while Baba patted its head. Then he spoke to it telling it not to roam in the vicinity of the ashram because it could frighten the inmates. The lion lay at Baba's feet for some time, enjoying Baba's affectionate patting. Then it rose, turned away, and ran into the forest.

The youths were relieved to see the lion go. They now realised that Baba was truly a realised saint, who was compassionate towards all beings and could communicate with all. The youths then emerged from hiding and went to Baba, fell at his feet and confessed their mistake. Baba forgave them and advised them not to roam around in night in these areas, as wild animals could attack them. He also asked them to give up their violent ways and explore true spirituality.

Feeding Ants

Baba's spirit of compassion encompassed all life, not merely human beings. Once, when a disciple wanted to enter his hut, he found it locked from inside and Baba called out, 'Hold on, I'm feeding my family.' After some time when the door opened, the disciple saw a stream of ants trickling out of a corner. Baba had been feeding them; he did not want to risk any of his disciples trampling them to death.

The Sound of Creation

Baba identified with all beings in the cosmos. Once, a pandit came to the ashram and was discussing spiritual topics with Baba when they were disturbed by the harsh and persistent sound of a crow crowing. The pandit kept trying to chase the bird away but Baba stopped the man and, to his surprise, Baba compared the crow's sound with the man's speech.

The Word of the Saint

There is a belief in India, that the words of a realised saint are truth itself. It is also believed that the orders of the saint should be followed and those who ignore it come to grief. Ishwar Chandra Ghosh, a devotee, stayed for some time in Baba's ashram. When he was leaving, the saint advised him to take a guide up to the river bank, where Ishwar's boat was waiting. Ishwar declined, as the river bank was just a short distance away, across the field. However, Ishwar surprisingly ended up losing his way that night and found himself going deeper and deeper into the forest. Eventually, he spent the night in the middle of the forest. In the morning, some villagers guided him back to the ashram.

When Baba saw him, he smiled and said, 'I told you last night to take a guide, but you refused and went deep into the forest. Had I not been present with you (in a subtle form), you would not even be here today.'

Once, a group of devotees from Dhaka came to Baba's ashram to seek his blessings. It was peak summer time and they were finding it tough to begin their journey back home, as Dhaka was roughly twenty miles away. The devotees could not undertake the journey on foot in the scorching sun. Baba understood their plight, yet he asked them to return. As they were about to take their leave, clouds appeared in the sky and the weather suddenly became conducive for walking. The devotees realised that the cloud formation was an outcome of Baba's grace, and they asked him till when the clouds would stay. He assured them that the weather would remain pleasant throughout their journey.

The group walked back to Dhaka and, all the while, the cloud cover remained. As they reached, the scorching sun came out again.

Freedom from the Law

A man was once caught in legal problems. He pleaded Baba to save him — claiming to be innocent, while he was not really so. The saint assured him he would be saved and no harm would come to him. However, someone else warned him that if he got Baba's grace by lying to him, he would eventually get into trouble. The man, therefore, confessed everything to Baba and asked for forgiveness. The saint responded, 'Now that you have confessed, will you do what I advise you?' The man agreed. Baba told him to confess his crime before the judge as well. Somewhat worried, the man agreed and did as was ordered by the saint – going against the advice of his lawyer. Strangely, the judge rejected the confession and the man was acquitted.

In another case, one Niranjan Roy was in prison, expecting a death sentence or at least life imprisonment. He had never seen Baba but had heard of him. He prayed fervently for Baba's grace. In a short while, he saw a luminescent figure in the cell; it was the great yogi himself. He assured the anxious man that the verdict won't go against him. The next morning, Niranjan Roy was relieved to hear the news of his acquittal.

Khichri for Sixty

Baba Lokenath, once, asked Gwalini Ma, the ashram administrator, to cook khichri for some visitors. However, when she began to gather material to cook, Baba ordered her to prepare the khichri for over sixty people. Nobody could understand why the saint wanted to waste so much food, when there were just a few visitors. Some thought Baba did not have a sense of proportion in material affairs. One disciple almost sarcastically commented, 'Who will eat so much khichri?'

However, Baba's word was law, and the khichri had to be prepared. Just as it was being cooked, a large group of devotees suddenly appeared unannounced at the ashram gates. They had travelled a long distance and were hungry. They were delighted to find hot khichri waiting for them. Just at this point, Baba remarked in the same tone, 'Who will eat so much khichri?'

The erring disciple realised his mistake and apologised.

Curing the Sick

Many people approached Baba Lokenath to cure diseases that were considered incurable at that time. Baba empathised deeply with the people who flocked to his doorstep, but held back dispensing an immediate cure, as he would test the persistence and devotion of the sufferer.

Sitanath Das, a rich man from Calcutta, had suffered a stroke, leaving him paralysed. As his health deteriorated further, he decided to surrender himself at Baba's feet. He was brought to the ashram and his bed was placed outside Baba's hut. He was determined to die at the feet of a yogi, if it had to be. Baba appeared oblivious of Sitanath's presence. Sitanath persistently continued to remain where he lay. However, after two-and-a-half days, in the early hours of the morning, Baba walked up to Sitanath, called him by his name and asked him to rise. Within a few minutes, Sitanath found himself miraculously cured. Baba told Sitanath that his heart had bled for him when he was lying outside his room. However, he now assured Sitanath that his health would be restored, and that he could continue to enjoy the rest of his life with a healthy body.

A Muslim devotee had once approached Baba asking for help for his small daughter. The girl was blind and he was hoping Baba could cure her. Baba affectionately stroked the girl's head and eyes and then he asked them to return the next day. The following day, when the man was approaching the ashram, the little girl began to describe the topography. The devotee realised that his daughter's eyesight had been restored due to Baba's grace.

Above Sectarianism

Baba Lokenath didn't believe in sectarian principles. He loved people of all communities and they, in turn, loved and respected his egalitarian outlook. In Baradi, Muslims had given up cow slaughter as a mark of respect for the saint, who had compassion for all living beings. Muslims would treat Baba with deep reverence and, even to this day, they are known to light lamps in his ashram and pray to him to fulfil their desires.

Baba was also well versed in *Koran*, just as he knew the *Gita* and other great spiritual books. Nobody questioned the source of his knowledge, as those in his presence were awed by his apparent spiritual stature. He, once, mentioned that he had travelled to Mecca thrice. He elaborated that Guru Bhagwan had accompanied him on one of the visits and that he had been treated with great respect in the holy city.

Divine Eyes

Baba had large unblinking divine eyes and anyone who saw him was captivated by them. On many occasions, his eyes would be open, but he would be lost in a deep, meditative state. But, the shape, characteristics and power of his eyes were divine.

Divinity of the Eyes: Saint's Recognition

Once, Baba's devotee went to attend the Maha Kumbh Mela in Allahabad[10]. On this particular occasion, a great saint who seldom came down from the Himalayas was also present. It was rare to meet such an enlightened soul. Baba's devotee, along with other people, decided to meet this saint, as it was a lifetime opportunity for them. Baba's devotee was also eager to meet the yogi, as his guru always encouraged his disciples to seek the company of saints. The next day, he reached the spot where the great yogi from the Himalayas was giving his blessings to the people. There was a huge rush and the devotee felt it would be impossible to see the saint, but instinct kept him going and soon he found himself in front of the Himalayan yogi.

The devotee bowed before the saint and Lokenath Baba's photograph dropped from his pocket. The saint reached out and lifted the photograph and exclaimed in a state of divine ecstasy: 'Who is this? What divine eyes!…It is rare indeed that such a great saint has come down from the Himalayas.' The devotee was thrilled to hear such praise for his guru.

Power of the Eyes: Courtroom Witness

On another occasion, Baba Lokenath was called as a witness to a court hearing because he had seen a crime in the vicinity of the ashram. His testimony would have resulted in the conviction of the defendant, whose lawyers were therefore trying to find a fault in Baba's account[11]. They challenged the fact that he could have clearly seen the alleged crime from such a great distance. Baba gently told them that his eyesight was very powerful; he then turned his gaze outside the courtroom and pointed towards a tree that was far away.

He asked the lawyers, 'Can you see that tree? Do you think I can see that tree clearly?'

Baba went on to describe the intricate details of the tree and its surrounding area. He also described how some ants were climbing up the tree in three streams. Everyone in the court room was stunned to hear his words. The judge then deputed a few people to verify Baba's description. Those people came back soon and testified that the it was correct. The case was finally decided against the defendant.

Baba and Sri Vijaykrishna Goswami

Sri Vijaykrishna Goswami—also known as Bejoy Krishna Goswami or Goswamiji—was a prominent saint whose fame had spread across India. He had initially been involved in the Brahmo Samaj Movement, where he was a preacher, but gradually, broke away from the organisation. He went on to become a great guru of yoga and spirituality and had many ashrams in the country.

Once, Goswamiji was meditating in a forest and was lost to the external world. He was completely unaware of the fact that a fire had broken out in the forest and, by the time he emerged from his meditation, it had turned into a blazing inferno. It seemed as if death was certainly on the cards, but before he could collect his thoughts and figure out what to do, a tall saint strode boldly through the blaze towards him. The saint had matted hair tied on the top of his head in a knot. He effortlessly picked up Goswamiji in his arms and carried him out of the blaze unhurt. Goswamiji did not recognise the saint and could not understand how he had appeared miraculously and just as he was wondering who this saviour was, the saint disappeared as suddenly as he had appeared.

However, the incident had left an indelible imprint on his mind. Many years later, he visited Baba Lokenath in his ashram and recognised him as the saviour – the one who he was indebted to.

In fact, the meeting in 1887 of the two saints in Baradi was a historic one. When Goswamiji saw Baba, he went into a trance and exclaimed that he saw the latter as the Lord of the universe. Goswamiji fell at Baba Lokenath's feet, who lifted and embraced him. Devotees saw a light emerging from Baba's eyes and entering Goswamiji's eyes, and Goswamiji behaved like an intoxicated individual for some time. Baba always addressed Goswamiji as Jiwan Krishna (the living embodiment of Lord Krishna), signifying the latter's high level of spiritual attainment.

CR ED

Sri Kuladananda Brahmachari, a disciple of Sri Vijaykrishna Goswami has written about Baba Lokenath in *Sri Sri Sadguru Sanga*, a biographical account of his own guru. He has mentioned that Goswamiji would often go into a spiritual rapture and would call out to some of the glorious spiritual masters he knew. One of the saints whose name he regularly recalled in his spiritual moods was *Baradi ke brahmachari*. Kuladananda and his two brothers, who were also devotees of Goswamiji, heard this name so often that they were intrigued and hence developed a desire to meet the *brahmachari*.

Goswamiji encouraged them to meet Baba, and also told them not to ask him any questions – he would guide them without their doing so. The brothers set off and reached Baradi late at night. Baba met them lovingly and it appeared he had been expecting them, as he had ordered the attendants to keep the ashram gates open well beyond the normal time. After inquiring about their guru's well-being, he gave them insightful spiritual advice. The advice given to each brother was different, and they realised many years later that the advice had great relevance in their life and reflected Baba's omniscient nature.

ଓଃ ଃ୦

Baba Lokenath had great affection for Goswamiji and also had a special liking for the latter's disciples. While Goswamiji always spoke reverentially about Baba, many of Goswamiji's devotees were disappointed to find Baba sometimes criticising their guru and belittling his spiritual attainments in front of them. Once, he vehemently abused Goswamiji's attainments and a devotee, Sridhar, ran towards him with a stick intending to attack him. Baba Lokenath's disciples restrained Sridhar, but this was the love for the guru that Baba wanted to see. Baba embraced Sridhar and explained that he criticised Goswamiji to confuse the disciples. Baba Lokenath also mentioned that Goswamiji was distributing yogic attainments to everyone and his intentions were to ensure that only true disciples received these treasures. Sridhar, then, had a spiritual vision of Goswamiji in place of Baba Lokenath, which showed him the unity between the two saints.

ଓଃ ଃ୦

Once, Goswamiji fell ill and his health kept deteriorating till eventually he was on deathbed in Darbhanga. Goswamiji's disciples did not know who to turn to, in that hour of crisis, but some of them had implicit faith in Baba Lokenath's capabilities. One of Goswamiji's disciples, Shyamacharan Bakshi, went to see Baba Lokenath and earnestly requested him to save his guru's life. Baba was always pleased to see devotion to the guru, but wanted to test Shyamacharan. At first, he asked Shyamacharan what he would do for his guru.

Shyamacharan instantly replied that Baba should take his life but save his guru. Baba persisted and said, 'So what if Goswamiji is going? I am here and I promise to look after all of you.'

Now Shyamacharan adamantly replied, 'We don't want you, we want Goswamiji. Please save his life.'

Baba was happy to see such single-minded devotion towards the master. Satisfied with Shyamacharan's reply, he immediately withdrew into a meditative state. When he returned to consciousness, he indicated that the disciples should wait for the following Tuesday to find out whether their guru would recover. At around the same time, Yogjiwan, Goswamiji's son, had a vision of Baba. Baba Lokenath assured him that he was on his way to Darbhanga to save Goswamiji's life.

On the following Tuesday, some of Goswamiji's relatives and disciples saw Baba's form beside Goswamiji's bed. Goswamiji's condition began to improve, gradually he regained his health. Goswamiji later mentioned to his disciples that he did not want to retain his body and was planning to 'move on', but Baba had appeared before him and had thrice forcibly brought him back to life and, the third time, Goswamiji relented.

The Chosen Few

Baba was a living embodiment of divinity to thousands of devotees and is still worshipped as such. A handful of devotees managed to imbibe the divinity and transform themselves into perfect instruments for the guru to distribute his grace to millions.

Gwalini Ma

Kamala, an elderly woman, took a vow that she would donate cow's milk to Baba if her barren cow gave birth. As soon as the cow gave birth to a calf, Kamala approached Baba with an offering of cow's milk. Normally, Baba would not rise to receive anyone but, in this case, he got up from his asana and greeted her. Baba Lokenath addressed her as his mother and asked her if she had brought milk for him and also how she could have stayed away from her son for so long. Kamala spontaneously felt maternal love for the yogi and embraced him. She shifted to the ashram and over time, Baba handed over the entire responsibility of the administration to her. Baba called her Gwalini Ma, as she used to previously support herself by selling cow milk. She was one of the most steadfast of Baba's devotees, having observed him from close quarters and being a witness to both miracle and grace.

Rajani Brahmachari

Sometimes, it so happens that in the last years of an individual's life, he meets dear people. It was certainly so with Rajani Brahmachari, who met Baba merely three years prior to the latter's *mahasamadhi*. During Rajani's first visit, he noticed a deep fragrance emanating from Baba's body – it was an enchanting divine fragrance[12]. He was entranced by the saint's large, unblinking eyes, and when he saw him lapse into the transcendental state of samadhi, he was completely inspired by Baba and became a lifelong devotee.

Rajani had always been of a spiritual bent. In their quest for spirituality, he and his wife had risen above the normal sexual relations between a man and a woman. His wife was no longer alive when Rajani approached Baba Lokenath. Due to Baba's grace and, by virtue of his intense sadhana, Rajani experienced a rapid transformation from within.

In India, it is considered impolite to smoke or drink in the presence of elderly people, particularly gurus and saints. Rajani was fond of smoking and, once, when he was with Baba, he thrice felt the urge to smoke. Each time the urge surfaced, Baba asked him to prepare tobacco and offer it to him. After tasting the tobacco, Baba would then offer it back to Rajani and would compel the latter to smoke it in front of him. The third time this happened, Rajani's habit of smoking disappeared forever.

Once, Baba Lokenath mentioned to Abhaya Charan, another disciple, that he and Rajani were one and the same. Hearing so much about Rajani made others curious – they wanted to see him. However, Baba soon began to criticise Rajani, accusing him of being a fake who was glorifying himself. Rajani did not react to Baba's words and, as a result, he progressed even further and more rapidly in his sadhana. It emerged eventually that Baba was only testing Rajani's sensitivity to criticism and devotion to the guru.

Finally, Baba recommended Rajani to sever all ties with the world and settle in a hut in a secluded place devoting himself entirely to meditation. Rajani eventually created his own ashram near Dhaka and went on to become a famous guru.

Janakinath Brahmachari

Janaki was a young boy whose parents had left him in a sick state in Baba's ashram in Baradi, hoping the saint would cure him, when doctors had given up hope. Baba commanded Janaki to perform service in the ashram. Over the next few days, Janaki perceived some improvement in his condition. He would wash Baba's feet and drink that water and smear the dust from the saint's feet all over his body – that was his cure. Eventually, he began to learn the science of yoga from Baba Lokenath and regained complete health. However, now that he had experienced a complete inner transformation, he refused to return to his family. He decided to dedicate his entire life to the service of Baba and the ashram. One day, Baba expressed his wish – Janaki must take over the charge of the ashram after the former's death. He assured him that he himself would support Janaki in the work. Baba lived up to his words and Janaki would find some money, hidden, every day in the ashram till the end of his life. Janaki went on to become a great *sadguru* in his own right and, after he took samadhi in 1912, a temple was built over the spot where he was buried, next to Baba Lokenath's samadhi.

Brahmananda Bharati

Tarakanta Ganguly, a lawyer, had heard about Baba through Sri Vijaykrishna Goswami. He along with his brothers went to see the great yogi. Baba instructed each brother in accordance with what was most suitable for him. Tarakanta expressed his distress at being stuck in the web of worldliness and the saint advised him to transcend it by worshipping the supreme principle underlying it. Over time, Tarakanta became a dear devotee of Baba – he initiated him into the path of yoga and gave him the name of Brahmananda Bharati. After Baba attained *mahasamadhi*, Brahmananda gave up his profession and left his home. He decided to settle in Kashi to further his quest for self-realisation. In his later years, he wrote a biography of Lokenath Baba in Bengali, entitled *Siddha Jivani* (Life of a Siddha or a Life of Perfection).

Ramkumar Chakraborty

Ramkumar Chakraborty was born in Baradi and lived the life of a householder. From the time he came in contact with Lokenath Baba, he began to yearn for deeper spiritual fulfilment. After fulfilling his family responsibilities, he surrendered himself completely at Baba's feet and the master took special care in guiding Ramkumar on the spiritual path. According to Baba's direction, Ramkumar travelled the country as a wandering monk, immersed in meditation. Before he left Baradi, he met Baba, who assured him that he would call Ramkumar to himself when the time came.

A few days before giving up his body, Baba summoned Ramkumar to Baradi. When Ramkumar reached the ashram, he spent some time in private communion with the saint. Baba disclosed his plan of leaving his body to Ramkumar and instructed the latter to perform his last rites. After Baba passed away, Ramkumar carried out the saint's wishes and then left for Kashi and took *mahasamadhi* there.

Giving up the Mortal Frame

Baba had crossed the age of 160. He decided the time had come to leave the mortal body. His health had been deteriorating ever since he had taken upon himself a devotee's tuberculosis.

Baba announced to his disciples that he was preparing to leave the body, and that he had fixed the date of his departure as 2 June 1890. The news sent waves of despair among the community of disciples and many of them beseeched Baba to give up his plan. Baba gently reassured them, reminding them not to confuse him with his body, and promised that he would always be with them in times of danger and distress.

The day that Baba had fixed for taking samadhi arrived, and devotees turned up in large numbers to pay their final respects to the saint who had touched their lives in so many ways. Baba again reminded his disciples that he was merely leaving his physical body, and repeated his promise of always protecting his disciples – his children. He made sure everyone who came to the ashram that day was well fed.

And then, consciously, he withdrew his spirit from the body, and continued his journey on the eternal plane. For the disciples, it seemed like Baba's normal samadhi, with unblinking eyes wide open. But this time, the samadhi did not end, and the disciples realised that the saint was indeed no more in body.

Despite Baba's assurance, most disciples wept bitterly, as on so many occasions he had saved them, guided them and loved them. Gwalini Ma, who had treated him as her own child, wept uncontrollably and repeatedly prayed for him to return to his body. But Baba had left his body and 'this samadhi was final'.

Devotees then placed his body under a large *bael* tree in the ashram and, subsequently, consigned it to the funeral pyre. Devotees from all over placed garlands and contributed ghee and sandalwood. Baba's dear devotee, Ramkumar, performed the last rites.

Living on

To this date, devotees from various parts of the world travel to Baradi to pay their respects at his ashram where Baba breathed his last. As he had promised his devotees, the limitations of the body did not apply to Lokenath Baba. His grace continues to bless those who look unto him.

In May 1941, Baba Lokenath appeared before the renowned saint Anandamayi Ma while she was in her ashram in Raipur. In 1978, years after he had breathed his last, Baba Lokenath appeared before Baba Shuddhananda Brahmachari and waved his hand around in a gesture indicating that Swami Shuddhananda should spread his word around the world. Swami Shuddhananda has since been working tirelessly to spread Baba's message and has set up a social service organisation for the upliftment of the poor.

As Baradi has become a pilgrimage spot, so has Chourasi Chakla, the birthplace of Baba. Devotees have erected an ashram in Chourasi Chakla as well. In one particular incident, some people had travelled to visit Baba's birthplace. A complete stranger miraculously directed them to the exact spot where he was born. It is claimed that Baba himself guided them to the spot and assured them that it was a very holy spot. There are reports that people regain health by consuming the dust of that place. Cancer, toothaches, brain tumour – no disease is considered incurable at Chourasi Chakla[13].

Those whose consciousness is of a very high order can perceive Baba, though he can manifest himself to whoever he wants. And, I firmly believe anyone can experience his grace if they have even a little yearning in their hearts[14].

CR SO

Endnotes

1. It is believed that the guru follows the disciple, life after life, until he ensures his liberation. Some believe that even if the guru exits the orbit of evolution, or does not take birth when the disciple is born, he ensures that the latter finds a master who can guide the aspirant to the state of liberation. However, the kind of loving service that Dengu provided to the saint is rare and is usually born of a karmic connection from a past life.

2. The Gayatri Mantra is one of the foremost mantras in Hinduism; it is said to inspire wisdom and awaken the life force or prana. It is both a mantra and a prayer. It is found in the Vedas and is believed that if it is chanted right, a knotted thread will open by itself; this is a result of the mantra's power to open 'knots', both psychic as well as phenomenal.

3. Vishwanath Mukherji, in *Bharat ke Mahan Yogi*, mentions that Baba was born in 1731; here we rely on the authoritative biography written by Swami Shuddhananda Brahmachari.

4. Hindu religious texts prescribe sixteen Vedic ceremonies or sacraments to be carried out during the life of an individual – the sacred thread ceremony is one of them. These ceremonies are called samskaras (not to be confused with karma *sanskaras* or impressions created in the past; though the sacraments seek to infuse good karma into the participant of the sacrament).

5. *Grihastha* saints are those who lead a householder's life, in contrast to those who embrace monkhood.

6. Another source mentions that Guru Bhagwan Ganguly had blessed the boy when still a small child. The scholar had predicted that the child would be a great yogi. He had further stated that when the boy would turn eleven, the former would personally perform the sacred thread ceremony and guide the young aspirant to a life of *sannyasa*.

7. Kalighat – literally, 'the bathing area on the river bank dedicated to the goddess Kali' – is one of the prominent temples of India devoted to the Divine Mother. According to Hindu mythology, Siva was roaming the world with the dead body of his beloved wife, Sati (the original incarnation of the Divine Mother), on his shoulders. The gods beseeched Vishnu to destroy her body in order to help Siva overcome his loss. Lord Vishnu used his discus to destroy her body, which was cut into sixty-three parts, that fell off in different parts of the Indian subcontinent. Each place became a place of pilgrimage for devotees of the Goddess. It is believed that the toes of the Goddess fell off at Kalighat.

8. The Kamakhya temple is a Shakti temple in Guwahati in Assam. It is the most important pilgrimage destination for tantric worshipers of the Divine Mother.

9. The *sookshma deha*, or *sookshma sharir*, is the subtle body. Great yogis can travel hundreds of miles in this state while their physical body remains in one place.

10. The Kumbha Mela is held by rotation in four cities considered holy by Hindus: Allahabad (also called Prayag or Triveni), Haridwar, Ujjain and Nashik, based on the zodiac positions of Sun and Jupiter. The Maha Kumbh is held once every twelve years and, every four years, a mini Kumbha Mela is also organised by rotation in these four cities. Many people from across the country, flock to these cities to participate in the mela. According to Hindu mythology, these were the four spots where amrit (ambrosia) spilled and fell from a pot being carried by celestial beings who were being chased by demons.

11. In this, they were assisted by Baba who, in response to the questioning, also told the court that his age was close to 150 years. To the court, such a reply was absurd and his testimony, therefore, came under suspicion.

12. It is said that fragrance emanates from the lotuses within the human body of enlightened yogis or sometimes even partially enlightened and purified beings. So many such fragrances sometimes emanated from the body of the great saint Vishuddhananda Paramhansa that he was also known as Gandha Baba (the Baba of fragrances). Once, I was in the presence of a saint – an advanced yogi and a devotee. Every once in a while, he closed his eyes, and tears of devotion filled them and rolled down his cheeks. At the same time, the whole room would fill up with a deep divine fragrance, something like a lotus or like the sea.

13. The popularly believed location of Chakla is in the Barasat district of West Bengal. However, Haripada Bhowmick's *Mahavishwa Key Lokenath* places the location of Chourasi Chakla as the village Kachua, in the Basirhat sub-division of the North 24 Parganas district.

14. I had read about Baba and I respected him as one of the most pure and inspirational saints in the world. Once, in 2001, when I was going through difficult times, I prayed to him, asking him whether he existed and whether saints existed, and why I should be in my predicament if they did indeed exist. I remember having tears in my eyes. Due to unforeseen circumstances, I was forced to get a lift to my office in a stranger's car. That day, I was surprised to see, on the car's dashboard, a statuette of Lokenath Baba. Never before had I come across photos of Baba outside Kolkata (where his devotees abound), and I had never (not even in Kolkata), seen his statuette. That was the only time I have ever seen a statuette of Baba. I perceived it to be Baba's way of communicating that he did indeed exist. I am certain that had my heart been pure or my consciousness evolved, he would have manifested himself in body before me.

MAHAYOGI GAMBHIRNATH
(Unknown-1917)

Shāntam dāntam samdrishtiyutam maunavātam nirīham
Swātmākrīdam nijasukhabhujām saumyagambhīrmūrtim
Shaktyādhāram paramakārudam jīvakalyānadīksham
Vande devam bhavabhayahāram sadgurūnām varishtham

He who is an embodiment of peace, is self-controlled, endowed with
equanimity of vision,
And who resides in silence and simplicity;
The one absorbed in the bliss of the play of the self,
The one who is of peaceful and pleasing appearance and is an
embodiment of silent grandeur –
The basis of shakti, ultimately compassionate,
The giver of blessings to all beings,
I sing praises to the great *sadguru* (Mahayogi Gambhirnath),
The Lord who overcomes the challenges in the lives of devotees.

Mahayogi Gambhirnath

Munni Kurmi was worried about his brother Akku, whose health was deteriorating rapidly. Relatives had given up hope that he would ever recover and felt that death was close. Munni and Akku were very close to each other. The patient realised that these were his last hours and expressed a desire to see his guru — a saint whom the brothers had served when he had stayed and meditated close to their hometown, Gaya. They used to look after the saint when he was immersed in deep sadhana and would meditate all day in a deserted mountain cave. Munni hoped that the saint would come and bless his dying brother.

Munni hurried to Gorakhpur, where the saint now was, hundreds of miles away from Gaya, and begged him to meet Akku in his final moments. All his life, this saint had abided by a principle that he would never visit the house of a householder, but this family was particularly special and close to him. They were extremely poor and simple, their only wealth in the world being the service they had rendered to this saint. For once in his life, the saint made an exception to his rule and accompanied his disciple to Gaya.

Unfortunately, before they arrived, Akku had breathed his last — his body was surrounded by grieving relatives. Munni was crestfallen. He could not believe that his brother had passed away, and that too when his guru was on the way to meet him. 'If only Akku had lived for a few hours more,' Munni thought, 'he would have died in peace.'

Only the guru was unmoved – he remained in the detached and deeply contemplative mood he was always known to be in. Ever so gently, he sat by Akku's corpse and began to stroke the body more lovingly than even a mother would. Within a short spell of time, the 'dead' body began to stir and showed signs of life. And to everyone's amazement, in a short while, Akku sat up, alive and completely healthy.

The saint, once again, relapsed into his detached mood and was lost to the world. While everyone had witnessed a miracle, the saint behaved as though nothing had happened, and, as if, whatever had happened had nothing to do with him. A short while later he left for his ashram in Gorakhpur. He would never discuss this incident, preferring instead to maintain a studied silence.

Detachment from the Miracle

On the path of yoga, aspirants routinely attain powers that can be used to perform miracles, but the performance of the miracle can lead to their spiritual downfall as well. Very rarely does one encounter an accomplished saint who is endowed with such complete powers and is yet completely devoid of either the desire to perform a miracle or take pride in such powers. This saint was completely detached from the act of executing miracles – he was Mahayogi Gambhirnath, saint of the Nath Sampradaya[1], and perhaps the most famous ever in the sect after the Nav Naths[2].

His simplicity deceived most people. It was said by Varadakant Bandopadhyaya that by seeing the simple manner in which he interacted with people, it was difficult to imagine that he was such an accomplished yogi.

Let us step back to the early years of his life and travel with him on his journey to spiritual fulfilment.

The Early Years

It is said that the spirit of renunciation and the thirst for spirituality rarely sprout in the heart of the young. When they do, it is either as a result of deep emotional hurt or the pangs of being insulted. Sometimes, this happens during a period of great material or physical difficulty, when the youth is exposed to the impermanence of the world. Yet, in some cases, they arise with the experience of a miracle or an induced spiritual experience. In the rarest of rare cases is one possessed by a burning spirit of renunciation that is spontaneous and is not sparked by any of the reasons mentioned above. Yogiraj Gambhirnath was one such rare case. Not much is known about his early days. When devotees and disciples asked him about his earlier life, he would dismiss their requests, asking what is the use of engaging in unnecessary gossip? He never even revealed his childhood name to his disciples.

What is, however, known is that he hailed from a province of Jammu and Kashmir. He was born in the lap of luxury and his family had, within reason, everything the material world considered desirable. He was physically fit, of attractive appearance and intelligent. Yet, for some reason since his childhood days, he would be lost in contemplation. Within himself, Gambhirnath, as a youth, felt a burning desire for a spiritual completeness, a thirst for true knowledge and a passion for a dispassionate state.

When such a fire burns within the heart of a man, it is inevitable that others around him get a glimpse of it. However, the youth ensured that nobody he interacted with, understood the storm that was raging within him. Neither in his sense of dress nor in his energy in carrying out daily activities, or in his conversations, did Gambhirnath let it appear that he would one day leave the materialistic world for a much higher purpose. The only worldly activity that really interested him was music; proficient in playing the sitar, he would sing melodious bhajans for long spells.

But, the storm raging within the young man kept deepening his spirit of detachment. He would prefer to spend his free time sitting in deep contemplation in deserted spots. The local graveyard became his favourite place, as it reminded him of the impermanence of life. Moreover, many sannyasis and yogis travelling through those parts would camp close to the graveyard, and the youth would serve them and engage in conversations on esoteric spiritual topics. However, every spiritual aspirant needs a guru in some form or the other, who will guide him into the realm of light and knowledge, and the young man had begun to yearn for such a guide.

Once, a great saint came to his village and camped close to the graveyard. He belonged to the Nath Sampradaya and appeared to be an accomplished yogi. He radiated divine energy. Word spread about this yogi and large crowds were drawn to him. Whenever he was not surrounded by villagers and had the time, he would be lost in a meditative state. The yogi stayed for close to a month in the village, during which time, the youth frequently interacted with him. He had the ability to answer most of the spiritual questions of the young man. Their interactions quenched some of the youth's thirst but, at the same time, also whetted his spiritual appetite.

One day, the young man begged the yogi to accept him as a disciple. The latter had already realised the potential of the youth, but he apologetically told him that he was not the guru destined for him. Instead, he instructed him to go to the Gorakhnath ashram at Gorakhpur, where the great yogi Gopalnath was the head priest. He told the youth to approach him to be his guru. He blessed the boy and prophesied he would one day be a great yogi. The next day, the villagers learnt that the wandering yogi had left the village and was nowhere to be seen. It was as though he had come to direct the youth to his spiritual destiny.

Guru Gorakhnath, the crown jewel of the Nath Sampradaya, has written:

Āpā bhanjibā, satgurū shojibā, jôg panth nā kariba helā
Phiri phiri mānisha janam na paib, kar ley siddha purush sū mélā

Destroy the ego, and search for the True Guru;
do not ignore the path of yoga.
One does not get the human body time and again,
(Now that you have it) seek out and meet realised saints.

It did not take long for the young man to make up his mind. In a short while, he set off for Gorakhpur, hundreds of miles from his home.

In the Guru's Ashram

The Gorakhnath ashram is a famous yogic centre in India, which also houses the Gorakhnath temple. The youth arrived in the Gorakhnath ashram and sought out Mahant Gopalnath. The residents of the ashram were curious to know the purpose of the youth's arrival. He was apparently from a well-to-do family. Some of the ashram residents imagined he was a newly married man, who was on a tour of holy places to seek the blessings of the Lord for a successful married life. The youth, however, neither appeared keen to move on from the ashram, nor keen to communicate. He did appear though to have a definite sense of purpose and was always in a contemplative state.

Mahant Gopalnath had an elaborate, private discussion with the young man. He was himself an accomplished yogi and could gauge at a subtle level the apparent suitability of the youth for a life dedicated to yoga. The yogic texts describe a lot of signs that denote spiritual advancement of an aspirant, many such signs were visible on the young man's body – his arms reached down to his knees, he had perfectly sculpted limbs and his hands and feet were soft and rosy. The fire of renunciation, the steadfastness of purpose and serious air of the aspirant had left no doubt of his qualification for initiation.

The Mahant accepted the youth as his disciple and initiated him in line with the rites of the Nath Sampradaya. He was initiated into Mantra Yoga, Sewa Yoga and Hatha Yoga. Gopalnath named his disciple Gambhirnath, meaning the Nath who is deeply serious. The name itself evokes a feeling of serenity, of peace, of seriousness and reflected the attributes visible in the disciple.

This was the first step of initiation, as per the rituals of the Nath Sampradaya. Gambhirnath received the mantras of Siva and Shakti and immersed himself in his daily practices. In addition, Gopalnath gave him multiple chores to do in the ashram, which Gambhirnath performed with devotion. Soon, he had become proficient in all the activities involved in running the ashram. In India, since the time of the ancient rishis, gurus have laid emphasis on *sewa*, the spirit of service in ashrams. This was considered an irreplaceable tool for self-purification and, even now, the tradition continues in many ashrams.

However, Gambhirnath was as unsuitable for the life of restricted sadhana in the ashram as he was of a householder. He would never be at ease until he attained self-realisation, through deep spiritual practices. He longed to spend more time on such practices.

However, he did not complain and, for three years, he diligently performed all the duties allotted to him. During this period, he did not waste time in unnecessary talk, even when others tried to draw him into idle conversation. He interacted with only those fellow residents in the ashram who could help him in his endeavour, for instance, he had frequent discussions on spirituality with Shivnath, a great yogi from Devi Patan. He had a single-mindedness of purpose that was feverish in intensity and astounding in constancy. During these years, Gopalnath taught him many advanced yogic practices and once the pupil had mastered them, he was initiated into *sannyasa*. This was the second stage of initiation in the Nath Sampradaya. Gambhirnath's head was shaved, his ears were pierced. He was given the *kaupeen* by the guru. Towards the end of this period, Gambhirnath had developed a burning desire to go into solitude and practise uninterrupted sadhana. Finally, Gopalnath allowed Gambhirnath to move on in his spiritual journey, to find a place where he could meditate in solitude and perfect the practices he had learnt from his guru.

The Nath Sampradaya considers the first two steps in the spiritual evolution of an aspirant to be external, which are those of the *kutichaka* and then the *bahudaka*. Beyond these are the stages of *hansa, paramhansa, avadhuta* and *turiyatita*, which describe the internal spiritual evolution of the aspirant. The ultimate attainment in the life of the aspirant is one when he is free of all bonds. This stage was the aim of Gambhirnath. He now sought his guru's blessings as he stepped out of the ashram on his spiritual quest.

Gambhirnath spent the next six years as a wandering monk. In his mind, the words of Guru Gorakhnath rang true:

> *Gyān sarīshā guru na miliyā, chitta sarīshā chélā*
> *Man sarīshā mélu na miliyā, tīthé gôrakh phiré akélā*
> One cannot find a greater guru than true knowledge,
> Nor can one find a greater devotee than the (dedicated) heart.
> One cannot find a greater companion than a (trained) mind.
> Gorakh therefore roams (on the spiritual path) alone.

Roaming in God Absorption: Sadhana in Kashi

Once, he left the guru's ashram, Gambhirnath vowed not to ask anyone for food or alms, resolving to subsist completely on the grace of the Lord. His desire for solitude prompted him to search for deserted routes. Sometimes, he would go hungry for a couple of days, but usually, someone or the other would miraculously turn up with food for him.

His first stop was Kashi, the holy city identified with Lord Siva. On reaching there, Gambhirnath bathed in the Ganga and offered his prayers to Lord Siva in a temple. Then, he began his search for a deserted spot on the banks of the river and on finding such an appropriate place, settled there and immersed himself in intense spiritual practices. For three years, he continued his practice of Mantra Yoga, Hatha Yoga, Raja Yoga, Bhakti Yoga and Laya Yoga and attained a very exalted spiritual state. Such a state is difficult to hide, and despite his best efforts, his popularity began to spread and more and more people began to visit him.

So far, Gambhirnath had avoided all human contact. The growing crowds convinced him that Kashi was no longer a location conducive to his sadhana. Without notice, one day, he set off in search of some other appropriate spot to continue his spiritual practices undisturbed.

In Allahabad

After a few days, he arrived in the ancient holy city of Prayag — Allahabad. He bathed in the confluence of the three rivers – Ganga, Yamuna and Saraswati (the third river is mythical and invisible). Once again, he set about searching for an appropriate place for his sadhana and on the outskirts of Allahabad, in Jhusi, he found a cave on the riverbank. The only problem was that this was in a desolate, deserted spot. Where would he get food in such a location? But, Gambhirnath was not worried about that, for he had left himself to the will of God. Help arrived from unexpected quarters. A Nath yogi called Mukutnath arrived at that spot and was very impressed with Gambhirnath's spiritual attainment and dedication. Mukutnath dedicated himself to serving Gambhirnath and making the atmosphere conducive for his sadhana. He begged for food in the neighbouring villages and fed Gambhirnath, who was now completely immersed in a steady, meditative state. In this manner, Gambhirnath spent three years in Jhusi, before moving on.

The Narmada

This time, Gambhirnath travelled as an itinerant monk for quite a long period. He traversed the entire country in all directions, visiting many famous holy cities and temples. He would stop at different places to continue his sadhana, sometimes for a day, sometimes a week, sometimes a month and sometimes for several months. His hair became long and matted[3], but his mind did not worry about the body. He continued to devote himself to his meditation. Soon, he developed a desire to spend time near the Narmada, one of the seven holy rivers of India. He decided to walk along the river and for many days remained in a state of spiritual stupor.

On one of these days, he found a small hut, quite appropriate to meditate in for a few days. This hut belonged to a *brahmachari*, who was not to be found. Gambhirnath settled down in the hut and began to meditate. He had a strange experience there. For three consecutive days, a snake would appear before him and stare at him for a long time and would then go around him thrice and vanish. For a yogi of Gambhirnath's stature, the snake did not instil fear. Instead, he was deeply influenced by its divine appearance and would lapse into a wondrous samadhi contemplating the snake. After a few days, the owner of the hut returned and Gambhirnath interacted briefly with him. He narrated the incident of the snake's appearance to the *brahmachari*, who was astounded. The *brahmachari* explained that it was reputed that an adept yogi inhabited these parts and that he assumed the form of a snake and would sometimes, though rarely, manifest himself before spiritually advanced yogis. The *brahmachari* himself had been living in the hut for the past twelve years in the hope of seeing the snake–saint, but had never managed to be successful.

Back to the Ashram, then on to Gaya

Returning to the Ashram

Gambhirnath decided to return to the Gorakhnath ashram, his guru's ashram, for some time. When he reached there, he found that his fame had spread; he was welcomed with respect and affection. His guru was also happy to see him. For a few days, he stayed in the ashram and then expressed the desire to move on, but his fellow disciples requested him to stay on a bit longer. Gambhirnath relented and stayed for a few more days, but the fire for complete attainment on the path of yoga was still burning strongly within him. He had not yet reached the pinnacle of attainment. He found the ashram not conducive to vigorous sadhana. More importantly, he was receiving a lot of recognition there and, though he remained unaffected by it, it made him uncomfortable. And, so one night, he ran away from the ashram.

Gaya and Kapildhara

He moved from place to place until, finally, he reached the hills surrounding Gaya. Gaya is one of the ancient holy places of India. This was the place where Siddhartha had become the Buddha and Ramakrishna Paramhansa's father had an intuition that a divine child would be born to him. Chaitanya Mahaprabhu also had first experienced the unfolding of his divine consciousness here. Since ancient times, Gaya had been the refuge of many monks, hermits and ascetics and, consequently, has a spiritual atmosphere. Gambhirnath reached the famous Kapileshwar Mahadev temple in Kapildhara, which is not very far from Gaya. Nestled in the Brahmayoni hills, the temple was an excellent spot for the yogi to go ahead with his sadhana; he decided to stay on there.

Disciples Appear to Serve

With renewed vigour, he began his meditations, unconcerned about his physical or material well-being. However, the Lord is more worried about the well-being of his devotees than the devotees themselves. The *Bhagwad Gita* mentions that the Lord protects his devotees who completely immerse themselves in him alone:

> *Ananyaschintayantô mām ye janā paryupāsaté*
> *Téshām nityabhiyuktānām yôgakshémam vahāmyaham*
> Those who worship Me with undivided attention,
> I take care of their needs and protect what they have.

Shortly after Gambhirnath settled at this deserted spot, some people again came forward to serve him. The first was an illiterate villager, Akku Kurmi, who saw Gambhirnath engrossed in deep meditation and was influenced by him. He began to look after the saint; he would clean the place and cook for him. Over time, Akku, his brother Munni and their entire family began to serve Gambhirnath. They were suffering from dire poverty but served him with as much as they could. Sometimes, though, they would come before him while he was meditating and narrate their woes to him. The saint did not even acknowledge their presence. However, in his later life, Mahayogi Gambhirnath never forgot the service of this family; he cared for their welfare till he lived.

After some more time, a young spiritual aspirant named Brahmachari Nripatnath appeared on the scene and began to serve Gambhirnath. The young man not only cooked food for his master but had taken it upon himself to ensure that nobody would bother him. He would angrily chase off people with a trident lest they disturb his master's sadhana. In fact, he was, sometimes, so harsh with visitors that Gambhirnath had to scold him, but it was the result of Nripatnath's protection and caring that the saint could continue his meditation undisturbed. Many times, he requested Gambhirnath to grant him spiritual initiation, but the saint did not want to become a guru and, therefore, refused. Finally, it was after Nripatnath had served him for close to fourteen years that Gambhirnath initiated him and that too at the request of other saints and disciples.

The attraction of a siddha yogi is immense. Two years after Nripatnath had arrived at Gaya, Gambhirnath went to Kashi at the time of the solar eclipse. There he met Shudhanath, a young seeker. The young man returned with Gambhirnath and began to stay with Nripatnath in a hut in Kharpar Bhairav, a spot below Kapildhara.

In addition, two rich residents of Gaya — Madholal Gayali and Motilal Ghosh — were also devotees of Gambhirnath. Madholal was initially involved in a court case, in which his conviction was certain. He probably hoped Gambhirnath would protect him. He served the saint with devotion, knowing fully well that the latter refused to perform miracles. However, one day, when Madholal was very disturbed by the legal dispute, the saint of his own accord asked him not to worry about the case. Madholal was amazed at the omniscience of the saint, but he could not imagine how the case could possibly go in his favour. But under the protection of such a spiritually attained guru as Gambhirnath, he need not have worried. Soon, Madholal, against his wildest expectations, found he had won the case in the High Court. He was extremely surprised and realised it was the saint's grace. This brought a great change within him and thereafter, he began to serve Gambhirnath without expecting a reward for his service.

The Meditation Cave and Mahasiddhi

Crowds had begun to build up to see the saint. Madholal decided to build a cave in Kapildhara for the yogi to enable him to meditate in peace and solitude. With Gambhirnath's permission, he constructed it, the design of which was in line with spiritual principles. The yogi performed his sadhana in the cave for close to thirteen years. Initially, he would stay in the cave all day long, coming out briefly only once during the day. After a short while, he began to extend his stay in the cave and would remain in a state of samadhi, coming out briefly once in two days.

When he did come out, people would be waiting to see him. He did not interact with them individually but would cast his gaze around, with a distant look in his eyes. The gaze radiated extraordinary brilliance, compassion and peace. People who saw him would feel strangely refreshed and their burdens lightened. Some people would come with materialistic wishes but the extraordinary environment that his presence created would compel them to forget their mundane desires. Others would insist on sharing their difficulties and problems, but the saint did not appear to be hearing anything and would not even acknowledge that he had heard their woes. It was as though he was between them all, yet alone. Many of the devotees would bring offerings of food and clothing, and Gambhirnath would get it all distributed as prasad to everyone.

After a while, Gambhirnath began to extend his sadhana and would come out of the cave once a week on Tuesday afternoons. This continued for two years till he again intensified his practice. He would now stay in the cave for an entire fortnight at a stretch before emerging, and later extended it to a month. His sadhana had now reached an intense state and would continue unbroken for long periods. During this time, his disciples used to sometimes worry about the master's well-being, but they were conscious of his control on his path.

In order to ensure that no one could disturb him, Gambhirnath had clearly demarcated his meditation spot within the cave. There was a point inside the cave beyond which no one was allowed. During the long stretches of sadhana, his disciples would leave some milk in a vessel at this point once a day. Gambhirnath would drink the milk and leave the vessel in the same place. That was all he would require for the entire day. He had reached a stage in his yogic practices when he did not even require to excrete at all. Gambhirnath would always emerge from the cave at a pre-nominated time and was never either late or early. This was due to his level of yogic consciousness that, despite being lost in samadhi for such long spells in the dark cave, he did not lose track of time.

Finally, he stayed inside the cave, meditating deeply for a long period of three months. When he emerged, he had attained *mahasiddhi*, or the ultimate state of yoga. He had gone beyond bonds, beyond good and bad, beyond the body and the mind, beyond time and space, in life but beyond it. As a *mahasiddh* and a *mahayogi*, he fulfilled his aspiration of perfecting all aspects of yoga. After this, he would meditate in the cave for no fixed periods and would come out at irregular intervals – there was nothing left to achieve.

While he had received initiation in Hatha Yoga, Mantra Yoga, Raja Yoga and Laya Yoga from his guru, Mahayogi Gambhirnath pursued the other facets of yoga, such as Bhakti Yoga and Gyana Yoga with equal vigour. He would, sometimes, say that the paths for attaining completeness in Raja Yoga and Kriya Yoga were hidden within Hatha Yoga. He had reached the pinnacle in all these paths and now he remained in a permanent state of bliss.

Mahayogi Gambhirnath stayed in Kapildhara for close to ten years after he reached the ultimate stage of yoga. He would, sometimes, wander off from his cave and spend some time meditating in neighbouring hills, or would go on a pilgrimage. During this time, the saint came into contact with two brothers who were advanced yogis. Gambhirnath considered them as *aughars*, who lived in a cave close to Kapildhara. The Mahayogi often visited them and they also came to Kapildhara. Sometimes, another great saint, Baba Thakurdas, would also join them. These four saints would often spend their time meditating together in a cave.

At this stage, it would have been very easy for Mahayogi Gambhirnath to completely retire from public interaction and spend the rest of his life in seclusion in the cave. However, he consciously interacted with common people to guide them, to teach them, to protect them in their journey to perfection.

Other Saints on Mahayogi Gambhirnath

Mahayogi Gambhirnath shied away from recognition, but recognition pursued him. The remarkable facet of this recognition was the laudatory manner in which saints and gurus across different schools of spirituality spoke of him.

Swami Vishuddhananda Paramhansa (Gandha Baba) was a great yogi and adept at tantra. He had received training in esoteric yogic practices in the mystical hermitage of Gyanganj, in the upper reaches of the Himalayas. He, once, mentioned that after he had received initiation from his guru, the latter brought him to Mahayogi Gambhirnath and made him bow before the saint.

Swami Bholananda Giri, an exalted saint of the Dasnami Sampradaya, had a lot of respect for the Mahayogi. Another great Vaishnav saint, Ramdas Kathia Baba, who epitomised the highest ideals of both Bhakti Yoga and Raja Yoga, considered the Mahayogi a *nitya yukta yogi* or a yogi who always remained endowed with the fullness of yoga.

Sri Vijaykrishna Goswami, a great saint of the nineteenth and twentieth centuries, held that Mahayogi Gambhirnath had reached such a high stage of yogic attainment that, if he wished, he could create, maintain and destroy the whole of creation in the blink of an eye. However, such yogis carry out their wishes completely within the bounds of the wishes of the Lord. Once, Goswamiji told a disciple that everyday he sought the blessings of seven exceptional living saints and when he remembered them, they would appear before him – one of them was Mahayogi Gambhirnath. Goswamiji was also very fond of the Mahayogi's disciples. He often repeated that it was rare to find a saint of the Mahayogi's calibre below the Himalayas.

Goswamiji lived in Gaya, in the vicinity of Akasha Ganga hills. Sometimes, when the Mahayogi would begin to play the sitar and sing devotional songs in the dead of night, the strains of the music would carry to Goswamiji's ears. He would realise that the Mahayogi was roaming in the hills, playing music and singing. He would go running barefoot to meet the Mahayogi. In those days, wild animals frequently roamed those forested hills and would attack humans, but this did not deter either the Mahayogi or Goswamiji from roaming in those hills. The attraction was spiritual.

The Mahayogi's Travels

There is an ancient Indian proverb that implies that travel purifies the spiritual aspirant. However, saints who have achieved perfection do not need to travel. If they travel, it is to spread their spiritual message, and sometimes, to fulfil the destiny of spiritual aspirants who they would meet during these tours.

After Gambhirnath attained perfection, he visited many places with his disciple, Nripatnath. Even when he travelled to the holy sites in the upper reaches of the Himalayas, he carried only a single blanket to protect himself from the severe cold. There are brief accounts of his passing through various holy places such as Gangotri, Yamunotri, Kailash Mansarovar, Pampa Sarovar, Badrinath, Kedarnath, Rameshwaram and Dwarka.

Once, when he was attending the Kumbh Mela at Allahabad, a fight broke out between some Naga sadhus and Nath yogis. The Naga sadhus were more in number and they ferociously attacked the Nath yogis, many of whom were seriously injured. Mahayogi Gambhirnath was in deep meditation at that point in time and despite the noise and violence all around, he remained in that state. Soon the Nagas began to approach the spot where the Mahayogi was meditating, and some Nath yogis let out an anxious cry for help. The Mahayogi then came out of his meditation and observing the melee all around immediately understood what was happening. He called out only once saying, 'Stop! Be calm, be calm.' Strangely, his voice was heard above the screams and the din. The single cry was enough to bring all action to a standstill. It was as though blood had rushed out of everyone's body. That was the power of the Mahayogi's voice. The offending sadhus immediately retreated and order was restored.

Towards the latter part of the Mahayogi's stay in Gaya, another well-known saint, Paramhansa Ratan Giri, came to Kapildhara and developed a large following there. When Mahayogi Gambhirnath had once gone for an extended tour of holy places, the disciples of Paramhansa Ratan Giri renovated and modernised the Mahayogi's cave. On his return, the Mahayogi did not find it appealing as he preferred to stay in more natural surroundings, suitable for renunciates and monks. The Mahayogi's disciple Madholal then constructed a hut and a garden in a deserted spot for the Mahayogi and, after that, whenever he was in Gaya he preferred to stay there.

Back in the Gorakhnath Ashram

In the year 1880, the Mahayogi's guru Gopalnath, the head priest of the ashram, passed away. According to the tradition of the Gorakhnath ashram, the post of the head priest should never be vacant. Baba Balbhadranath succeeded Baba Gopalnath, but he too passed away in 1890 and Baba Dilbarnath assumed the post. In 1896, Baba Dilbarnath also passed away without nominating a successor and a search was launched for one. Various people came forward to invite the Mahayogi to assume this position.

Mahayogi Gambhirnath was not keen to be involved in running the day-to-day affairs of the ashram, as it involved extensive interaction with the material world. In addition, the head priest was considered a living embodiment of Gorakhnath, the central figure in the sect. He was, therefore, worshipped ritually and had substantial exposure to the public. For the Mahayogi, living in the wild and getting lost in the bliss of samadhi was far more appealing than being the master of one of the most prestigious and wealthy seats of religious authority in India. The Mahayogi was, therefore, unwilling to assume this position. He supported Baba Sundarnath, a disciple of Baba Dilbarnath, who was then nominated as the head priest. The Mahayogi instructed Baba Sundarnath on the responsibilities that the latter was assuming, and then returned to Gaya. Unfortunately, Baba Sundarnath did not turn out to be a capable head priest in the pure tradition of the Gorakhnath lineage. As one of the perfect masters in the Nath Sampradaya and a widely respected saint, Mahayogi Gambhirnath began to receive complaints regarding the manner in which his guru's ashram was being managed. After a great deal of urging, the Mahayogi went to Gorakhpur and stayed at the ashram for a short while, ensuring that the administration returned to capable and honest hands. However, he again turned down requests to become the head priest, and ensured that Baba Sundarnath remained at the post. After a short while, when the ashram administration had stabilised, the Mahayogi returned to Gaya.

However, very soon, the affairs deteriorated again, and the Mahayogi's earnest intervention was required. Baba Sundarnath's responsibilities as a head priest were now curtailed; he lost the right to initiate disciples. The Mahayogi permanently shifted to the ashram to ensure that the administration was efficient and honest. He, however, remained the ashram's administrator and did not assume the post of the head priest till the end of his life. This decision probably stemmed from his disinclination to accept ritual devotion from lay disciples.

Despite the fact that the Mahayogi was perennially lost in an ocean of bliss, he was an excellent administrator. His capability to comprehend a situation and determine its requirements in an instant flowed from his state of yogic attainment. His instructions were brief but infallible. In addition, his interactions with people reflected a soft heart full of intense compassion for mankind. He was fondly addressed as *boodha maharaj* (the old master) by the residents and visitors to the Gorakhnath ashram. The Mahayogi emphasised service to guests, the poor and the needy and demonstrated the same by personal example.

The Mahayogi's *Leela*

Saints often possess supernormal capabilities and supernatural powers. The Mahayogi also possessed such powers and capabilities, but was extremely reluctant to display them. Very seldom would such incidents come to light.

Animals

Mahayogi Gambhirnath deeply loved the entire creation and the recipients of his love reciprocated. Even snakes and lions would come and lie down at his feet with love and the saint would pat them. It was widely known that the lion in Gorakhpur zoo would, sometimes, escape and the Mahayogi had to intervene to get the animal back to its cage. The Mahayogi would pat the lion and 'convince' it to move inside the cage. This lion had a strange connection with the saint, for the day the Mahayogi finally left his body, the animal also died.

During his stay in Kapildhara, a tiger would often come to the Mahayogi and would spend some time sitting at his feet, looking at him. It would walk around the saint and eventually run off. While usually it came when he was alone, it once arrived when the Mahayogi was surrounded by sadhus, some of whom got frightened. The Mahayogi reassured the sadhus that the tiger would not harm anyone. The animal sat for some time and then left peacefully.

When Mahayogi Gambhirnath lived in Gorakhpur, it was noticed that cows returning from feeding would rub themselves lovingly against him. Often when he was sitting outside the ashram precincts, stray dogs would sit near him. If a disciple tried to chase them away, the saint would restrain him.

He even fed chappatis with his own hands to rats. He avoided wearing silk and when pressed to explain why, he confessed that he did not want to wear garments that were made at the cost of the lives of silkworms.

Unaffected and Undisturbed: State of Bliss

From his young days, Gambhirnath would, sometimes, smoke tobacco. Some of his disciples would prepare a chillum, light it and offer it to him. The Mahayogi would be in a permanent state of bliss, with eyes half-opened. The pipe would smoulder in his hand for hours until it burned out and then the disciple would make a fresh pipe. This would go on for hours. It was evident to the disciples that the Mahayogi permanently resided in such a state of blissful communion.

The Mahayogi would often sit amid a group of sadhus, some of whom would, sometimes, get into nasty, abusive, shouting matches with each other. Mahayogi Gambhirnath would completely ignore the disturbance and remain in a state of bliss. Only if he was approached to broker peace would he volunteer his opinion. At other times, he would gently and sombrely scold the sadhus in as few words as possible, before, once again, lapsing into his state of bliss.

Simple and Childlike

Mahayogi Gambhirnath was like a child with regard to his physical needs. He would allow himself to be taken care of by his disciples and devotees. He was neutral to most things about himself – neither liking nor disliking anything.

Once, a disciple approached the saint and asked him to give a spiritual discourse. The Mahayogi replied with genuine humility, saying that he did not know enough to do so. To the disciple, this attitude was in itself a discourse, as it came from a realised master.

Adherence to Principles

The Mahayogi had a principle that he would never visit the house of a disciple. Only once in his life did he deviate from his vow and that was to visit the house of Akku Kurmi, the dying devotee.

The Mahayogi, once, travelled to Udaipur with a group of sadhus and camped in an open field on the outskirts of the city. Soon, Udaipur along with its surrounding areas was inundated with heavy rainfall and the only dry places were the field and its adjoining areas, which were strangely spared by the rain gods. The residents of Udaipur saw this as a miracle and many flocked to see the sadhus and, in particular, Mahayogi Gambhirnath. The news of this event reached the king, who became anxious to meet this saint and sent for him a couple of times. When the king realised that the saint would never come to his court, he announced the plan to visit the saint the subsequent day. Mahayogi Gambhirnath, however, did not wish to interact with royalty, in keeping with the principles of lay monks. He and the accompanying sadhus left Udaipur that night itself.

Curing a Madman

If a siddha abuses or beats someone, it is said to lead to enormous benefit – spiritual and material. Shunnulal Ghariwala, a Gaya-based businessman had lost his mental balance and become completely incapable of taking care of himself. He would run around from place to place and would also suffer from fits of insanity, during which he would attack and harass people. Nothing seemed to cure him. He, once, came to the area close to the Mahayogi's cave and began to heckle some sadhus there. The saint held his hands and gave him two hard slaps on his cheeks. This appeared to calm him down, not just at that point in time, but forever. Shunnulal resumed managing his business and remained free of neurological ailments for the rest of his life.

The Effect of his Company

Many disciples of different gurus came to visit Mahayogi Gambhirnath, as he was known to be a realised saint. Some of these visitors had already received initiation into a mantra from their own gurus. Many of these visitors attested to the fact that in the Mahayogi's company, they experienced spontaneous and continuous internal repetition of the mantra their guru had initiated them with.

Reflections of Yogic Attainments

Once, a huge crowd of Brahmins had gathered in the Gorakhpur ashram to participate in some festivities. The temple administration was worried – the crowd was over twice as large than what had been expected, and it was now certain that the food supply would fall short for a ritual meal. In those days, sending back a hungry Brahmin would result in a bad name for the institution. The people at the ashram in charge of preparing and distributing the food rushed to Mahayogi Gambhirnath, who was then the administrator of the Gorakhnath ashram and described the problem to him. The saint quietly went to the kitchen and instructed the cooks to cover the food with a fresh sheet of cloth, and begin the feeding ritual from under one side of the edge of the cloth. The feeding commenced and continued satisfactorily until all had been fed. Finally, the food turned out to be enough for the ashram inmates as well, and it lasted till the next day!

Varadakant Bandopadhyaya, a disciple of Vijaykrishna Goswami, once, came to the Gorakhnath ashram with a desire to hear the Mahayogi play the sitar, since he had heard so much praise of the saint's skills. Yet, he was too shy to voice his wishes. But a surprise awaited him. Without being asked or without it being indicated, the Mahayogi asked a disciple to bring his beloved sitar, which he played for a long time. The Mahayogi would also prepare excellent tea and Varadakant, once, developed a desire to drink tea in the ashram, but could not tell anyone about it. Tea was not ordinarily prepared, but the moment Varadakant came to see him, the Mahayogi spontaneously decided to have the tea prepared for him[4].

Once, a worried lady approached Mahayogi Gambhirnath. Her only son had gone abroad and there was no news of him. She begged the saint to help her. Communication channels were poor in those days and, thus, her feelings of helplessness. Moved by her plea, the Mahayogi meditated for a few moments. He then assured her, that her son was on a ship bound for home and would return the following Monday. The lady went back home happily and his prophecy came true. Later, she came back to meet the saint with her son. The son was surprised to see the saint. He claimed that he had seen him on his ship, outside his cabin, the day before his ship reached Bombay — now Mumbai — he even had a small chat with the saint for five minutes. The boy couldn't believe his eyes, as he had boarded a train bound for Gorakhpur immediately on landing in Bombay, and he was certain that the Mahayogi was not on the train. The saint disassociated himself with the incident, but it was found he had indeed appeared outside the boy's cabin the day when his mother had met the Mahayogi.

However, Mahayogi Gambhirnath considered miracles to be meaningless in the world of yoga. He would assert that miraculous powers could easily be gained with the practice of yoga, but the true miracle was the power to suffer, to persist, to serve and the power to transform.

As a Master

Till the year 1909, the Mahayogi had very few direct disciples, but during his trip to Calcutta that year, he began to receive many requests for initiation. Consequently, he initiated many disciples until his passing away in 1917. Initially, he would turn away some aspirants, but he would do so with apparent sadness. In his later years, he seldom turned away an aspirant, but it was noticed that only those destined to receive initiation would end up asking for it. Some aspirants would come to him determined for initiation but would end up discussing mundane topics and return without initiation.

By the time of his death, Mahayogi Gambhirnath had initiated a large number of aspirants into mantra, but he rarely initiated aspirants into *sannyasa*. Many disciples would approach him for *sannyasa* initiation, but he would advise them against it and, for those who persisted, he would lovingly convince them to change their minds. Some aspirants spent many days at the ashram, hoping for *sannyasa* initiation, but he would send them back to continue living as householders. He was essentially against the practice of initiating raw aspirants into *sannyasa*. In his opinion, not everyone could face the rigours of *sannyasa* – physical, emotional or spiritual – and many sannyasis had failed to surmount them and had fallen from grace.

One remarkable disciple of his was Baba Brahmanath, whom the Mahayogi had initiated into the Nath Sampradaya. Brahmanath was a committed devotee of the Mahayogi and would serve him with dedication. He went on to become the head priest of the Gorakhnath ashram after Baba Sundarnath passed away. Other initiates into *sannyasa* included Baba Shantinath and Baba Nivrittinath, both of whom were considered exceptional yogis.

Another notable disciple of the Mahayogi was Kalinath Brahmachari, an ex-police officer who had left home in search of spiritual solace. Kalinath had only one focus – the service of the saint and the Mahayogi would meekly accept the service and allow himself to be bound by Kalinath's loving care.

Rasik Behari Bandopadhyaya was another disciple of the Mahayogi. A noteworthy aspirant and a householder, he was initially a Vaishnava devotee. Rasik Behari had many spiritual experiences, including *bhava samadhi*; subsequently, he became a devotee of Kali, the Mother Goddess. However, after hearing about the Mahayogi, he went to Gorakhpur and received initiation. He practised the mantra for long hours and attained a very high state of spirituality and himself became a master who could initiate aspirants. Though, till the end of his life, he remained a householder and did not adopt *sannyasa*.

Mahatma Pranavananda, considered by many as a divine being, was also initiated by the Mahayogi. It is reported that the Mahayogi initially had told him that he did not need initiation as he was a perfect being, but eventually agreed. After Mahayogi Gambhirnath passed away, the Mahatma took *sannyasa* and established the Bharat Seva Sangh. He dedicated his life to serving the people of India.

Attracting Disciples

The Mahayogi had a miraculous way of attracting disciples. There were cases where some future disciples had seen him in their dreams, some had heard his name and yet others had visions of him or sensed his form. Some had also received spiritual initiation in their dreams from him, even before they actually met him. When they would finally meet the saint to thank him for his grace, he would acknowledge the initiation but avoided discussion on the miracle.

There was certainly an element of destiny in being accepted as a disciple by Mahayogi Gambhirnath. Once, when the saint was in Calcutta, he was asked by his disciples to travel to Dhaka, where a large number of spiritual aspirants wished to be initiated by him. These aspirants were poor and could not afford to come to Calcutta. The Mahayogi was normally more kind and caring towards the poor but, in this case, he remarked that those who were destined to come to him would find a way to reach him. He did not travel to Dhaka.

Once, a Bengali youth was meditating on his heart centre, one of the body chakras, when he had a vision of the Mahayogi's radiant form. He had neither met the Mahayogi, nor heard of him, so he could not determine who the person in the vision was. Some days later, he was surprised to see the Mahayogi's photo at a friend's house and recognised him as the same person he had seen while meditating. In course of time, he went to Gorakhpur and became a disciple of the Mahayogi. After the saint passed away, he dedicated himself completely to spiritual pursuits.

A married couple wanted spiritual initiation from the Mahayogi, but the wife could not go to Gorakhpur. However, when the husband returned from Gorakhpur, the wife told him that she had received initiation from the Mahayogi in a dream. She had dreamt that she had sought initiation from another saint, but he refused and directed her to the Mahayogi, who initiated her[5]. Later, when she met the Mahayogi in person he initiated her again, and she realised it was the same mantra as the one he had given her in the dream.

Another lady desiring initiation could not accompany her family to Gorakhpur, but she received mantra initiation in a dream. When her family returned, she shared the mantra with her mother and, to her surprise, her mantra was the same as her mother's.

The path of sadhana is long and difficult and aspirants often go astray, attracted by the accomplishments of miracle mongers. Once, a yogic siddha[6] began to attract a large number of disciples with the promise that he would appear (materialise) before aspirants who revered him and chanted a particular incantation. He would appear before such aspirants and then initiate them. Once, a disciple of the Mahayogi was curious, and he followed this siddha's direction. The siddha actually appeared before him. The yogi then began to force the disciple to accept a mantra from him, which put the Mahayogi's disciple in a dilemma, as he had already received one from the Mahayogi[7]. His mind turned to the master and he mentally prayed to him to relieve him of this distress. The very next instant, the master appeared before the disciple and began staring at the siddha, who seemed to lose his composure and then disappeared. The Mahayogi also then disappeared, but the disciple had learnt his lesson. After that incident, he remained steadfast in his devotion to the Mahayogi.

A unique characteristic of Mahayogi Gambhirnath was that he would also initiate small children along with their parents. In some cases, he predicted that as the child would grow up, the mantra would emerge in his consciousness while, in other cases, he told the parents to remind the mantra when the child came of age.

For devotees and disciples, the Mahayogi appeared to be a divine embodiment of love and grace. As disciples would serve him out of love and respect, he would serve them even more out of love. He was always conscious of their smallest requirements. His eyes were always moist and his gaze tender. Leaving him and returning from Gorakhpur would be ever so difficult after they saw his compassionate form, like that of a loving mother bidding them goodbye.

The Final Journey

The Mahayogi was a firm believer of addressing material problems with material solutions instead of wasting creative spiritual energy to solve them. For instance, if there was a physical ailment, he would approach a doctor, or for legal problems, recommend legal help. His disciples too had varying degrees of powers but, by his own example, he had taught them not to fritter away spiritual wealth in meaningless outlets. Once, when he was very ill, his disciples pleaded with him to cure himself, but he refused, saying he did not wish to interfere with God's will.

In Calcutta

Towards the end of his life, Mahayogi Gambhirnath developed a problem in one of his eyes. In December 1914, doctors advised him to go to Calcutta for surgery. A house was taken on rent and the saint was shifted there along with some of his key disciples. It was during this trip that his followers from Bengal — and specifically from Calcutta — multiplied and his existing disciples also had the good fortune of having long periods of interactions with him. It was as if the Mahayogi had planned the trip for reaching out to these disciples in the last leg of his life. The house was transformed into an ashram and was always full of devotees and disciples.

The Mahayogi's disciples had a very tough job at hand — all the visitors were to be fed. The fluctuating number of the crowd used to confuse the disciples further. Finally, they devised a clever scheme. They would approach the Mahayogi to discuss the menu for the day, and he would casually ask them how many guests they were expecting. He would then suggest a change in their estimates, and it was found that they were invariably correct, reflecting his clairvoyant capabilities.

After the operation on his eye, the doctors prescribed complete rest for the Mahayogi and devotees were not allowed to meet him for a few days. On strict instructions from him, disciples had to be careful not to hurt the sentiments of visitors they had to turn back. After a few days, the Mahayogi began to meet visitors, but mostly he would stay in a partial state of samadhi.

Visitors would often bring fruits, sweetmeats and money that they would leave at the Mahayogi's feet as a token of devotion. Disciples would take the money and separately account for the same. Accounts were also maintained for necessary daily expenditures. When the Mahayogi was on his way to Gorakhpur, both these accounts were tallied, and it was found to the surprise of the disciples that the amounts spent and donated were exactly the same, to the last digit!

Gorakhpur and the Haridwar Kumbha

After spending a few days in Gorakhpur, the Mahayogi left for Haridwar, the site of the Kumbha Mela. In Haridwar, he accepted the request of Nath yogi sannyasis to put up with them at Gorakh Dalicha, a crowded spot full of sannyasis. Most saints would stay in houses close to Gorakh Dalicha, as that place was crowded and noisy, not conducive to their meditation. The Mahayogi, however, had no problem and would stay in a meditative semi-external state. Even in this state, he was fully conscious and aware and showed full attention to detail in administrative matters and was careful in recognising visitors and greeting them with love and humility.

Around this time, cholera broke out in the Kumbha Mela. Mahayogi Gambhirnath's disciple, Umesh, had come with his family to join the celebrations. His son became sick with cholera and was on the deathbed. Umesh was very worried and approached the saint to intervene. He prayed to the Mahayogi, offering his own life or the life of his wife in exchange for that of his son's. This appeared to anger the saint, but Umesh subsequently prayed with all humility and the Mahayogi nodded and assured him that his son would recover. True to the blessing, the son recovered, and Umesh and his family returned from the Kumbha Mela safe and healthy.

The Mahayogi returned to Gorakhpur. For two years, until his passing away, he received many disciples. He would stress on two critical teachings – 'keep the faith' and 'keep up the contemplation'. He assured devotees that he was indeed with them, even when he was physically far away.

The Very End

The Mahayogi's health began to deteriorate and he progressively withdrew deeper into himself. When asked how his health was, he would respond positively, saying, 'I'm fine.' As the administrator of the Gorakhnath ashram, it was his job to look after the properties of the trust that were scattered in the neighbouring villages, hence, he would, sometimes, go on such tours. While planning for one such trip, he felt it was time to leave the body. His disciples meanwhile wondered how his health would permit him to travel, but he put off their objections by saying that the air and water at the place he wished to visit were pure. Finally, he decided the date of his departure as 21 March 1917. The great saint had actually decided the date of his passing away, but he camouflaged it as his date of commencing the tour.

The disciples were unaware of his true travel plans and nobody could guess what his intentions were – the Mahayogi did not wish to share it with them. He even used ambiguous words to describe the place of his visit, putting the disciples in dilemma. The reason is unclear, but it probably lay in the fact that they would insist on him deferring his ultimate plan, or use his spiritual power to cure himself. Neither of these options was acceptable to him.

As the date approached, his health deteriorated further. His disciples, once again, asked him to reconsider his travel plans, but he insisted that where he was going, there would be peace and happiness and no ailment. Due to his failing health, his closest disciples were with him, serving him in whatever manner they could – Brahmanath,

Yagyeshwar, Varadakant, Shantinath and Nivrittinath were all with him. The last two were actually not in Gorakhpur, but were recalled on some pretext.

On the nominated date of travel, Mahayogi Gambhirnath sat on his bed in a meditative posture at eight o'clock in the morning, as was his normal routine. He spoke to no one after that, and stayed in the state of samadhi till he merged finally into the Absolute.

For his disciples, this came as a shock. Only then did they understand the significance of his travel plans, the decision of the travel date and the insistence of their master to travel despite his failing health. Only then did they decode his abstruse and ambiguous references to the place of travel. In hindsight, his references and descriptions of the travel destination started to make sense. They realised with regret why he did not clearly discuss where he was going, and what he meant when he said that the air and water at the destination were pure.

The Mahayogi Lives On

A glorious saint had left his body. Words cannot describe what he was, or what he is. His devotees built a marble platform in his honour, near his place of samadhi. In course of time, a temple was erected in the saint's memory in the compound of the Gorakhnath ashram and a life-sized idol, a replica of his form, was installed there.

Till today, devotees throng the temple and pray to the saint. Almost a century after he passed away, the Mahayogi lives on in the hearts of his devotees, disciples and their descendants. He answers their calls in times of distress and guides them in times of confusion. And to those who look to him for answers, he responds with love, compassion and grace, fulfilling desires both material and spiritual.

CR 80

Endnotes

1. The Nath Sampradaya is one of the famous sects of ascetics and yogis in India, made famous by Guru Gorakhnath, considered by some as a potent reincarnation of Siva, the eternal yogi.
2. Nav Naths, or the nine famous Nath saints—though the names differ across sources. One of the prominent sources lists them as Machhindra, Goraksha, Jalandhar, Kanif, Charpat, Nagesh, Bharat, Revan and Gahini Nath.
3. Years later, when he assumed the position of the manager of the Gorakhnath ashram, disciples cut his hair and repeatedly washed and oiled it to make his appearance more conducive to public interaction.
4. Varadakant wrote a small booklet entitled *Mahatma Baba Gambhirnath* on the life of Mahayogi Gambhirnath. This was based on his own experiences and the accounts of the Mahayogi's and Vijaykrishna Goswami's disciples; it is currently unavailable.
5. The saint who refused was Sri Vijaykrishna Goswami.
6. In this case, a person who had attained some occult powers as a result of yogic or tantric practices.
7. It is considered extremely inauspicious and harmful for an aspirant's spiritual progress to receive mantra initiation from more than one master; especially when the master is alive. Hindu tradition requires disciples to be committed to their masters and the mantra, or else a psychic confusion may be created, hindering the aspirant's spiritual evolution.

SAI BABA OF SHIRDI
(Unknown-1918)

Ajanmādyamekam parambrahma sākshat,
Swayamsambhavam rāmamekāvatirnam
Bhavaddarshanādsampuneetah prabhôham,
Namāmeeshwaram sadgurum saināgham

O Unborn One, O Primordial One,
the Embodiment of Ultimate Divinity
O Self-Manifested One,
The incarnation of the Lord
The One who is the Lord,
Who purifies me with the vision of his form
I bow to thee, O Sai Nath, embodiment of the Lord.

Sai Baba of Shirdi

It was the night of Diwali, the Indian festival of lights. Everyone in the small village of Shirdi was involved in ritual prayers and celebrations. People were decorating their houses with small lamps and the village was looking extremely beautiful. At this time, Sai Baba, the mad fakir, was sitting lost to the world in Dwarakamayi, the broken masjid which in those days served as his home and meditation room.

Baba's daily routine included going around Shirdi, begging for alms, often asking merchants for goods to fulfil his needs. Many a time, he begged for oil from them to light lamps in the masjid. He kept these burning throughout the night. But, many in the village considered Baba a madman and the merchants were waiting for an opportunity to refuse his requests for oil. All of them had discussed that, the next time he came there, they would all refuse in a coordinated manner. Apparently, this decision was motivated by Bhate, an official of the village administration of Shirdi. He considered the fakir to be a fraud. When Baba went around to the merchants asking for oil, all of them refused, saying they did not have any. Some of them gave an excuse — they were worshipping Goddess Lakshmi, the goddess of wealth, and it would be inauspicious to give away oil on that day. Others chased him away roughly. When Baba returned empty-handed, some merchants followed him back to the masjid, wanting to see whether anyone else would give him oil.

Baba was unruffled and remained half lost, as usual, in deep contemplation of the Divine. He picked up a pot that had a few drops of oil and filled it with water. He then drank some of that water and spat it back into the pot. After that, he filled all the oil lamps with water from the pot. The merchants smiled to each other over the antics of the madman. After that, Baba lit the lamps and, to the surprise of the onlookers, they began to burn brightly. The entire masjid looked like a beautiful ornament, sparkling with a hundred diamonds and the lamps burnt throughout the night.

Word spread of the latest miracle of Baba and the merchants were both awed and scared. They gathered together and approached Baba, seeking forgiveness. Baba accepted their apologies but asked them to be honest in future.

And soon after that, he was, once again, deeply absorbed in the experience of the Self, with no apparent recollection of the incident.

Origins of the Saint

Who was this saint? Where did he gain such powers from? And did he enjoy demonstrating such magical powers, when most saints have been known to shun miracles?

The origins of the saint and details of his early days remain unknown. No one even knew his real name; they all called him 'Sai'. Nobody could even firmly ascertain whether he was a Hindu or a Muslim by birth, though there were compelling arguments in favour of both. Some evidence points to his birth in a Hindu Brahmin family in Pathri, in the Parabhani district of the state of Maharashtra. A fakir apparently brought him up and instilled in him the purity and perfection of yoga. Sai Baba's life after the age of sixteen is documented, but there is no account of the spiritual practices he followed. No literature written by him has been formally recorded. Often, he used to speak to his disciples on the subject, recollecting his earlier days as a seeker. Till the end, Baba led an austere lifestyle, untouched by the material wealth and power of thousands of devotees.

The Guru

Sometimes, Baba had mentioned to a few of his disciples that his guru (the fakir), with whom he had spent twelve years of his life, was a complete saint, an *aulia*. His guru did not blow any mantra in his ear, nor did he give any *upadesh* (lesson), but treated him with so much love that he considered him 'love incarnate'. Baba would always feel his guru's loving protection, irrespective of whether he was physically present or not. In yogic tradition, the guru is entitled to demand of his disciple *dakshina*, or some specific material donation. According to Baba, the guru only asked him for two paise of *dakshina*, namely *shraddha* (faith) and *saburi* (patience and perseverance). Faith, not only implies unwavering faith in God, but also in oneself. Patience and perseverance are essential in spiritual life, when one takes refuge in a path, a form or a master. Those without patience and perseverance keep questioning their sadhana and also keep moving from one master to another and never attain fulfilment in this life.

Baba served his master wholeheartedly. He attributed all that he was and all that he had attained to his guru and emphasised that he never felt the need to look elsewhere for guidance. Unfortunately, nobody could discover any details of the guru's identity, undoubtedly a great master, a Sufi fakir or yogi.

Hatha Yoga and other Yoga Practices

Baba never taught Hatha Yoga to his devotees and disciples, but he himself used to practice yoga. He was sometimes observed cleaning his intestines (*dhauti*) in a novel way by taking them out of the body and washing them. Baba would also practice Khanda Yoga, or separation of the various parts of the body and would remain in that state for some time. Once, a visitor came to the mosque to meet Baba, and found his body parts strewn all over the place. He thought someone had killed the saint and was worried that the police would arrest him for the crime. He ran away from the spot, but later found the saint hale and hearty. Baba never performed these practices publicly and no one understood why he performed them at all.

Baba was apparently also an adept of Shabda Yoga, or the yoga of the eternal sound. Once, Swami Sai Sharan Anand, a great devotee, mentioned that *nama smaran* (the echo of the divine name of the Lord) always continued in the saint's heart. The *anahata* (unstruck) sound always poured out of his body.

Learning and Education

Abdul, one of Baba's closest Muslim disciples, wrote in his unpublished works that the saint had a profound knowledge of Islamic religion and civilisation, including the *Koran*, the *Sira* (life of the prophet), the *Hadith* (the guiding traditions), the *Sunnah* (code of conduct), the *Shariat* (religious law) and the *Tariqat* (spiritual observances). He was well versed with the works of Sufi shaikhs, the masters of popular Sufi orders – the Chishtis, the Naqshbandis, the Qadiris and the Suharawardis. In fact, Abdul considered Baba's depth of knowledge on these subjects truly amazing. Though Baba possessed deep knowledge of both Hindu and Islamic scriptures, for many years, his simple and unassuming attitude, his ragged clothing and general demeanour led people to assume that he was a mystic without any formal knowledge. But that impression changed over time, and one particular incident was responsible for it.

This happened at a time when devotees were not yet swarming by the thousands to see Sai Baba. Very few individuals used to be by his side. Once, Nanasaheb Chandorkar was massaging Baba's feet and simultaneously chanting some Sanskrit verses under his breath. Baba asked Nana what he was muttering and the latter dismissively responded that he was repeating verses from the *Bhagwad Gita*. Baba then asked Nana to speak out aloud and give him an explanation. Baba was not satisfied with what he heard from Nana and requested him to repeat the exercise, this time going word by word. In the ensuing discussion, Nana realised that Baba was well versed with the intricacies of Sanskrit grammar. Sanskrit was a language that few had mastered, and even fewer could speak, but the saint appeared to have a strong command over it. While that was in itself amazing, since Baba had not revealed any sign of formal learning till then, Nana was further surprised by his interpretation of the verse. From that day onwards, Nana firmly believed that the saint had an impressive mystical and intuitive understanding of the scriptures.

Technique of Instruction

Baba would often resort to storytelling as a medium of instruction. The stories used to be very specific and relevant for some listeners while others heard them only out of devotion. He had no intermediary and would instruct each disciple personally. In most cases, as the devotees increasingly contemplated on him, he would reveal greater knowledge and inspire even more devotion. The process of expansion of consciousness was spontaneous. The saint also enjoined his devotees to follow the virtues of *shraddha* and *saburi*.

Above Sectarianism

Arthur Osborne, author of *The Incredible Sai Baba* narrates a tale of his neighbour, Ms Dutton, a devout Christian. She had given up the life of a nun as she found it difficult to cope with the strict convent life. Though she had been given permission to leave, she was worried about how she would manage her life. She had a nephew in Calcutta, but was hesitant to contact him; she was unsure whether he would welcome her after so many years without contact, or whether he would even recognise her. Just then, a saint appeared in her room. He did not appear to be a Christian saint and his presence surprised her since the door was locked.

The saint reassured her, asked her to leave for Calcutta and then requested for some money. She told him she had none, but he reminded her of the money in a box she had forgotten about. When she turned to recover the money, he vanished and true to his words, Ms Dutton did find some money in the box. She then joined her nephew in Calcutta and lived a happy life with him. When she narrated this tale to her neighbour (Arthur), he instinctively felt that the saint was none other than Sai Baba.

He showed a picture of Sai Baba to Ms Dutton and the lady exclaimed that it was indeed the same saint who had blessed her!

Sai Baba's outward appearance was that of a Muslim fakir, but he had a large Hindu following. In fact, Hindus, Muslims, Jains, Parsis and Christians, all flocked to him for blessings, and he instructed each person in accordance with the tenets of his own path. He constantly chanted *Allah Malik*[1], a very Muslim term, but he always sat by the *dhuni*, which he considered a holy fire, a concept alien to Islam.

Once, a burly Muslim devotee objected to the Hindu practices that Baba was following. When he complained to the saint, the latter didn't pay him attention. Out of sheer anger, the Muslim devotee tried to attack Sai Baba with a big stick. However, the saint calmly held his hand and looked into his eyes. The devotee fell powerless on the ground and could not get up even with the help of two people.

Mhalsapati, a devout Hindu, would offer his prayers to the saint daily by visiting the mosque. Once, a group of armed Muslims tried to stop this practice. Mhalsapati saw the crowd and hesitated, but Baba called him and instructed him to perform the puja. With Baba's visible support, the devotee continued his routine fearlessly.

Sai *Leela*

Once, Sai Baba said, 'I give people what they want in the hope that they will begin to want what I want to give them.' Baba was all powerful and his *leela*s are innumerable. Some of these took place when Sai Baba was physically present and, in fact, even today there are instances of the saint blessing his devotees through these gestures. Only a few of the beautiful incidents are mentioned here.

The Hathayogi

Once, a practitioner of Hatha Yoga visited the saint, hoping to receive the latter's blessings to overcome some obstacles that he was experiencing in his sadhana. In those days, Baba was not surrounded by large crowds, and so the practitioner had the opportunity to join him and Nanasaheb Chandorkar for a meal. Baba was eating rotis and onions, which seemed strange to the Hathayogi, who believed that onions belonged to the tamasic category of food and should be strictly avoided by spiritual aspirants[2].

As the thought crossed his mind, Sai Baba spoke out loudly, 'Nana! Only they can eat onions who can digest them.' The yogi was startled by Baba's faculty to read his mind, and his doubts were replaced by devotion. Eventually, he received the saint's blessings and returned home to pursue his sadhana.

The Mosque and the Plank

Throughout the day, Baba used to sit beside the *dhuni*, nobody knew for how many hours he slept, as even at five in the morning, he could be spotted in his favourite position. For many years, the saint slept within the premises of the mosque. He used a wooden plank as his bed. The arrangement was fragile, as the plank was suspended on both sides from the roof by flimsy rags. Nobody could understand how Baba managed to climb up on the plank or get down from it and many people were curious to see him do it. One day, Baba broke the plank into small pieces as he could sense the increasing curiosity among the villagers.

The Plague

In 1911, an epidemic of bubonic plague ravaged the area. The son of Dadasaheb Khaparde — a devotee — had developed high fever and was in pain. One day when the saint was on his daily rounds, the boy's mother approached him and asked him to bless her son. Sai Baba lifted his *kafni* and showed her four buboes on his body. He assured the woman that her son would be fine. He was suffering for her child. Baba suggested applying burnt cotton wool dipped in ghee on the buboes. During this time, seven to eight buboes appeared on the saint's body and he, too, developed high fever. But he refused to give up his daily routine and assured everyone he would be fine.

Dakshina

Usually, devotees flocked to Baba's doorstep to offer him money; from some, he used to accept this gesture and from others, he refused to even take a penny. At times, the saint used to request for *dakshina* to test the devotee's faith in him. Often, people promised to donate a sum of money to a temple, or a deity, or even the saint himself, in return for supernatural grace to fulfil a material desire. Generally, once the desire was fulfilled, the devotee would forget his promise, but Sai Baba would then remind him of his oath. He never hoarded money; whatever he received, he gave away and lived on alms. Once, Baba said that when he took alms from anyone, he would also take upon himself that person's material difficulties. In fact, according to Chakranarayan, a police constable, Baba would distribute much more than he received, something that completely baffled him. Usually, whatever Baba took from a devotee, he returned manifold.

Once, Somnath Deshpande, son of Nanasaheb Nimonkar, a great devotee, visited Sai Baba. The saint requested the young man to part with ₹10—a very large sum in those days—the devotee immediately obliged. Somnath then went on a pilgrimage. He returned home after many days. When he resumed work, he was surprised, he had been sanctioned a monthly increment of ₹10 in his salary with effect from the day he had handed over the money to Sai Baba!

Then, there were others who were wary of donating money at all to the saint. Once, a certain gentleman gave his entire money to a friend to avoid giving *dakshina* to Baba. He thought that if Baba would request him for *dakshina*, he could genuinely claim he did not even have a penny. As the gentleman had presumed, Baba approached him and asked him for ₹2. He conveniently told the saint that he did not have any money. Baba smiled, and then asked him to take it back from his friend and give it. The gentleman realised he could not outwit the all-knowing saint.

Seedless Grapes

Kaka Mahajani, a resident of Bombay, was a great devotee of Baba and would speak about his miracles to as many as would listen. This prompted Thakkar, Kaka's employer, to visit the saint in Shirdi.

When he reached Dwarakamayi mosque, he saw Sai Baba busy in distributing grapes to everyone; he also gave some to Thakkar. Those were grapes with seeds, and Thakkar could neither swallow the seeds nor could he spit them out. He found it very inconvenient to hold the sticky seeds in his hand. He began to wonder why Baba gave him these grapes if he was truly a saint, since a true saint would know of Thakkar's discomfiture. Just as he was nursing these thoughts, Baba distributed the same lot of grapes again. Strangely, this time the grapes were seedless! Thakkar asked the person next to him whether he had received seedless grapes or grapes with seeds, and found that his neighbour had received grapes with seeds. Thakkar concluded that it was within Baba's power to convert grapes with seeds into seedless ones if he wished to do so.

The Blacksmith's Daughter

Once, when Baba was sitting in the mosque stoking the *dhuni*, he consciously put his hand in the fire and sat quietly as it burned. Seeing this, a devotee rushed to Baba's rescue and dragged him back. By this time, some people had gathered in the mosque and everybody was anxious to know about the saint's well-being. When devotees asked him the reason for his action, Baba informed them that he had to take this step to save the life of a baby girl. She had fallen from her mother's lap into the fire and he had pulled her out of it successfully. A few days later, it was learnt that at the same time in Shirdi, a blacksmith's daughter had fallen into the fire, but miraculously nothing happened to her!

Control over the Elements

Baba had complete control over Nature, and he demonstrated this capability many a times to protect his devotees and disciples.

A devotee's farm was on fire, and other devotees beseeched the saint to help. Baba walked towards the yard, sprinkled some water on a stack of sheaves and, strangely, the fire died down. In another incident, the fire in Baba's *dhuni* blazed high in an uncontrolled manner, with the flames reaching up to the ceiling. Devotees sitting in the mosque got worried. Baba picked up his short stick and began to hit a pillar, shouting at the fire to subside. With each stroke of his stick, the flames calmed down. In a short while, the *dhuni* was normal again.

Another time, Baba was sharing a meal with his devotees in the mosque. Suddenly, in the middle of his meal, he looked up and shouted, 'Stop,' pointing at the ceiling. After the meal, when the group stepped out, large pieces of the ceiling fell on the floor, exactly where they had been sitting and eating. Baba had obviously stopped the chunks from falling while they were all sitting inside the room.

Insight

Incidents of the saint's omniscience were common, but that did not cease to amaze his devotees. Cholkar, a very poor devotee living in Thane, near Bombay, longed to travel to Shirdi but could not afford the trip. He decided to forego sugar in his tea, as it was very expensive in those days. This way, he managed to save some money to travel to Shirdi but did not mention this to anyone. After he had met the saint, Baba requested another devotee, Bapusaheb Jog[3], to take Cholkar to his home and serve the latter many cups of sugared tea. Cholkar was moved.

The saint's omniscience also covered his disciple's dreams and he, sometimes, discussed the key parts of the dream in a casual manner. Once, Baba appeared in the dream of his devotee Professor Narke, along with a man who looked like a labourer. In the dream, Baba pointed at the man and informed Narke that they had been close friends in the previous birth. The play of karma was responsible for the two being in different conditions in the present life. Narke awoke with a clear memory of the dream and as he pondered over it, he felt certain he had never seen the man before. Strangely, few days later, Narke paid a visit to Baba in Shirdi and was sitting in the mosque with him when he saw 'his friend' entering the premises. The man had come with a bundle of firewood and Baba suggested Narke to pay 'his friend' ₹2 for the wood. When the latter hesitated, Baba asked him, 'Don't you know him from your previous life?' Narke's doubts were dispelled.

Baba could also predict the future of his devotees and their families. Mhalsapati's wife gave birth to a son in 1897. When the couple took the child to the saint for his blessings, the latter asked them to take care of their son for the next twenty-five years only. Mhalsapati was baffled by the saint's words. In 1922, exactly twenty-five years later, Mhalsapati passed away.

Baba's Blessings

Once, someone donated a good variety of mangoes to the saint. Sai Baba decided to share the crop with Damodar Rasane (Damya), a close devotee. He kept eight pieces aside for Damya. Damya was on his way to Shirdi, but nobody had any news of his planned trip. Meanwhile, some children couldn't resist and stole four pieces from the share that Baba had kept hidden away. When Damya arrived, Baba gave him the mangoes and asked him to feed them to his second wife. Over the years, his wife gave birth to eight children, but only four survived, probably representing the four mango pieces that were not stolen.

Dream Appearances and Remote Materialisations

On many occasions, the saint's devotees would recount how he had blessed them in their dreams, by giving them an object that fulfilled their wishes. Once, a woman dreamt that Sai Baba was offering her a coconut, promising her she would give birth to a son if she ate it. Next morning, when she awoke, the woman found the coconut beside her! Needless to say, she followed Baba's words. In due course of time she was blessed with a son.

Another incident was of Raoji Upasani, a devotee from Dhulia in the state of Maharashtra. When his son was very sick, he dreamt that Baba had applied holy ash, *udi*, on his son's forehead with assurances of quick recovery. Baba also instructed the father to bring the child to Shirdi once he was well again. The child was in a critical condition but, to the surprise of the doctors, he recovered rapidly. Upasani followed Baba's words and came to meet the saint with his son. Baba hugged the boy and told him that he (Baba) had visited their home when he was very sick.

Uddhavesh, another devotee, was on a pilgrimage to Girnar, where he fainted due to exertion. A holy man with a pot of water revived him. By the time Uddhavesh regained consciousness, his saviour had disappeared. The next time he met Baba in Shirdi, the latter reminded him that he had once given him some water to drink!

Nanasaheb Chandorkar, one of Sai Baba's prominent devotees, had many mystical experiences. Once, he went to see a saint, Govind Buwa, who stayed deep in the forest near the Padmalaya shrine, close to the town of Pachora in Jalgaon district of Maharashtra. Govind Buwa normally retired at ten o'clock at night and refused to meet anyone after that. Nana started out from Pachora on foot in the evening, walking through hilly and forested roads. Unfortunately, Nana misjudged the time of the journey, and he walked through the forest reaching way beyond ten, completely exhausted. Nana lost hopes of meeting Govind Buwa. He was worried about even finding a safe place to rest at night in the jungle. He somehow managed to reach Govind Buwa's ashram, where a big surprise awaited him. Govind Buwa sought him out and told him that Sai Baba had appeared before him and asked him to keep a pot of hot tea ready. Tea was just what Nana was longing for at that time!

A very interesting incident occurred when Nana was living in Jamner in Jalgaon. His daughter was due to deliver a child, she was going through acute labour pains for the last three days. Nana was worried for both her and the child. He was constantly praying to Sai Baba for divine intervention. Just then, Baba decided to send Ramgir Buwa, another devotee, with holy ash to Jamner. Ramgir was perplexed; he had just ₹2 on him and was worried how he would manage the journey from Shirdi with so little money. Noticing Ramgir's discomfiture, Baba assured him that he would definitely make it to his destination, as he had enough to pay for the train's fare. Ramgir reached Jalgaon, the nearest railway station to Jamner and was wondering how to make his way to Nana's house, when he saw a horse carriage waiting.

The driver was calling out his name loudly. The driver told him that he had been sent by Nanasaheb and the two set off for Jamner. In the course of the journey, the driver also fed Ramgir. When they were very close to Nanasaheb's residence, Ramgir stopped to relieve himself. When he returned, he found that the carriage and the driver had vanished. A bit surprised, he made his way to Nanasaheb's house and handed over the holy ash to Nana, just in the nick of time, as the girl was about to deliver. After some time, Ramgir narrated the entire episode of the carriage and the driver to Nana. Nana was clueless, as he had not sent anyone to Jalgaon at all. Ramgir Buwa then realised this was Sai Baba's grace, as he had promised him that the Lord would take care of him.

Once, a devotee, B.V. Dev sent Baba an invitation to grace an occasion at his home. The saint acknowledged it. He also mentioned that he would be accompanied by two more people. On the nominated day, a group of three people came to Dev's house. One of them was a sannyasi who had been pursuing Dev for donations, but he reassured the latter that this time he had not come for money. He was hungry and was looking for food. Dev readily fed the three. Everything in the ceremony went well, but Dev was unhappy that Sai Baba had not come. So he wrote to the saint, complaining of the breach of promise. Baba asked a devotee to write back declaring that he had indeed come with two companions as he had promised. He explained that it was Dev who had failed to recognise him. Dev then realised that Baba was indeed present on that day. He was the sannyasi who had appeared on his doorstep with two companions.

Acceptor of Offerings

Often, people would send their offerings to the saint through the devotees travelling to Shirdi. If the devotee carrying the offering forgot to give it to Baba, the saint would ask for it. Sri Vasudevananda Saraswati also known as Tembe Maharaj, a great saint of the Datta Sampradaya[4] – once requested Pundalik Rao to give a coconut to Sai Baba, who Tembe Maharaj addressed as his 'brother'. By mistake,

Pundalik Rao and his friends consumed the coconut before they even reached Shirdi. When they met Sai Baba, he immediately asked them to hand over what his 'brother' had given them for him. Pundalik begged Baba's forgiveness and offered another coconut as a substitute. Baba refused to accept it, claiming that the coconut given by Tembe Maharaj was far more valuable to him. He, however, forgave Pundalik and told him that since they were his children after all, they were right in consuming what was meant for him.

Once, Sai Baba decided to have a meal at his devotee Purandare's house, but he requested the host to serve only simple food. On the nominated day, Purandare arranged for everything. He anxiously waited for the saint to arrive. But instead of Baba, groups of fakirs kept coming to his home and demanded food. Purandare's family was worried that the food would run out but, surprisingly, despite the crowd, the vessels remained reasonably full. Finally, Purandare's patience ran out and he personally went to remind the saint of his promise. Reaching the mosque, he requested Sai Baba to come along and eat the food that had been prepared for him. However, the saint surprised Purandare by saying that his stomach was already full and, unfortunately, would not be able to oblige him. The devotee left for his home, but a question kept on nagging him, how could Baba say that? Then he realised that the streams of fakirs demanding food at his doorstep was nothing else but Sai Baba's miracle.

Snakes and Scorpions

Shirdi, in those days, was infested with snakes and scorpions. There were many instances when Sai Baba had warned the villagers to watch out for such creatures. The people, thus forewarned, were careful and managed to evade a potential crisis. Even if someone reported a case of snake or scorpion bite, Sai Baba would cure it with his blessings.

Once, his devotee, Shama, was bitten by a snake and the poison seemed to be spreading quickly. Instead of seeking medical aid, he told his friends to take him to Baba. However, as the group was climbing the steps of the mosque, Baba appeared before them, his eyes red in anger and shouted, 'Down! Down! Don't come up!'

The devotee was deeply hurt. He couldn't believe that, in his time of distress, Sai Baba had turned him out of the mosque. His friends then urged him to seek medical aid in earnest but Shama declined. He remained glued to the spot; soon, he heard Baba's voice calling out to him, assuring him that the merciful Lord was still gracious to him. Shama was glad to hear this. He realised that Baba had been addressing not him but the poison, asking it not to rise (come up). Miraculously, nothing happened to Shama, despite the fact that he had not used any medication; the saint's divine presence cured him.

In another incident, Bapusaheb Jog was bitten by a scorpion and was in intense pain. He rushed to Sai Baba to seek a cure. Baba asked the devotee to go home and assured him he would be all right. The minute Baba said these words, Jog felt the pain subsiding completely.

The Protector of Virtue

Hari Vinayak Sathe, a devotee, developed a desire to meet a woman of questionable moral character. When he was with Baba, the saint perceived the latent desire of his devotee and indirectly warned him, but Sathe did not understand his indication. Later that day, when Sathe went to meet the woman, all of a sudden, the saint appeared before him, gestured his displeasure and vanished. This shook Sathe out of his mood and he resolved never to interact with the woman again.

The Word Was the Cure

Baba also had the powers to heal people suffering from incurable diseases; his word alone became the cure. Whatever he advised them – even if it was irrational or, in some cases, could have worsened the ailment – it resulted in a miraculous cure when followed.

Once, Bapusaheb Buti was down with cholera and Baba prescribed a bowl of *kheer*, a sweet dish made from milk, rich in dry fruits. This would certainly have worsened the ailment, but Buti ate the *kheer* and recovered.

Leaving Shirdi with Baba's Blessing

Sai Baba always used to caution his devotees before commencing their journey back home from Shirdi. If the person was too bent on doing things his way, he would invariably meet a mishap. Once, Baba told a person not to be in a hurry to catch his train, as there was plenty of time. The individual thought he knew better, but when he reached the station, he found the train delayed.

Once, Kaka Mahajani came to Shirdi with the intention of staying a full week with the saint, but when he arrived, Baba asked him to leave the next day. Mahajani was disappointed, but complied. On his return, he found a crisis had arisen in his office and his presence was needed to sort the matter out. In fact, a letter to that effect had already been despatched from his office, but Mahajani had returned even before it could reach Shirdi.

Indifference to the Material

Arthur Osborne describes another incident, which reflected Baba's indifference towards all organisations in the phenomenal world. A thief had been caught in the neighbouring town of Dhulia and to confuse the police, he claimed Sai Baba had given him the stolen jewellery. Summons were issued to Baba to appear in the court, but when they reached Baba, he ordered a disciple to throw them into the *dhuni*. This resulted in a warrant for Baba's arrest, but he also got it thrown, this time into the commode.

Fearing that things were spiralling into a needless crisis, some devotees petitioned the government to hold the court hearing in Shirdi, since the person being summoned was a saint, dear to one and all. The petition was approved and a first-class magistrate held the court in Shirdi, but Baba's demeanour confounded the authorities. The magistrate would ask him straightforward questions, but he would reply in philosophical terms.

The magistrate asked Baba if he knew the alleged thief. Baba responded, 'Yes, I know him,' but before this assertion could be considered seriously, he added, 'I know everyone.'

When the magistrate asked him if he had given the thief the jewels, Baba again nodded in agreement, and then characteristically added, 'Who gives what? And to whom do they give?'

The magistrate was exasperated and tried to explain to him the seriousness of the matter. Baba finally lost his patience and said, 'What is all this about? And what has this to do with me?' He stomped out, leaving the magistrate frustrated and angry. Once again, things had become extremely serious and Baba's arrest could not be ruled out. Fortunately, some glaring holes were found in the thief's testimony and the matter ended.

Dwaita and Adwaita (Duality and Universal Identification)

Baba, sometimes, showed the principle of duality in his nature. On one hand, he insisted he was but the servant of God, and often repeated God is the Master, but on the other, he completely identified with God.

Sometimes, he was a picture of humility and would gravely say, 'We are blessed by your presence,' or 'Brothers, I deem myself fortunate that I came to know you, and I am grateful to God for it.' He would not hesitate to consider himself lucky to have seen the feet of some visitors and would equate himself with an insect in their presence.

At other times, he equated himself with God to the extent that he said with authority, 'If one meditates on me, repeats my name and sings about my deeds, he is transformed and his karma is destroyed. I stay by his side always.'

Sai Baba had undoubtedly attained the Vedantic stage or ideal of complete universal identification and, from many of his utterances, it appeared that he had attained this state even before this life. He, once, described the state of his birth thus, 'My mother was greatly rejoicing that she had got a son...I was wondering at her conduct. When did she beget me? Was I begotten at all? Have I not been already in existence?'

Baba, sometimes, consciously and sometimes accidentally, demonstrated his state of universal identification through his actions and teachings. He, once, told a lady that he was hungry and requested her to cook for him. She went home and prepared a meal, only to find a stray dog trying to run away with the food. She chased the dog away angrily and took some of the remaining food to Baba. Only she now found him in no mood to eat. 'You chased me away when I wanted the food and now I no longer want it,' was what he said.

In a similar vein, another lady, once, fed a dog and a pig and went to meet the saint. He told her, 'Eating that lovely bread, I am heartily content and still belching. The dog...is one with me, so also other creatures are one with me. I am roaming in their forms. He who sees me in all these creatures is my beloved. So abandon the sense of duality and distinction, and [always] serve me as you did today.'

Once, Baba felt hurt when a bull was surreptitiously sold to a butcher in a neighbouring village. He decided to save the animal and appeared in the dream of his devotee, Bayaji. In the dream, he told Bayaji that he (Baba) was tied to the door of a butcher and that he should rescue him. Bayaji understood Baba's words and with this timely intimation, he, along with some others, managed to rescue the bull.

Identification with Deities, Gurus and Saints

Baba identified himself completely with various deities and gurus. Often, he would remind visitors of promises they had made to their chosen avatar of God or a saint or their guru. At other times, he would appear before some visitors in the form of their guru or chosen deity.

A doctor, a devotee of Sri Ram[5], visited Shirdi, but told the person on whose bidding he had come that he would not bow before a Muslim fakir. Suddenly, Sai Baba appeared before him as Sri Ram and the devotee was delighted to see the Lord. He forgot his prior resolve and bowed before Baba, as he now realised the unity between Baba and the Lord.

In another instance, Muley Shastri, a devotee of the famous saint Guru Gholap, hesitated to meet Sai Baba in the mosque, for fear of ritual pollution[6]. Muley had come to meet Bapusaheb Buti, a millionaire devotee of Baba, who was then in Shirdi. Baba, who normally wore an off-white garb, hinted to others he would wear *geru*[7] that day, though he did not change his clothes. The reference was probably to Guru Gholap, who normally wore *geru*. Baba sent Bapusaheb Buti to bring Muley Shastri to the mosque and since Muley Shastri could not refuse Buti, he reluctantly accompanied the latter to the mosque. The *aarti* was being sung when they arrived and, to Muley's amazement, he saw his guru, Guru Gholap, sitting where Baba normally sat. Muley prostrated himself before Baba and once the ritual was over, he, once again, saw Sai Baba sitting where he normally did.

Many also considered Baba to be an incarnation of Lord Dattatreya or an incarnation of Sri Swami Samarth of Akkalkot, the great yogi. Close to the day of his *mahasamadhi*, Sri Swami Samarth had disclosed to his devotees his plan to leave the body. He was approached by Keshav Naik, a devotee, who was distraught with news of the saint's planned departure. Keshav asked the yogi who he and his son should look to for guidance after his departure. Swami Samarth directed him to go to Shirdi, where his own incarnation existed in human form.

Megha, a devotee of Lord Siva, considered Baba to be an incarnation of Lord Siva and expressed his desire to bathe the saint with water from the Godavari on a particular holy day. Sai Baba would normally bathe once in eight to ten days, though he was always clean. He was reluctant to allow Megha to bathe him, but when he persisted, Baba agreed. He requested Megha to put only a little water on his head, as the head was considered a representative of the body. However, Megha got carried away and began ritual chanting of 'Har Har Gange' while pouring the water from the pot all over Baba's head and body. Strangely, only the head had become wet. Not a single drop of water was found on the saint's body, which remained completely dry.

The Devotees

While Baba arrived in Shirdi around 1868, it took time for his popularity to spread beyond Shirdi. Over time, thousands of devotees swarmed to Shirdi to see Baba and seek his blessings, particularly after 1910. He had very close relationships with some devotees, including Mhalsapati, Swami Sai Sharan Anand, Abdul, Upasani Maharaj, Bayajabai, Tatya Kote Patil, Shama, Dadasaheb Khaparde, Nanasaheb Chandorkar, Kakasaheb Dixit, Megha, Das Ganu Maharaj, Govindrao Dabholkar, Bapusaheb Buti and Hari Vinayak Sathe, to name a few.

Nanavali, a great devotee, loved the saint so deeply that on the thirteenth day after the latter's *mahasamadhi*, he himself passed away. Nanavali appeared to be slightly mentally deranged, but Baba maintained he was actually a realised saint of a very high stature. There were also some miracles attributed to Nanavali. His samadhi is situated near the eastern entrance door of Lendi Bagh in Shirdi.

Sai Baba would often mention that his link with his devotees was across many births. Once, he told Nanasaheb Chandorkar that their relationship spanned four previous births. Baba would also describe the previous lives of devotees. For instance, he once told Balram Mankar and Swami Sai Sharan Anand that they had lived and performed penance in caves opposite each other. He also spoke of Chandrabai Borkar as one who always searched him out in every life wherever he went. Baba also told Dadasaheb Khaparde that he (Baba) and some of his devotees (Dadasaheb Khaparde, Bapusaheb Jog, Kakasaheb Dixit, Shama and Dadabhat Kelkar) had lived together in a previous life along with their guru.

Once, R.B. Purandare's mother approached Sai Baba and requested his grace on her son. Baba assured her, 'Mother! I know your son from several last births. From his childhood, I have protected him. Without that, I do not even eat food.'

To explain the blessedness of the devotees, brief overviews of the lives of some select disciples and devotees are given here.

Swami Sai Sharan Anand

One of Sai Baba's foremost disciples, Swami Sai Sharan Anand, was born as Vaman Patel in 1889, in Mota, in Surat district of Gujarat.

At the age of five, he was severely ill due to bouts of diarrhoea and it was not expected that he would survive long. Just then, a fakir appeared out of nowhere, and told his mother that her child had auspicious signs on his body and pointed them out, which surprisingly she had never noticed before. The mother told him that those signs meant little to her, as she was worried for the child's life. The fakir told her not to worry. He gave her some *udi* to feed the child. Vaman recovered and, when he was older, his mother recounted this incident to him.

When he turned seven, Vaman started visiting a temple daily. Everyday, on his way, he would meet a fakir who would lovingly tease him. Many years later, in 1911, when Vaman finally met Baba, he realised that the fakir was none other than Baba himself. How was this possible, when in the years 1894 and 1895, Baba lived continuously in Shirdi? Baba's ways were mysterious. The mystery deepened when Baba told Kakasaheb Dixit that he knew Vaman since the time he was very young.

Since his childhood, Vaman had memorised various *stotras* (prayers), such as *Aditya Hridaya*, *Ram Raksha* and *Vishnu Sahasranam*, which he repeated daily. However, he lost his faith in rituals over time, but continued to chant some prayers out of habit. He read the *Bhagwad Gita*, and also the *Vairagya Shatak* and *Neeti Shatak*, written by Yogiraj Bhartrihari, and these books infused him with the spirit of renunciation. He became obsessed with the objective of seeing God face to face and also unravelling the mysteries of the universe. It was with this aim that he finally came to Shirdi.

The first meeting made an impact on Vaman and he kept visiting Sai Baba, until the latter's passing away in 1918. Sai Baba made him undergo various austerities and Vaman had many spiritual experiences. Gradually, Vaman became fearless and would meditate even in the middle of a forest at the dead of night. Once, in Shirdi, a heavy stone fell on his head. Though Vaman survived, he was grievously wounded. Sai Baba sent an ointment that immediately alleviated the pain and in the course of the next few days, Baba completely awakened Vaman spiritually. The periods with Baba led to a break in Vaman's professional career, but each time, with the saint's grace, the latter's career always got back on track.

Vaman was a prolific writer and wrote many books of religious significance, some of which were published posthumously. His wife died in 1951, which freed him from material obligations and, in 1953, he took *sannyasa* as per Sai Baba's directions. He spent the rest of his life in complete meditation and had reportedly developed various supernatural powers that he used sparingly. He passed away in 1982.

Abdul

Abdul was born in 1871, in Nanded (in Maharashtra), and was of a deeply religious temperament since childhood. Apparently, his parents entrusted him to the care of Amiruddin Faqir of Nanded for training in Sufism.

Abdul lived with his teacher till 1889, and after that, he spent the rest of his life with Sai Baba. Apparently, Sai Baba appeared before Amiruddin in a dream and gave him two mangoes. Baba told him to give them to Abdul and requested him to send the boy to Shirdi. Next morning when Amiruddin woke up, he found the two mangoes before him. He handed over the fruit to Abdul and sent him to Shirdi. When Abdul entered Shirdi, Baba mentioned, '*Mera Kabla Aala*' (my crow has arrived)[8].

Abdul immersed himself in Baba's service and, in a way, completely became one with him. Abdul was obviously an inseparable part of Baba's *leela*. Many years later, when Amiruddin Faqir requested Sai Baba to send back his disciple, Sai Baba flatly refused and even Abdul showed no inclination to go back to his teacher.

Baba would, sometimes, beat Abdul in anger. He would beat other devotees as well. He usually did this to cleanse them[9]. Sai Baba would ask Abdul to read from a copy of the *Koran* in his presence and would explain the concepts to the young disciple.

130   *Yogis of India*

Abdul diligently wrote down Sai Baba's instructions, including his random pronouncements. After Sai Baba's death, Abdul, sometimes, used the jottings to solve people's problems with miraculous results. In one case, villagers dug a well in Shirdi only to find hard water in the source. They decided to consult Abdul on this issue. Abdul flipped open a page of his diary and found that Baba indicated to carry out the digging further. Abdul advised the people accordingly and, as predicted, they did find sweet water several feet below. In another case, based on the jottings in the diary, he told an advocate that his son would eventually return from the U.K. Surprisingly, the son who had married an Englishwoman and had attractive prospects of settling abroad did return to India with his wife.

Abdul's complete identification with Baba and his saintly personality created an atmosphere of reverence towards him. For many years, Abdul took care of Baba's samadhi, including cleaning and decorating it. He passed away in 1954 and his hut and *mazaar* (grave of a saint) are, to this day, open to visitors.

Bhagat Mhalsapati

Mhalsapati was a devotee of Khandoba[10] and a priest at the local temple. He and his family lived in dire poverty. He also doubled as a goldsmith to supplement his income. However, there was little income as a goldsmith in Shirdi. Mhalsa's real wealth was his devotion to God. He would sit in front of the idol the whole day, completely absorbed in meditation. As a result, he had developed the capability to see into the future.

When Sai Baba first arrived in Shirdi, some say it was Mhalsa who addressed him as 'Sai', an epithet that stuck. Mhalsa probably thought Baba was a Muslim saint, so he reportedly directed him to go to the dilapidated mosque, where he eventually settled. Mhalsa was an orthodox Hindu Brahmin. Due to his conservative views, it took time for him to develop devotion towards the fakir, but once he committed himself, he remained in his service for the rest of his life. For many years, he slept in the mosque with Baba and was one of his closest companions. Mhalsa was also the first to perform ritual worship of Baba in the traditional Hindu fashion.

Once, Mhalsa and his companions decided to go to Jejuri, in Maharashtra, on a pilgrimage. When they reached their destination, they found that the town was in the grip of plague. Mhalsa was wondering what to do as he rested against a carriage. Suddenly, Sai Baba appeared before him, but even before he could react, the saint vanished. He realised that they were safe and cajoled the group to stick to their plan. Eventually, all the members returned safely, having completed their pilgrimage successfully. Mhalsa wondered about the vision he had of the saint and speculated whether it had been his imagination at play. But, when Mhalsa met Baba, the saint said, 'I saw you in Jejuri, leaning against a carriage.'

Once, in 1886, Baba fell grievously ill and was suffering from asthma. He decided to take samadhi for three days. He asked Mhalsapati to take care of his body. He then withdrew his prana from his body and merged himself into samadhi. The body showed no sign of life – no heartbeat and no pulse. Soon after, some people gathered around the mosque and insisted that Baba was dead, and it was inauspicious to keep the dead body in that state. They were the ones who strongly opposed Sai Baba's philosophy and actions. It was a ripe opportunity for them to be rid, once and for all, of this 'so-called' saint. As time passed, they strengthened their opinion and Baba's devotees felt helpless. But, Mahalsapati refused to give in, insisting that the master would give up the samadhi soon. Eventually, when some members of the crowd tried to force the issue, Mhalsa hugged his master's body and began to call out to him to return. Shortly thereafter, the body began to show signs of life and people realised that Baba was not dead.

Mhalsa often had visions and dreams in which Lord Khandoba would direct him, or resolve his problems. Once, he had a dream in which the Lord asked him to give up the work of a goldsmith.

Mhalsa complied with the command and began to subsist on alms and lived the life of a monk while still being a householder. Several times, Baba tried to give Mhalsa some part of the *dakshina*, but Mhalsa was firm that all he wanted was permission to remain devoted to him. He preferred a life of poverty over everything else.

A few days before Baba's death, when Mhalsapati was lighting lamps around the mosque, Baba told him, 'Mhalsa, in a few days, I will go somewhere. After that, you keep coming here in the nights for two to four years.' Baba passed away shortly thereafter and Mhalsa followed almost exactly four years later in September 1922.

Shama

Shama, whose full name was Madhavrao Deshpande, was born in 1880, in the village of Nimone. His parents shifted to Shirdi when he was still a child. Though he was not highly educated, he became a teacher in the local school.

Once, some devotees came to Shirdi to see Sai Baba. They had been guided to Shirdi by a saint who lived in the temple town of Bhimashankar[11]. They asked Shama where the 'great saint of Shirdi' could be found, and he innocently replied that there was no 'great saint' in Shirdi. However, he explained that there was a 'mad fakir' who lived in the mosque. The devotees went there to see the fakir. Sai Baba angrily told the group to go away, shouting that he was a 'mad fakir'. He asked them to return to the saint in Bhimashankar. The visitors were amazed at Sai Baba's omniscience and bowed before him. Incidents like this convinced Shama that Baba was a great saint. Shama was later influenced by the views of other great saints such as Anandanath and Gangagir Baba. Both of them considered Sai Baba as an exceptional saint.

Shama grew up to be a straightforward and strong-willed person and Baba loved him like his own child. He referred to Baba as *Deva* (Lord). The extent of the saint's love for Shama became evident to others over time. Kakasaheb Dixit and Nanasaheb Chandorkar, once, came to invite Sai Baba to some family functions in the cities of Nagpur and Gwalior, respectively. The saint asked them to take 'his Shama' as his representative. Another time, Kakasaheb asked Baba to keep him forever under his protection. Baba told him to always keep Shama with him and consider him as his own self. Kakasaheb adhered to Baba's guidance and always tried to be with Shama.

Shama was also proficient in the traditional Indian line of medicine, Ayurveda. He would prescribe medicines to ailing people which, by the grace of Baba, would turn out to be particularly potent.

Shama behaved roughly with Baba at times but he also equally loved him dearly. Once, he developed a severe eye infection that would not cure, despite all attempts. He approached Baba at the mosque and began to loudly criticise him. He blamed the master for not showering his grace on him. Shama warned him that he would drive the latter out of the mosque if he did not cure his eye within a day. Baba was an embodiment of peace, so he did not get disturbed at Shama's ranting. He calmly asked him to apply the paste of black pepper and water on his eyes. Shama was not to be pacified and he questioned Baba, 'Deva, what do you mean? Won't I lose my eye completely if I apply black pepper on it?' Logically, black pepper should have irreversibly damaged the eye, but since Shama had implicit faith in Baba's words, he applied the paste as directed and miraculously the eye healed.

In his later years, Shama spent time in continuous remembrance of the saint and would often lament at the rough manner in which he had sometimes treated him. Shama was over eighty years when he passed away in 1940.

Tatya Kote Patil

Tatya was the son of Baijabai, the lady who took care of Baba when he first arrived in Shirdi. Baijabai was one of the first devotees of Baba who, in the early days, would seek out and forcibly feed him wherever he was. The saint referred to her as his 'sister' and remained indebted to her throughout his life for the loving care she had bestowed on him.

He was by her side when she breathed her last. He had promised her that he would consider Tatya's life as his very own.

Tatya remembered an episode from his early life when he was barely a child of seven or eight. At that time, Baba had just come to Shirdi and having no fixed place to stay would end up in the mosque more often. Tatya and his friends would mischievously trouble the fakir and the latter always responded likewise. Baba, sometimes, pinched Tatya, covered his eyes, changed the direction of his body while he was sleeping or covered his body with a warm blanket in summers. Mhalsapati and Tatya were also the only two who slept in the mosque with the saint.

In 1918, Tatya fell grievously ill, and his condition worsened day by day. Two years before this, when his devotee Ramchandra Patil was unwell, Baba had appeared in Ramchandra's dream and had blessed him with good health. He had warned Ramchandra, 'Tatya will pass away on Dussehra day two years later.' As Tatya's health worsened, Ramchandra became convinced of Sai Baba's prediction. However, Baba stood by his promise to Tatya's mother, Baijabai. He took Tatya's ailments upon himself. Tatya began to recover and Baba began to lose his health, until eventually, Sai Baba died in 1918 and the disciple passed away in 1920.

Kakasaheb Dixit

Hari Sitaram Dixit, popularly known as Kakasaheb Dixit, was born in 1864, in Khandwa, in the Central Provinces – now the state of Madhya Pradesh – in a learned and progressive family. He graduated in law and, in a short span of time, became one of the most prominent lawyers of Bombay. He also held many elected positions and was on the board of many institutions. He executed all his responsibilities proficiently. In 1906, aboard a ship on a trip to London, he hurt his leg, which never recovered despite all his efforts. This injury affected Dixit's productivity at work and also became a cause of embarrassment for him[12]. He gradually detached himself from the worldly affairs and became increasingly spiritual. In 1909, he was introduced to Sai Baba by a friend, Nanasaheb Chandorkar, who suggested that Baba could cure his leg. Kakasaheb however found Baba as his guru, and instead requested him to cure his worldliness.

In a couple of years, Kakasaheb built a grand rest house in Shirdi so that he could spend long stretches of time with the saint. He kept a small room for himself, where he could meditate and pray in solitude, while the rest of the rooms were opened to other devotees who used to visit Shirdi, so that they could have a convenient place to stay in.

Kakasaheb was then an extremely wealthy, influential and respected man. As his devotion to Baba increased, he became increasingly detached from the material life. As a result his legal practice suffered.

Kakasaheb's life was full of miracles because of Baba's grace. Baba intervened to protect and care for his family. Kakasaheb also experienced Baba's omniscience a number of times. Once, when he was going to meet Baba, he had a garland with him, which he planned to give to the saint along with ₹25 as *dakshina*. However, when he handed over the garland, he forgot the money. Baba looked at the garland and said simply, 'This garland is seeking ₹25.' Kaka was wonderstruck and he immediately gave the money.

Baba once declared, 'I will personally take "my" Kaka in a ship,' implying he would take him across *Bhavsagar* (the sea of worldliness) and grant him liberation. Baba also assured him that he would take care of Kaka's material needs. In his later years, Baba gave Kakasaheb a *kafni* to wear and allowed him to eat food in the same group as Baba and other Hindu and Muslim renunciates. The saint, thereby, acknowledged Kakasaheb's spiritual status to be the same as that of the other renunciates.

After Sai Baba's *mahasamadhi*, when the Shirdi Sai Sansthan was set up to take care of the saint's samadhi, Kakasaheb was appointed the honorary secretary, a role he performed with diligence. He also published several articles about Sai Baba, his teachings and the experiences of devotees in the *Sai Leela* magazine.

He strongly believed that the devotees of the Lord pass away on *ekadashi*, the eleventh day of the lunar month by the Hindu calendar, and he too desired to pass away that day. It was eventually on the *ekadashi* in July 1926 that Kakasaheb passed away, when he was deep in the blissful contemplation of his Lord, Sai.

Leaving the Body

In June 1918 — four months before his passing away — Sai Baba sent some money through a messenger to a fakir, Shamsuddin, in Aurangabad, with the message, 'On the ninth day of the ninth month, Allah will take away the lamp he lit. It is his will[13].' The fakir was instructed to organise food for a large gathering and to make arrangements for devotional singing to the Paigambar and *aulias*. Baba also told the messenger to give the same message to the saint Banne Mia along with a garland of flowers. When Banne Mia received it, he looked towards the heavens and shed tears. It was a clear indication from Sai Baba that according to the Muslim calendar, he would leave his body on the ninth day of the ninth month. On the predicted day, 15 October 1918, when people were celebrating Dusshera in Shirdi, Sai Baba cast off his mortal coils.

A few days before his passing away, Abdul was cleaning the mosque, when he accidentally dropped Baba's brick. Some sources claim that the brick was given to Sai Baba by his guru. The brick broke into two pieces and Baba cried out that it was not the brick, but his own fate that had broken. The brick had been his companion all his life in Shirdi.

A few months earlier, an incident occurred that laid the foundation for Baba's plans for the future. Bapusaheb Buti, a devoted disciple, had moved with his family to Shirdi. One night, Baba appeared in his dream and instructed him to construct a rest house and a temple in Shirdi. Bapusaheb awoke with a distinct memory of the dream and, on waking up, he saw Shama, who was also sleeping there, crying. When Bapusaheb asked Shama why he was crying, the latter replied that he had dreamt of Sai Baba. In the dream Baba had asked for a rest house and a temple to be constructed in Shirdi. Bapusaheb felt blessed and he firmly resolved to build the rest house and the temple. He decided to dedicate the temple to Lord Krishna.

Sai Baba also gave his permission and preparations began in earnest. Baba abstrusely mentioned to Shama that he himself would move into the temple once it was ready. Soon after spending almost a ₹100,000, the temple was ready and the idol of Lord Krishna was being prepared when Sai Baba breathed his last in that very temple.

The Body and Beyond

The news of Sai Baba's death spread like wildfire. Hindus and Muslims began to argue over last rites, with both communities insisting they would dispose off the body in line with their own customs. In the meantime, Baba appeared before some devotees in a vision. He appeared before Laxman Bhat and asked him to perform the daily worship rites, explaining that Bapusaheb Jog, who normally performed the ritual worship, was not doing the same under the mistaken notion that he (Baba) was dead. He also appeared before Das Ganu in the holy city of Pandharpur in Maharashtra. He told him that he had left his body and that he should come to Shirdi and cover it with flowers.

Finally, the quarrel between the communities was resolved and both agreed that the saint's body would be buried in the temple where he had passed away. Strangely, even after three whole days, Baba's body looked bright and remained soft, without a trace of rigor mortis.

Casting off the body has never interfered with Sai Baba's ability to appear before his devotees in visions or sometimes physically.

We close this chapter with his own words, 'Believe in me, though I pass away, my bones in my tomb will give you hope and confidence. Not only myself but my tomb would be speaking, moving and communicating with those who would surrender themselves wholeheartedly to me. Do not be anxious that I would be absent from you…but remember me always, believe in me with your heart and soul and then you will be most benefitted.'

And, these words have proved true to the hundreds of thousands of seekers who approach him for grace in Shirdi.

CR ℘

Endnotes

1. 'Allah Malik', literally, 'the Lord is the Master', is a term that is used to signify surrender to the divine will of the Lord.

2. It is believed that of the three categories of food, only sattvic food is suitable for practitioners of many spiritual practices. While consuming tamasic food encourages evil thoughts in the mind, rajasic food leads to materialistic or passionate thoughts.

3. Bapusaheb Jog (Sakharam Hari) was part of Sai Baba's close circle of devotees. He was given the task of performing ritual devotion to Sai Baba daily (leading the *aarti*). When Bapusaheb first came to Shirdi, he received a divine vision of the great saint Swami Samarth of Akkalkot in Sai Baba. With Sai Baba's permission, Jog and his wife settled in Shirdi. Sai Baba would, sometimes, beat Jog physically, but Baba's beatings were always accompanied by material benefit, or spiritual advancement.

4. The Datta Sampradaya is a sect devoted to the worship of Lord Dattatreya, an incarnation of Lord Vishnu who is part of the holy trinity of the Hindus — Brahma, Vishnu and Siva. The key inspirers of this path, such as Sripad Srivallab, Narasimha Saraswati and Swami Samarth of Akkalkot, are themselves believed to be incarnations of Lord Dattatreya.

5. Sri Ram or Ram is one of the ten principal incarnations of Lord Vishnu.

6. Though Hinduism was coming out of a state of orthodoxy, most Hindus believed even then that interacting with people from other faiths or the so-called lower castes would 'pollute' them, resulting in losing their faith, or worse, that they would be treated as outcastes by others. Entering a mosque was similarly regarded as a potential source of ritual pollution.

7. *Geru*, or ochre, is the colour associated with renunciation and *vairagya*, and is the colour of clothing donned by Hindu monks.

8. Nobody knows why Baba referred to Abdul as 'his crow', but he referred to him thus more than once. Another time, Baba promised Dr Pillay that he would be cured of guinea worm by a crow that would peck out the worms. Eventually, Abdul accidentally stepped on Dr Pillay's leg, and the guinea worms were forced out and he was cured. Baba told Dr Pillay that Abdul was the crow. Since Abdul provided personal service to Baba, including cleaning, Baba often called him his *halalkoor* (scavenger).

9. Yogis have been known to beat their disciples, often without cause. It has been known to lead to spiritual purification of the disciple or some material benefit. A disciple was once hit with a stick by Paramhansa Satyananda on his back; the beating permanently cured a spinal defect!

10. In Maharashtra, and in some of the adjoining states, Khandoba, or Mhalsapati, is a popular god, considered to be an incarnation of Lord Siva.

11. Bhimashankar is one of the twelve *jyotirlinga*s of India; *jyotirlinga*s or *jyotirlingam*s are shrines where Lord Siva is worshipped in the form of a *lingam* or a volume of light. These *jyotirlinga*s are supposed to have been spontaneously manifested, and not discovered or created.

12. There used to be a strange tradition in some parts of India according to which people looked down upon those who were blind in one eye or hobbled due to a foot problem. Such people were considered cunning and evil. This obviously played on Dixit's mind.

Yogis of India

13. Another version mentions that a day before Baba sent the messenger, at two o'clock in the morning, a brilliant ball of fire entered the masjid and exploded into many lights and lit up the entire place. After that, Baba spent around fifteen minutes chanting something in Arabic; this scene was witnessed by Appa Bhil and Imambhai.

Bhagwan Ramana Maharshi
(1879-1950)

Antaryascha bahirvidhūtatimiram jyotirmayam shāshvatam
Sthānam prāpya virājate vinamatām ajnānamunmūlayan
Pashyan vishwam apīdam ullasati yo vishwasya pāre parah
Tasmai sri ramanāya lokagurave shokasya hantre namah

He is resplendent, having arrived at the eternal state of light,
Which chases away the darkness both inside as well as outside,
He strikes at the root of ignorance of those who bow down to him.
Even when he perceives this universe, he is beyond it,
On its other shore, shining.
We offer our salutations to Sri Ramana,
World preceptor and destroyer of grief.

Maharshi Ramana:
Silent Sage of Arunachala

Paul Brunton was a disappointed man. He had come to India seeking mystics and spiritual adepts, who could uncover for him the secrets and traditions that he knew lay hidden in the country. In the course of his travels, he met many great saints and sages, but none who could fulfil the desire of his head and heart. In 1930, after many days of fruitless travel, he met the great saint Sri Chandrashekhar Saraswati, the Shankaracharya of Kanchi, in Chengleput—Chengalapattu in present-day Tamil Nadu. He told Brunton that he himself would not be able to guide him, but forcefully insisted that the latter should meet another great saint in the nearby town of Tiruvannamalai. This place was a good hundred miles from Madras—now Chennai—and Brunton was in no mood to prolong his journey. Yet, he decided to leave the very next day. Little did he realise that destiny had inextricably linked his life with that of a saint, and he had a special role to play in introducing him—and facets of Indian mysticism—to the Western world.

Later that night, Brunton had a vision. He saw a glowing form of Sri Chandrashekhar Saraswati in a dark room. He closed his eyes but the vision of the acharya persisted, making him realise that this was truly a mystic vision and not his imagination. 'Be humble and then you shall find what you seek!' the acharya said with a smile and disappeared. But Brunton still had some doubts. He pondered over acharya's words and finally resolved to follow his advice but allotted merely two days for the visit.

When he met Bhagwan Ramana Maharshi — as the saint was called — in Tiruvannamalai, he felt he was engulfed in an ocean of peace. Disappointingly though, the Maharshi spoke little and sometimes nothing at all, an attribute that did not help Brunton's troubled state of mind. The Maharshi did guide Brunton, but the latter was not yet prepared for it. He had not surrendered completely to the master and was interacting at the level of the intellect. There was an element of impatience to receive what he had set out to achieve within the short span he had planned to be in Tiruvannamalai. Brunton, eventually, extended his trip, and was sufficiently impressed by the Maharshi, but his lack of patience drove him to travel again to other parts of India. This time also his travels were as disappointing as those prior to meeting the Maharshi. Finally, when Brunton was in Bombay, all set to go back to England, he had an intuition to return to the Maharshi's ashram.

This time, he came as a disciple. His impatience had receded, and he built a small cottage within the premises of the Maharshi's ashram and spent a lot of time with the saint. Each day appeared to bring about a greater change within him, as he was drawn closer to the sage. And then, one night, when Brunton was with the Maharshi, he found himself in a state of spiritual trance, a state he remained in for close to two hours.

Brunton returned to England a changed man and, for years, he felt the Maharshi's presence in his meditations. Brunton then began to pen down his experiences with the saint. He wrote the best-selling *A Search in Secret India*, which introduced the sage to many seekers around the world.

He admitted, forty years after his departure from India's shores — while other memories of that era had faded away, the vision of the Maharshi was as vivid as when he had met the sage for the first time.

Years later, when he was planning to sail to Egypt, he received a mystic vision of the Maharshi and, on his command, Brunton wrote *The Secret Path*, describing the grace he had received.

Birth and Childhood

Venkataramana[1] was born in the town of Tiruchuli, Tamil Nadu, in 1879, as the second son of Sundaram Iyer and Alagammal. The couple was of a simple and deeply religious disposition. During Alagammal's pregnancy, she would often have a burning sensation in her body, which no medicine could cure. However, she got relief when she consumed the juice of the *bilwa* leaves, which are traditionally used in the worship of Lord Siva.

A blind woman in the neighbourhood perceived the newborn to be enveloped in great light and declared him to be an avatar of a divine being. The blind lady's perception may have surprised or impressed the family, but the description was soon forgotten. It was to be remembered decades later when Venkataramana, the child, had become Bhagwan Ramana Maharshi — world preceptor and yogi par excellence.

Two generations before Venkataramana was born, a wandering monk had cursed the family. He had been refused food at their doorstep and had proclaimed that as a result of this insensitivity to the needs of an ascetic, henceforth, one member of each forthcoming generation would embrace monkhood. The implications of this curse finally came to light when Venkataramana decided to follow the path of sainthood.

Venkataramana had three siblings, two brothers and a sister. Nagaswami was his elder brother, while Nagasundaram and Alamelu were his younger brother and sister, respectively.

Venkataramana was a normal child of extremely attractive appearance. As he grew up, he would spend hours playing all sorts of games with his elder brother and their band of friends. There was nothing to set him apart from other children, except his astounding memory and the depth of his sleep. His memory — he could remember exactly anything he had read, heard or seen — served to cover up for his laziness in academics. And, his sleep was so deep that nobody could wake him up, no matter how hard they tried. His friends who had to settle a score with him would, sometimes, drag him off and beat him to their heart's content but he would remain completely unaware. No matter what they did to hurt him, he would not wake up. On one occasion, his parents got worried; they kept shouting and banging on the door, but Venkataramana who was sleeping inside failed to wake up and open it. They finally had to arrange for a substitute key. Again, nobody could correlate this habitual state with samadhi until Venkataramana became a realised saint.

He was very active in sports and, as a result, grew up to be a healthy lad. He was also sensitive and caring. He would often assist his mother and aunt in their daily chores, despite the fact that others considered him effeminate. Sri Krishna Bhikshu in *Ramana Leela* considers Ramana Maharshi to be a perfect synthesis of masculine and feminine qualities. He opines that only such a person can become a true redeemer of humanity.

The Evolution of Consciousness

While Venkataramana was growing up, there were four incidents that triggered the unfolding of his consciousness. These incidents progressively led him on the path of realisation and finally took him to a state of complete enlightenment.

The first incident leading to his awakening was the death of his father in 1892. Sundaram Iyer was only forty-two years old and a widely loved person. His early demise was a major loss, resulting in much mourning in the family. Amid all this, Venkataramana spent several hours trying to understand the nature of death. After some contemplation, he concluded — the 'I' that they had associated with his father's body had left it. This was the first recorded rational process of contemplation in Venkataramana's life that was centred on the concept of the relationship of the soul and the body.

After the last rites were over, Venkataramana and his elder brother went to Madurai with their maternal uncle, Subbu Iyer, as the latter assumed responsibility of their upbringing. Their mother and two younger siblings stayed back with Nelliappa Iyer, their younger maternal uncle. As time passed, Nagaswami became more responsible towards his studies, but there was no change in Venkataramana's behaviour. In fact, this was the phase when he learnt swimming and would sneak out with his friends at night and swim till the early hours of the morning.

The second incident took place when Venkataramana was sixteen years old. One day, he met Ramaswami, an elderly relative, who told him that he had come from Arunachala. An inexplicable thrill passed through Venkataramana, and he exclaimed excitedly, 'Arunachala? Where is that?' Ramaswami responded indignantly, 'Don't you know? It is in Tiruvannamalai!' Venkataramana had often heard the name Arunachala, a hill held sacred by the Hindus as an embodiment of Lord Siva, but wasn't aware of its exact geographical location.

Venkataramana lapsed into a sheepish silence but his heart was full of joy. Why was it that hearing about Arunachala affected him so much, whereas, earlier it meant little to him? Arthur Osborne calls this a 'presentiment of his destiny'. As events unfolded later, the world realised, it was his destiny to spend his spiritually awakened life in the holy land of Arunachala, in communion with universal consciousness. That would be where thousands of aspirants would seek him out. That was where he would issue his message, asking seekers to absorb themselves in the enquiry of the self, asking themselves, 'Who am I?'

A couple of months after this, Venkataramana chanced upon a copy of the *Periyapuranam*, a work dedicated to the biographies of the Nayanmars, great devotees of Lord Siva. Venkataramana experienced great joy in reading the book and the more he read, the more he got involved in it. The extent of devotional fervour he found in the book amazed him. He rejoiced in the fact that the consummation of a divine life was indeed a reality experienced by the subjects — and by extension, could therefore be experienced by him. He became deeply absorbed in it and an emotional storm seemed to take over him, until he finished reading it. Osborne writes that it was in this period that the, 'Current of awareness [or]…meditation began to awaken in him…', and stayed as a continuous state of transcendental consciousness, yet which allowed him 'full use of physical and mental faculties'. He quotes the Maharshi that the feeling of this awareness began during the visits to the Meenakshi temple in Madurai. Initially, Venkataramana thought it was some kind of fever, but he felt that even if it were so, it was a pleasant one. This was the third of his awakenings and laid the foundation for the final one.

The Final Awakening

The final awakening took place a few months later in July 1896. Venkataramana was sitting in his room, preparing for the examinations. All of a sudden, and without any apparent reason, he was overcome with a violent fear of death. He became obsessed with the thought that he was about to die and began to think deeply on what he needed to do to avoid it. Venkataramana thought for a few seconds and decided to simulate the experience of death, in order to overcome it. He stretched out himself, stiffened his limbs and stopped his breath and lay as a corpse would. He then rationalised the experience of death and tried to understand who he — as consciousness of himself — really was. He realised that when he would die, the body would be cremated but he, as the spirit or consciousness — that he experienced as separate from the body — would continue to live.

Shri Krishna Bhikshu describes Venkataramana's experience, 'Even if the body died, the sense of "I" did not go. The consciousness of individuality was very much there. When the body was taken to the graveyard and reduced to ashes, "I" did not perish because "I" was not the body.'

This event barely lasted for half an hour. But in this short span itself, Venkataramana realised that he was not the body and that consciousness was the force that survived it. This was not an intellectual understanding of the concept, but a throbbing vibrant experience.

From then on, he was completely aware of and one with that state of consciousness.

This was the final awakening. After this, throughout his life, he lived in this state of constant and complete communion. There was no further striving for realisation. His external life did change, but by his own admission, there was no change in his state of consciousness.

The Transformation

Venkataramana had little training in spirituality prior to the realisation. The only religious texts he had read were the *Periyapuranam* and the *Holy Bible*, and bits of *Thayumanavar* and *Thevaram*, but no philosophical text described the *adwaita* state that Venkataramana was experiencing. Only much later in life did he come across such books in Tiruvannamalai, where he read about descriptions of the state he had come to spontaneously experience. He realised that the ancient seers had also gone through such a state.

Venkataramana did not share the details of his discovery or his realisation with any of his friends or family.

The event of realisation resulted in transforming Venkataramana's external behaviour. Earlier, he was always busy in playing games with his friends but now preferred to spend his spare time in contemplation, experiencing the Self. He avoided his friends, some of whom ridiculed him, while others in turn avoided him. He became indifferent to food. His former sensitivity gave way to resigned humility. He continued to help in household chores, but now only as a matter of routine. His indifference towards his education increased, which resulted in reprimands and punishments. His family did not take his behaviour seriously, in fact, his brother and uncle would bemoan his new state of being. His brother would often pass sarcastic remarks about Venkataramana's new spiritual orientation — suggesting that he should leave the house and go to the forest like the sages of yore.

Venkataramana's visits to the Meenakshi temple increased and now he went alone. Earlier, his attitude towards religion wavered between detached ritualism and often irreverence, but not anymore. Now, he would stand before the deities and waves of emotion would overcome him and a steady stream of tears would flow from his eyes. Often, he would pray for his devotion to increase and become perpetual like that of the sixty-three devotees described in the *Periyapuranam*. Osborne writes, 'The soul had given up its hold on the body when it renounced the "I-am-the-body" idea and it was seeking some fresh anchorage; hence, the frequent visits to the temple and the outpouring of the soul in tears. This was God's play with the soul.'

For now, Venkataramana was unconsciously awaiting God's command or a sign that would take him towards his destiny.

The Command and the Journey

Finally, the call came. On 29 August 1896, Venkataramana was punished by his grammar teacher for not memorising a lesson properly. He was asked to copy it three times in his notebook. He had copied it twice, but then the futility of the exercise struck him. He gave it up and instead sat in a meditative pose, contemplating on the Self.

His elder brother commented angrily, 'What is the use of all this for someone like this?' Nagaswami meant that material comforts were not for one who intended to live a life of a monk. His brother had not realised the depth of the spiritual upsurge within Venkataramana. Nagaswami hoped his taunts would prompt Venkataramana to focus more on his studies.

Venkataramana was generally indifferent to his brother's jibes, but this time, he thought to himself, 'Why not? I have no interest in studies or the pursuit of material attainments.' At the same time, he wondered where he would go and who would support him. In a flash he realised he would go to Tiruvannamalai, to the holy Arunachala, his eternal father. The thought was accompanied by the same torrent of emotion he had experienced a year ago when his relative had told him about Arunachala. Was it a sign, a command from the Father?

If his Father was indeed calling him, what could then stop him? A thrill flooded him and he resolved to leave home at once. But, he decided not to disclose his intention to anyone, since he was sure his family would thwart his plans.

The next day, when he was getting ready for school, his brother reminded him to deposit the school fee and instructed him to take ₹5 from the money box. Venkataramana took this as another sign that his Father was facilitating his journey. He consulted an old atlas and found the details of travel to Tiruvannamalai. He estimated that it would take him roughly ₹3 to cover the journey. He decided to take only that much for his legitimate requirements. He hurriedly ate what his aunt had prepared, took the money and left home for ever.

Before he went, he left a note, informing his family that he was leaving in search of his Father. The note was written in an impersonal manner, referring to himself in the third person as 'this'. At the bottom of the note, he did not append a signature, but instead put three dashes, indicating his disassociation with his name in the form of the human ego.

The Journey

Venkataramana finally arrived in Tiruvannamalai on 1 September 1896, after a long journey of almost three days. He had travelled by train and had also walked for long stretches on foot, overcoming fatigue and caring for food and sleep only when it was truly unavoidable. Venkataramana had also run out of money and pledged his earrings to cover the expenses. He had to change trains because he had mistakenly assumed that there was no direct train to Tiruvannamalai. The grace of the Lord was evident, as someone or the other would help him out when he needed it. On the way, some people willingly offered him food while others refused to feed him. Strangely, his hunger would vanish as soon as he ate the first mouthful. Whenever he got the opportunity, he would settle down in meditation.

Those who helped him were awed by this youth who was evidently in the grip of intense *vairagya*. This is evident from an incident that took place a day before he reached Tiruvannamalai. A couple took pity on the wandering youth and invited him to join them for a meal. They were enamoured by his bright eyes and spiritual radiance. They took it as a good omen that on the festival of Gokulashtmi[2], an enlightened soul had appeared at their doorstep.

At Tiruvannamalai

Venkataramana eagerly entered the Arunachaleshwara temple in the early hours of the day. Strangely, that day, all the doors were open and the large temple premises were completely empty. He entered the sanctum sanctorum almost in a state of stupor and stood speechless in front of the deity. Tears streamed down his cheeks. The burning sensation he felt in his body since the day of realisation began to subside. This day was the culmination of a phase in his life in which he had experienced spontaneous spiritual awakening.

'Father! I have come!' Venkataramana said, surrendering and (re)dedicating himself to his spiritual father. Then he left the temple and returned after getting his head shaved. He had thrown away all his remaining belongings, keeping only a small *kaupeen*. A sudden downpour bathed him as he stood outside the temple. He entered the premises, but did not again enter the sanctum sanctorum. He did not need to, as he was one with the Father. The next time he would visit the inner shrine would be three years later.

Penance

Venkataramana looked around for a suitable place to settle down in meditation. He finally found a raised stone platform in the thousand-pillared hall in the temple. In a short while, he was lost to the world, deep in contemplation. This stage continued unbroken for weeks, and he remained deep in communion with Truth, without moving or speaking. Even after the initial period, he walked a little and never spoke. He appeared to have lost track of time, of day or night. He did not seem

Yogis of India

to rise for either eating or bathing. If someone offered him food, he would silently accept it, otherwise he had no need – food was rare but that was of no consequence. Often, he was forcefully fed by a devotee who had developed deep reverence towards the meditating youth.

However, children could not understand his elevated state. Initially, they were curious. Gradually, their curiosity got better of them, and they began to tease him, pinch him and throw stones at him.

In these circumstances, Seshadri Swamigal, a great saint, decided to look after the young *tapasvi*. Seshadri Swamigal was a realised soul, an *avadhuta*, and was intuitively aware of Venkataramana's evolved state of consciousness. But, in his peculiar state of divinity, Seshadri Swamigal would often behave like a small child and, to the common people, he often appeared to be a madman. Children in Tiruvannamalai commonly teased and troubled him. Now they found him taking care of a youth, who seemed to be doing nothing but sitting all day with his eyes closed, caring not at all for the world around him. The children turned their attention on the meditating youth and they began to trouble this 'small Seshadri'.

Venkataramana remained unconcerned and detached from the disturbance, continuing in his state of deep contemplation. His body bled and bumps caused by the injuries appeared. Seshadri Swamigal would chase the children away, but they thought that it was yet another game that the saint was playing with them. They returned at periodic intervals to trouble Venkataramana. Finally, to escape the disturbance, Venkataramana moved to the *patalalingam*, the underground cellar, in the corner of the thousand-pillared hall.

Much has changed now, but a hundred years ago, the cellar was damp, dirty, musty and received no sunlight[3]. Large rats, insects and mosquitoes infested the cellars. Rats and insects would walk over Venkataramana's immobile body, often nibbling at and biting him, but he remained unmoved and undisturbed. His thighs soon bore bleeding and pus-filled sores. Many weeks passed like this.

But even in this state the children would harass him. They were scared of entering the cellar but threw stones at him from the entrance. Venkatachala Mudali, a devotee, was once enraged when he saw children throwing stones in the temple premises. He chased them with a stick. When he returned, he was surprised to see Seshadri Swamigal emerge from the *patalalingam*. He asked the saint if he was hurt. Seshadri Swamigal replied in his characteristic childish innocence, 'No, but you must take care of the little swami,' pointing to the cellar below as he walked off.

Mudali went into the cellar a little apprehensively. It was very dark but he saw the 'little swami' after some time. With the help of some devotees, he carried this young 'Brahmin swami' out of the cellars and took him to the Subrahmanyam shrine within the temple premises. All this while, Venkataramana neither moved nor appeared to know that he was being shifted. The devotees were awed to see his state and they bowed in reverence.

The change in venue resulted in slightly better food intake—a glass of milk was offered to him daily—but there was no interruption in his meditations. Over the course of the next eighteen months, the 'Brahmin swami' was moved to different venues, but he continued to remain absorbed in silence and inner bliss. Even in winters, he would usually sleep in the open, with little to cover himself. He often found it difficult to stand up on account of weakness and cramps in his legs. His vocal cords weakened because of disuse. He became terribly constipated due to irregular, inappropriate or inadequate consumption of food and water. Years later, the Maharshi recollected that at that time, he used to excrete very hard faecal matter, just like blocks of steel. But, all this mattered little to him, as he stayed absorbed in the state of bliss.

Venkataramana moved frequently within the Arunachaleshwara temple compound, searching for suitable places for *tapasya*. He stayed for long stretches at each place. Initially, he stayed in the thousand-pillared hall, then the underground cellar, later he shifted to the

Subrahmanyam temple, then the flower garden, the large vehicle hall, the Sivaganga tank and finally under some trees in the compound. By now, his fame had begun to spread and many onlookers would come to have his darshan or to stare in wonderment. The urchins still harassed him sometimes, when nobody was there to guard or protect him. It was here that a devotee called Uddandi Nayanar began to serve and take care of him with Uddandi himself sleeping under a tree.

Seeing the difficulties, Uddandi and another devotee, Annamalai Tambiran, requested Venkataramana to move to the nearby shrine of Gurumurtam. This place, unfortunately, was infested with ants that would crawl all over the swami's body and bite him, but his meditation continued undisturbed. It was here that streams of devotees became a regular feature and managing them a difficult task. Some came for darshan, some to pray and others to seek boons. Many devotees came with offerings of food, but Venkataramana would eat just a little bit and only once a day. It was also here that he had to reveal his identity, on the stubborn insistence of a devotee — an incident that led to the swami's eventual discovery by his family.

After spending a year at Gurumurtam, Venkataramana moved to a neighbouring orchard. He was joined by Palaniswami, a devotee who took care of Venkataramana's needs. Before this phase, the saint remained completely indifferent to his surroundings. It was only then that Venkataramana began to sometimes acknowledge his companions and the environment. He would also take pity on some of the close devotees and explain abstruse philosophical concepts by reading from the books that they themselves could not completely understand. Venkataramana would rapidly read the text and explain the concepts on the basis of his real experience[4]. He was already blessed with a photographic memory, and the reading he did for the benefit of the devotees would later help him in performing the role of a world preceptor. The reading and explaining in different languages also helped in polishing his knowledge of English, Tamil, Telugu and Malayalam.

Venkataramana finally moved into a cave on Mount Arunachala in 1899. The cave, in the shape of the mystic symbol Om, was known as the Virupaksha cave, after Saint Virupaksha who had lived there. Venkataramana still abided in the Self and silence was his perennial characteristic.

The Family

Venkataramana's departure had come as a major shock to the family, and particularly to his mother. The family had tried its best to locate him, but to no avail. Then, almost two years after his leaving, they received news of Venkataramana, but were uncertain if the information was authentic. Venkataramana was apparently in Tiruvannamalai. Nelliappa Iyer, his uncle, accompanied by a friend, Narayanaswami, immediately set out to find their way to Gurumurtam temple. They were initially not allowed to meet the young swami but after Nelliappa Iyer wrote a note to Venkataramana, the latter asked the devotees to let the visitors in.

Venkataramana showed no sign of recognition and continued to sit in a state of dispassionate contemplation. More than the youth's lack of recognition, it was his physical form that shocked Nelliappa; he was dirty and unwashed, his hair matted and finger nails horribly overgrown. With great difficulty, Nelliappa recognised his nephew and even that by a mole on his foot. For a few days, Nelliappa and Narayanaswami tried to convince Venkataramana to return with them, but he did not acknowledge either their words or their presence. Narayanaswami wanted to use force but as he approached Venkataramana, he felt a burning sensation in his own body. It receded only when he stopped walking towards him further.

The duo, thus, returned unsuccessfully and informed Alagammal that they had indeed found Venkataramana but the boy had refused to return. At the first opportunity, the anxious mother and Nagaswami went to Tiruvannamalai and tried their luck at persuading Venkataramana to return. To say Venkataramana was steadfast in his decision not to return would be inappropriate, since he remained detached even from the discussion on the subject.

Like Nelliappa before her, Alagammal too returned unhappily. She had already lost her husband and her elder brother, and her middle son (Venkataramana) had left home for a life of asceticism. More tragedy awaited her in the coming years. Her elder son, Nagaswami, passed away and after some years, her brother Nelliappa also died[5] and then her younger daughter-in-law (Nagasundaram's wife) passed away too. Now Alagammal began to spend more and more time with Venkataramana. In 1914, when she was staying with him, she became grievously ill. Venkataramana gave up his dispassion and nursed her back to health. He also composed a beautiful set of verses dedicated to Arunachala, beseeching the Lord to save his mother's life, but it could also be interpreted as a prayer to free her from the clutches of the endless cycles of rebirth. Alagammal recovered and with the recovery, her bent towards spirituality intensified.

Eventually in 1916, Alagammal, and in 1918, Nagasundaram, moved in with Venkataramana. By then, a regular ashram had been established around the realised yogi, who was already being addressed as Bhagwan Ramana Maharshi. Nagasundaram embraced the lifestyle of a sannyasi and was renamed Niranjanananda Swami. In the ashram, however, he was known as Chinnaswami (small swami).

Ramana Maharshi and the Path of Self-Enquiry

Venkataramana becomes Bhagwana Ramana Maharshi

In 1907, Venkataramana broke his public silence in response to questions posed by Ganpati Muni – a renowned ascetic, scholar and an authority in the science of mantra. He had a large following and had performed many austerities. Still, he was not satisfied and felt he had not succeeded in his *tapasya*. He decided to approach Venkataramana to seek answers for unresolved queries. He hesitated since he needed time alone with Venkataramana. It was the festive season with the Karthigai festival on, and Venkataramana was usually surrounded by thousands of seekers.

Strangely when Ganpati Muni approached Venkataramana, he found him all alone. He surrendered mentally and physically to the yogi and asked him the meaning of *tapas* and why his sadhana of so many years had not borne fruit.

Venkataramana looked at the ascetic and Ganpati Muni felt the gaze bathing him in a 'soothing stream' of compassion. Venkataramana broke his characteristic silence and said, 'When the mind enquires from where the notion "I" arises and dissolves right there at the origin of its birth, that is *tapas*. On the enquiry as to the exact origin from where the sound of mantra arises, the mind dissolves at the origin (of the sound) itself and that is *tapas*.'

Venkataramana had finally spoken after eleven years in Tiruvannamalai. He had succinctly enunciated the doctrine of self-enquiry. Far beyond the words, the ascetic felt that the grace of the guru had flowed to the disciple. Ganpati Muni was in a state of bliss for a long time after that, and he meditated at Venkataramana's feet throughout the day.

Ganpati Muni realised Venkataramana's stature as a world preceptor – leading seekers on the direct path of self-enquiry and seeking the answer to the fundamental question of 'Who am I?' The questioning, both at an experiential as well as an intellectual level, resulted in attainment of the ultimate objective of human existence. The ascetic christened Venkataramana as Bhagwan Ramana Maharshi and he spread his glory to seekers and devotees far and wide. The name stuck.

The Path and the Literature

Ramana Maharshi was an embodiment of knowledge and dispassion. He prescribed the path of self-enquiry, the constant questioning of 'I'. In the nomenclature of yoga, he was thus a *jnana* yogi. Many questioned whether they were ready for such a path, as *jnana* yoga is considered fit only for the more-evolved souls or people with an intellectual temperament. But the Maharshi recommended this path to all, and those who sought refuge in him – irrespective of evolution or temperament – achieved progress and results. With his grace, many devotees experienced their true self.

However, the Maharshi was also an embodiment of *bhakti* or devotion. His writings reveal deep devotion to the Lord in the form of Sri Arunachala. There were several instances when the Maharshi tried to read a devotional text, and he would become so overwhelmed with emotion that he found it difficult to continue reading – his eyes would overflow with tears.

In terms of writing, Ramana Maharshi ended up creating a large volume of literature, in both Sanskrit and Tamil. Most of the works he created were on account of requests of devotees. Books such as *Who am I?* and *Self-Enquiry* were compiled out of his teachings by devotees. There were two works, however, that he himself created spontaneously – *Eleven Stanzas to Sri Arunachala* and the *Eight Stanzas to Sri Arunachala*. In general, the Maharshi did not encourage writing of poetry, since he felt that creative energy could be better utilised in sadhana. However, he would listen attentively and graciously to compositions of devotees. Of the Maharshi's works, the *Marital Garland of a Hundred and Eight Verses to Sri Arunachala* was one that combined the epitome of both devotion and knowledge. When he was writing it, tears would start to flow from his eyes, often 'blinding his eyes and choking his voice'. The work was spontaneous, surprising anyone who saw the cleverness in the writing, where each verse began with successive letters of the alphabet. A clever poet with considerable skill in language and grammar would find it difficult to create such verses, in spite of hard work, creativity and devotion.

The Maharshi was an adept of Kundalini Yoga, a fact that not many were aware of. A large part of the *Uma Sahasram* – thousand verses in praise of the Mother Goddess – written by Ganpati Muni was inspired internally by the Maharshi. In the words of Sri Sundaresa Iyer, the text, 'Is *pasyanti vak* – revealed by the Divine Mother in Her own words to one who is accomplished in the Kundalini Yoga.'

Ganpati Muni composed and dictated the *Uma Sahasram* in one day itself and, at the end, the Maharshi asked him, 'Nayana[6], has all that I said been taken down?' From Sri Ganpati Muni came the ready and grateful response, 'Bhagavan, all that Bhagavan inspired in me has been taken down!'

The essence of the Maharshi's teachings on the path of self-enquiry is contained in three literary works. These are the *Upadesha Saram*, written at the request of Muruganar, a devotee, the *Forty Verses on Reality* and its supplement.

The Ashrams

Skandashram

Soon after his mother moved in with the Maharshi, they shifted to a much-larger cave above the Virupaksha cave. This was called Skandashram. On the Maharshi's directions, the devotees dug in a damp patch and found an abundant supply of water, enough for the growing needs of the small ashram. The continuous stream of visitors kept increasing over the years, particularly so during festive times. Alagammal helped in cooking for the increasing requirements of the inmates. This was the foundation of the ashram's kitchen.

Alagammal was an exalted soul and Ramana Maharshi had taken it upon himself to ensure her complete liberation. He therefore directed her, openly and subtly, with the intent of expanding her consciousness. At times, he would poke fun at her orthodox ways. Sometimes, he gave her visions to show that he was now one with the supreme soul and he belonged to all equally and not to her alone. In one such incident, he disappeared and in his place, she saw a column of light. Another time, she saw him externally take on the form of Lord Siva. Gradually, she gave up her traditional notions and also the pride in being his mother and redirected her consciousness to self-enquiry. In her last hour, the Maharshi was with her, one hand on her head and the other on her heart. When she breathed her last in May 1922, the Maharshi was happy and he declared that she had not 'died' in the traditional sense, but had taken *mahasamadhi*[7]. She was therefore buried in the fashion of liberated souls and not cremated.

Ramanashramam

A temple was constructed on Alagammal's samadhi and a *lingam* was installed there. This was at the foot of Mount Arunachala. Everything was done on the Maharshi's instructions and he closely guided the work. For many days, the Maharshi would visit the samadhi daily and after about six months, he shifted to the spot and began living there. The Maharshi mentioned that an irresistible power had dragged him down, an ashram sprung up around him here as well. He got some digging done and an underground spring was discovered, which helped the ashram's inmates in overcoming the water shortage. Initially, just a few thatched huts came up and, gradually, the construction was completed.

However, by 1930 – eight years after the Maharshi settled there – there were still doubts whether the ashram would survive. Then with the appointment of Niranjanananda Swami as the chief administrator of the ashram, its development caught pace.

Ramana *Leela*

Bhagwan Ramana Maharshi was widely known for his dispassion and love for silence and would mostly be found sitting with a tender but granite-like face, detached from what was going on. Only his eyes shone with grace and compassion. His detachment did not indicate indifference to the difficulties of those who sought refuge in him. Ramana Maharshi also possessed supernatural powers, which were demonstrated from time to time, but he tried his best to hide them. As a saint and a guru, he exhibited his grace in miraculously transforming the nature of devotees and disciples and comprehensively responding to their queries on material or phenomenal difficulties.

The Word of the Sadguru

The Maharshi spoke very sparingly, but each word was full of meaning and was a channel of grace.

A devotee, once, mentioned to Ramana Maharshi that his boss often teased him that he was overpaid, at ₹150 a month. 'What will he say if your salary is raised to two hundred?' the saint retorted. The very next month, the devotee's salary was inexplicably raised to ₹200.

Food Arrives

There were times when financial difficulties would arise in the ashram, yet food was always available for the residents and the visitors. Even if a particular food item was not in stock, it would miraculously appear — someone or the other would offer it. The Maharshi, once, wanted to feed plantains to a cow, Lakshmi, in the ashram but the entire stock had been consumed. When this was reported to the Maharshi, he didn't respond. In a short while, someone appeared at the ashram's gates with huge sacks of plantains. He wished to donate the crop to the ashram. The stock was replenished and Lakshmi ate to her heart's content!

Once, two devotees, Cohen and Chadwick, arrived in Tiruvannamalai to meet the great saint. In the middle of a discussion one day, they expressed their ignorance about Indian food habits. The saint decided to help them. He tried to describe a local fruit — a grapefruit — to Cohen and Chadwick, but both of them could not understand what it was. Maharshi was finding it difficult to go on, he thought that a specimen may be of some help, but soon realised that it was not the season for that fruit. That evening, a devotee came and offered three grapefruits – one for the Maharshi and one each for Chadwick and Cohen. The two were amazed at the Maharshi's grace.

Once, a devotee visited the Maharshi in his ashram, but it was already very late in the evening and he resolved to stay overnight. He was hungry, but did not reveal this to anyone. However, the Maharshi knew about this and instructed the kitchen staff to feed the devotee. Skandashram was far from the town and all the food received during the day had been equally distributed and consumed, as was the practice in the ashram. So, not even a morsel was available in the kitchen. The cooks were in a fix, when strangely, someone discovered a coconut and informed the Maharshi, who ordered to make gruel with it. But cooks felt a little embarrassed as they had also run out of sugar – there was no hope to feed the hungry devotee. However, in a short while, two devotees knocked at the ashram's doors. They had sacks full of sugar and plantains, which they wanted to donate to the ashram. The hungry devotee did not need to reveal his hunger and was relieved to consume the gruel and plantains.

Doctor of Doctors

There are innumerable incidents of Ramana Maharshi curing devotees of their ailments, where medical science had given up. The 'cure' was often a response to prayer, but very often, it was spontaneous, owing to the Maharshi's maternal nature. In either case, the cure was swift. When devotees approached the saint with a request for a cure, he would usually express his inability to do anything, asking, 'Am I a doctor?' But, if the devotee persisted, a miracle would certainly follow.

Once, a six-year-old boy was bitten by an insect and he fell ill and began to sweat profusely. His condition deteriorated rapidly and the doctor could not cure him. The mother brought him to the Maharshi on the suggestion of the boy's aunt. By then, the boy's body had begun to turn blue. The saint passed his hand over the child and the boy was fine in a short while.

It has been recorded that the saint had cured two devotees of terminal cancer. The first was Jagadeeswara Sastri, who was cured during Ramana Maharshi's lifetime. Jagadeeswara lovingly but obstinately compelled the saint to cure him. He wrote a moving poem to the saint, requesting him to change the course of destiny. Suri Nagamma, the other devotee, was cured of terminal cancer by the saint's grace many years after he had left his body.

In another episode, a devotee had unbearable pain in his index finger, but did not disclose this fact to anyone. Sometime later, he saw the Maharshi stroking the same finger in his own hand. Strangely, the pain in the devotee's finger subsided immediately. The Maharshi had intuitively sensed the pain and was curing it in his own way without letting anyone know.

A young man had developed leprosy soon after his marriage. He came to Tiruvannamalai to meet a saint who could cure diseases with occult powers. The saint turned out to be a fake, but people redirected the youth to the Maharshi. The sage heard his story and gave him some sacred ash. He asked the youth to apply it on his body daily, for roughly three months. He followed the saint's directions, and after three months, he was completely cured.

A devotee who was afflicted with dyspepsia approached the Maharshi. He could hardly digest anything other than light gruel. The saint asked him to ignore the ailment. Many days later, a picnic was organised by his disciples. The Maharshi forcefully and repeatedly asked the devotee to eat the heavy food. As it was the guru's command, he had to follow it. While he was eating, he felt no discomfort in the stomach; he found he was fully cured of his problem.

Once, a devotee was on his deathbed due to tetanus; his limbs had stiffened and doctors had given up hope. He saw the Maharshi in a dream and felt an electric current flowing through his body. He recovered shortly, much to the surprise of the doctors and anxious family members.

In another incident, a two-year-old child died due to failure of all the vital organs. The mother, however, could not believe the doctor's words, and she immediately sent a telegram to Ramana Maharshi. The post office assured her it would be delivered by seven o'clock that evening. At exactly that time, a series of coincidences took place. A stranger appeared at her door and gave her a packet of prasad, saying that Bhagwan Ramana Maharshi had sent it for her child. The lady tried to put some morsel in the 'dead' child's mouth. Later, two Ayurvedic physicians she had desperately been looking for in the morning also landed there and together they administered a successful cure. The 'dead' child recovered.

The Maharshi could also cure himself, but he was reluctant to do so, as he did not want to interfere with the body. He would cure himself only at the behest of a devotee. Ramana Maharshi, once, developed severe eczema and, even though he tried his best, the doctor could not cure it. The doctor was disturbed as he had to leave Tiruvannamalai the next day, but wished to see the saint in fine health as well. That night, the doctor silently prayed to the Maharshi to cure himself. The next morning, the eczema began to respond to the treatment and in a short while, the cure was complete.

The saint would, sometimes, help his physicians during crises by revealing to them an appropriate medicine used in traditional methods to cure an ailment. Once, the Maharshi was not responding to Dr Krishnamurthi Iyer's treatment, the doctor also happened to be the saint's devotee. One night, he had a strange dream. He saw the saint leading him into a forest, describing a particular herb that would prove beneficial in the treatment. In the dream, the saint also explained the process of administering the herb. The anxious doctor woke up in the middle of his sleep, picked up a lantern and decided to venture into the nearby forest, all alone in the dead of the night. To his surprise, he found the herb at the exact location, as he had dreamt. He picked up the herb and went back to his house. The next day, he followed the saint's guidelines, prepared a medicine out of the herb and went to see his ailing guru. Seeing the doctor, the Maharshi said, 'Give me what you have brought.' The cure worked and the Maharshi recovered completely in a few days.

The last days of the Maharshi's bodily existence were spent in great suffering and pain; he had become very weak. All through the day, his devotees used to serve him. Once, accidentally, a devotee spilled boiling water on the Maharshi's body. He was terrified and woke up another devotee. They immediately wiped the Maharshi's body. Strangely, he was not harmed at all, and his body showed no sign of scalding. The devotee realised that the Maharshi had cured himself in an act of kindness to save the former from the feeling of remorse.

Animals

Animals were not scared of the Maharshi. He would fondle and caress them—even speak to them as he would with a human. In the early days, many wild animals roamed in the areas around the ashrams. Ramana Maharshi would communicate with wild animals and they would obey him. Snakes would crawl over his leg and he would remain in his state of dispassionate grace. Monkeys would often share the Maharshi's meal; they were never a nuisance. A peacock, sometimes, followed the Maharshi as the latter walked around. Once, a black cobra appeared before the peacock and both the creatures were ready to attack each other when the saint intervened. The Maharshi asked the cobra why it had come there and urged it to go away. The cobra slithered away immediately. Squirrels would crawl over his body unafraid. A mongoose once ran into the ashram and went up to Ramana Maharshi, ignoring everyone, and sat for some time in his lap. And shortly after that, it went away without paying attention to anyone.

Who is Ramana?

> When Ganpati said, 'Mother is mine,'
> And sat in the lap of Parvati,
> Kumara retorted, 'Never mind,
> Father is mine,'
> And got into Siva's lap and was kissed by him on the head.
> Of this Kumara…Ramana is a glorious manifestation.

> — Vashistha Ganpati Muni, *Ramana Gita. 18.9*

Ganpati Muni had various experiences, on the strength of which he claimed that the Maharshi was an incarnation of Skanda, or Lord Kartikeya, and there were many subscribers to this view. He had also composed verses in praise of his guru. On the other hand, mother Alagammal saw him as Lord Siva and Muruganar worshipped Ramana Maharshi as Lord Siva himself. Once, a devotee approached

Ramana Maharshi with a query. He wished to know more about the saint's incarnation, specifically, of which divine being was he an avatar? To this, the saint replied that he was an embodiment of pure consciousness.

A follower of the Theosophical Society of India[8] would often come to the Maharshi, but always found him surrounded by devotees and could not get the privacy to discuss his queries. One day, he resolved to ask the Maharshi for three things, namely: whether the Maharshi could meet him in private, whether he approved of the activities of the Theosophical Society and whether he could give him a vision of his (Ramana's) true form. It turned out that he did not need to ask. Soon after he reached, the crowd miraculously disappeared and he was alone with the Maharshi. The Maharshi saw a book in the devotee's hand and asked him what it was. On finding it was a book published by the Theosophical Society, he nodded approvingly and told him that the organisation was doing good work. The first two wishes of the devotee had been accomplished without asking!

Now, the devotee was emboldened and he requested the Maharshi for a vision of the yogi's true form. The Maharshi did not speak, but in a short while he disappeared, and after some time reappeared. For a month, the devotee was in awe of this experience, later he requested the saint to explain him the meaning of this experience. The Maharshi said, 'You wanted to see my real form. I am formless.'

How Many Ramanas?

Once, Ganpati Muni decided to leave the guru's ashram for some time. He wanted to perform penance and requested the saint to permit him. The yogi not only gave him permission but also blessed him. After reaching the town of Tiruvottiyur, miles away from Tiruvannamalai, Ganpati Muni settled down in the Ganpati temple for his meditations. After eighteen days, he felt some obstacles in his penance and was hoping for the Maharshi's grace. He suddenly saw the master standing beside him in flesh and blood! The saint blessed the devotee by touching him and an electric current passed through Ganpati Muni's body. And then Ramana Maharshi disappeared. All this while, the Maharshi was far away in Tiruvannamalai, but at that very moment, he indicated to another devotee that he had been to Tiruvottiyur and had met Ganpati Muni. Though Ramana Maharshi had never been to Tiruvottiyur, many days later, his description of the Ganpati temple and the town itself was corroborated by Ganpati Muni.

The Maharshi would attract disciples and devotees from across the world through various means. He, once, appeared in flesh and blood before an Australian lady, while she was relaxing at home. For some time, he gazed intently at her and then disappeared as suddenly as he had appeared. She was mystified, but the next day, a friend gave her a book on the Maharshi, which contained a photograph of him, in the same form as she had seen in her home. She went on to become a devotee.

A very poor Peruvian couple heard about the saint and felt he was an embodiment of Christ. They wanted to meet him in person but they didn't have enough budget to cover the expenses of a sea voyage. It took them months to arrange for the journey by saving some money. Finally, their wish came true and they landed on the Indian shores. When the Maharshi saw them, he commented that they need not have come physically—as he was always with those who thought of him. The couple only understood the true meaning of his words when, later that evening, he described the beach of their town and the spot where the couple would often sit. They realised he had been with them in spirit all the while when they were thinking about them.

A spiritual seeker who had met various saints in India came to the ashram and saw Ramana Maharshi. He thought the saint was yet another yogi like the ones he had met. He then visited the Arunachaleshwara temple. Strangely, unlike other devotees, he could not see the *lingam* in the temple. In its place, he saw the Maharshi. In fact, wherever he looked, he saw hundreds of forms of the Maharshi in the same pose. The seeker realised the state of unity that the Maharshi experienced with the Lord. He hurried back to Ramanashramam to meet the Maharshi again before leaving Tiruvannamalai.

Devotees

Bhagwan Ramana Maharshi guided many seekers over half a century during his stay in Tiruvannamalai. Many of these souls, it appears, were linked to him from previous births. Ramana Maharshi's message and guidance, however, were universal, meant for all seekers — the realised and the novice. Yet, many of his disciples were advanced souls, as it often happens when saints of Ramana Maharshi's calibre incarnate in a human body. Outlines of two of these seekers' lives are given in this section.

Vashistha Ganpati Muni

In November 1878, Nrisimha Sastry was on a pilgrimage to Kashi, while his wife, Narsamamba, was at home. She was in an advanced stage of pregnancy. The anxious father-to-be was fervently praying before Lord Ganesha's idol in the Dunti Ganpati temple, when he had a vision of a boy emerging from the statue and crawling towards him and climbing into his lap. Nrisimha Sastry intuitively felt that the Lord had taken birth in his house as a child. He returned home and found that, at the time he had the vision in the temple, his wife had indeed delivered a baby boy. The parents recalled that nine months ago, Narsamamba had a divine vision in the temple of Surya, the Sun God, after which she had conceived the child. They, therefore, considered the child a blessing of Lord Surya and an avatar of Lord Ganesha, the embodiment of knowledge and devotion. Thus, they named their son Surya Ganpati.

However, the boy, unlike Lord Ganesha, turned out to be rather unintelligent and suffered from various illnesses until the age of six, when, following a traditional remedy, he miraculously turned into a brilliant child. His ability to learn was matched only by his extraordinary health and photographic memory. In a matter of a few years, he had mastered many of the complex traditional texts. He would compose devotional hymns to various deities extempore. Whatever he prophesied would come true.

In 1888, Ganpati's mother was expecting again. When the time of delivery was near, she asked Ganpati whether it was auspicious to deliver a child that day. Ganpati responded innocently, 'Twins will be born, but neither the mother nor the children will survive.' True to the prophecy, she delivered twins, but both the children and the mother passed away. Ganpati was deeply moved by this event and, for two months, he refused to speak to anyone when he contemplated on the true nature of the world, the soul and the body. It was then that he decided to devote his life to *tapasya* and after that, he adopted a lifestyle of intense austerities. At the age of twelve, Ganpati was married to an eight-year-old girl, Vishalakshi. Instead of becoming an obstacle to his *tapasya*, Vishalakshi became a supporter and partner in his austerities. In 1899, Vishalakshi gave birth to a son, who they named Mahadeva.

Over time, Ganpati became an adept in the science of mantra and *ashtavadhani*, one who can pay perfect attention to eight simultaneous interactions. It was said when he initiated an aspirant into a mantra, the aspirant had nothing more to do as 'the voice of the muni [Ganpati] who articulated the mantra continued to reverberate ever afterwards in the heart of the disciple'. By nature, Ganpati was a *tapasvi* and he revelled in *tapasya*. He had been initiated into several mantras and had repeated his favourite, the *Om Namah Shivaya* mantra, millions of times. Yet, he felt that he had not got the fruit of his penance as prescribed by the traditional texts. He approached Ramana Maharshi and surrendered to him. The rest is history as the Maharshi gave him a discourse on the doctrine of self-enquiry. Later, Ganpati Muni had many divine visions. In one of them, a light descended from the heavens and touched Ramana Maharshi's head six times. It was also on his insistence that the Maharshi composed verses, such as *Deham Naham Koham Soham*, in Sanskrit. Ganpati Muni himself composed verses in

Sanskrit in praise of the master (*Ramana Chatvarimsat*), which were arranged by the Maharshi. Even today these are sung in front of the Maharshi's samadhi.

In 1926, Vishalakshi passed away. After that, Ganpati Muni devoted more time to the propagation of his guru's teachings. Till the end of his life, he spread the glory and the message of his master. Throughout his life, after he 'discovered' Ramana Maharshi, Ganpati Muni lived for long stretches in Arunachala with his guru, though he would go away for long periods to perform *tapasya*. A patriot, he was involved in social and political reform activities until 1930 after which, he wholeheartedly devoted himself to *tapasya*. Initially, he stayed in his guru's ashram but the climate did not suit him and his health failed. Therefore, his disciples decided to move him to Sirasi and then later to Kuluve, both in the present-day state of Karnataka. In 1932, Ganpati Muni was moved to Kaluvarai, in the present-day state of Andhra Pradesh, where he stayed until 1934. In the same year, he moved with a devotee, Maruvada Pasad Rao, to his house in Kharagpur (now in West Bengal).

His devotees built an ashram for him in Kharagpur in 1935. He breathed his last in 1936, in this ashram. Ramana Maharshi dearly loved Ganpati Muni; on hearing of his passing away, the saint was overwhelmed with emotion.

Muruganar

Muruganar was born in 1890 and named Subrahmanyam by his parents. As his father had died when Subrahmanyam was still a small child, he was raised by his mother. He had a deep love for Tamil, his mother tongue, and changed his name from Subrahmanyam to Muruganar, by adopting the Tamil version of the Sanskrit name Subrahmanyam. He grew up to be a learned and devout individual. He was held in high esteem by the royal family of Ramanathapuram, the place of his birth, but he did not at that time have the guidance of a *sadguru*. Then one day, his father-in-law gifted him two works by Ramana Maharshi, which influenced him a lot. The first, *Aksharamanamalai*, contained devotional poetry, while the second, *Who Am I?* was a compilation of questions and answers covering the saint's path of self-enquiry.

Muruganar intuitively realised the greatness of the saint and accepted him as his guru and guide. He met Ramana Maharshi in 1923, and it was a momentous meeting. Muruganar approached him with some devotional verses that he had written in the saint's praise, but was so overwhelmed at seeing Ramana Maharshi that he choked with emotion and all that flowed forth were tears. The saint gently took the sheet of paper from his hands and read the verses himself.

Muruganar was completely drawn to Ramana Maharshi. The devotee was an embodiment of love for the saint. After the first meeting, Muruganar stayed for long spells with his guru, but would always return to his mother, till she passed away in 1926. She was his only bond with the material world, and shortly after her demise, Muruganar shifted permanently to Tiruvannamalai. He initially stayed elsewhere, but eventually shifted to Ramanashramam.

Muruganar wrote excellent works in Tamil on his guru and his path. They are a beautiful confluence of devotion to Ramana Maharshi and the path of self-knowledge. Muruganar would spend the entire day in the Maharshi's presence, except when the former had to beg for food. He would note down the master's responses to seekers, convert them into verses and have them approved by the guru himself.

Muruganar had a special place in Ramana Maharshi's heart and the master would ensure that any special dishes cooked in the ashram were shared with him.

Muruganar was deeply disturbed by Ramana Maharshi's passing away in 1950. Muruganar could speak for hours on his master, his path and his grace. When someone would sing a devotional verse in praise of Ramana Maharshi, Muruganar's face would be streaming with tears. He continued to inspire aspirants and seekers to tread the twin paths of devotional surrender to Ramana Maharshi and that of self-enquiry.

His poetic compositions after 1950 reflect the continuing presence and grace of the Maharshi.

Muruganar passed away in 1973, in Ramanashramam, amid the chanting of devotional verses. He was considered a liberated soul and was, therefore, not cremated but buried in line with tradition.

Letting the Body Go

Echammal was a great devotee of the Maharshi. In 1945, when his disciples informed the Maharshi about Echammal's demise, he said with sadness the mysterious words, 'Yes, it is so. I am also looking forward to go, but the time has not yet come.'

In a few years, when the Maharshi reached the age of seventy, his physical condition had deteriorated considerably. This was strange, given his generally excellent state of health since childhood and the pure, carefree attitude he had towards life. However, some people think his condition worsened towards the end because he had neglected the body in the early days of intense *tapasya*. But, the reason more commonly accepted was that he had absorbed the karma of those who sought refuge in him. There are numerous instances where the Maharshi took over the ailment of the disciple on himself.

Towards the end of 1949, disciples noted a small boil below his left elbow. A few months later, the doctors removed it by surgery, but it reappeared after sometime, larger and higher on the arm. Another operation took place, and yet it reappeared. It was diagnosed as sarcoma.

Doctors suggested amputation of the arm, but the Maharshi refused. He had been completely indifferent to the treatment and the surgery, submitting tenderly more on account of his disciples' insistence. Various non-invasive treatments were tried, including Ayurveda and homeopathy, with some providing temporary relief, but the ailment would ultimately worsen. The sarcoma destroyed his health and sapped his strength.

Though the Maharshi was in extreme pain, he kept on emphasising that 'the body is itself a disease', and that everything will become all right eventually. He would always refer to the body in the third person. When he was asked which treatment he would like to follow, he categorically stated that he desired none. Once, a devotee couldn't control his emotions and burst out crying in front of the saint. To this, he responded, 'Why are you so attached to the body? Let it go.' He maintained equanimity in front of the sobbing devotee.

The Maharshi would not hear of dissipating spiritual force to cure himself. In the same vein, he refused to 'give' the ailment to a devotee, by asking who 'gave' it to him (Ramana)? He suggested obliquely, though gently, that it was the devotees themselves who had 'given' him the ailment.

On 12 April 1950, when one of his relatives tried to give him some medicine, he refused, gently telling him that it would be all over in two days. Indeed, it was. All through this period, hundreds of people would throng to Ramanashramam to receive his darshan. This continued till his last day in the body. On 14 April 1950, the doctors knew it was his last day. Large crowds had assembled for his darshan. The Maharshi had, in his own words, expressed gratitude to his attendants. He asked his attendants to help him sit up.

Some devotees began devotional singing of *Arunachala-Siva*. The Maharshi opened his tender, luminous eyes and smiled. Then, tears rolled down the outer edges. For some time, he was quiet, breathing audibly. He breathed once deeply. And then he was gone.

At precisely the same moment, an extremely bright star was observed rising in the sky, and then moving towards the peak of Arunachala and disappearing.

The build-up of the ailment and the knowledge of his imminent departure had cushioned the impact of the passing away. But it did leave many of the close devotees shattered, despite their faith in his assurance that he was not the body. His words, 'Where could I go? I am here,' could not assuage their feelings of shock.

The following day, when the prescribed rituals were over, the Maharshi's body was lowered into a pit dug close to the Matrabhuteswara temple. The pit was filled with sand, camphor and other aromatic material. The spot for the samadhi had been identified by the Maharshi himself in a devotee's dream. Later, a grand temple was built on the samadhi, and a *lingam* was also installed there.

Ramana Maharshi Lives On

'...I exist everywhere and always.'

These were the Maharshi's words and countless devotees and seekers have found the truth in them, across time, all over the world. Devotees, many thousands of miles away, have been drawn to an unknown face, which they discover to be Ramana Maharshi's. The impact of the Maharshi's presence in their lives is as complete as it would have been during the period when he was present in body — the same flow of grace, the melting effect on the ego, the maternal protection and the unfolding of knowledge and experience.

Many have experienced the Maharshi's grace at the samadhi. Carl, a devotee from Germany, came to Ramanashramam and sat by the samadhi. In a flash, he received the grace that melted the ego, uncovered the glorious state of self and understood the true meaning of love. A businessman in the US felt compelled to enter a book shop, go to a shelf and pick up a specific book. The first thing he saw in the book was a photograph of Ramana Maharshi, who drew the businessman to himself.

The Maharshi's ways are mysterious. He draws some to himself through his photographs, others through books or devotees, yet others through spontaneous internal messages. Many throng every year to experience that bond at his samadhi in Tiruvannamalai, where they can still feel the living presence. This is why they call him 'The Living Guru' even after more than half a century of his passing away.

CR 80

Endnotes

1. Though he was named Venkateswara after Lord Venkateswara, the presiding deity of the Iyer family, his name was changed to Venkataramana when he was admitted to school; Venkataramana is another name for Lord Venkateswara.
2. Gokulashtmi is the festival marking the birth of Krishna, the divine child.
3. The cellars, the *tapobhumi* (the place of penance and meditation) of Bhagwan Ramana Maharshi, have since been cleaned and renovated and a picture of the Maharshi has been placed there.
4. He would, however, not speak but would write on a slate or some other flat surface.
5. Nelliappa Iyer, Venkataramana's uncle, for long felt deeply unhappy that the boy had ruined his life; this regret was deepened when he heard a sadhu criticising Venkataramana's lack of knowledge of Vedanta. He felt Venkataramana had lost out on both material and spiritual life. It was only when he visited Ramana Maharshi in Skandashram, while the saint was giving a rare discourse on the *Dakshinamurti Stotra*, he realised the spiritual eminence his nephew had achieved. Finally satisfied with the state of affairs, a few days later, Nelliappa breathed his last.
6. The Maharshi called Ganpati Muni 'Nayana', which was an expression of both respect as well as endearment.
7. In another case, he tried to release one of his earliest devotees, Palaniswami; the Maharshi mentioned that he was not entirely successful, but declared that Palaniswami would have an auspicious re-birth.
8. The Theosophical Society was formed to create a universal brotherhood of humanity without any distinction. It promoted the study of the scriptures of the world's religions and sciences, particularly the Eastern religions.

SWAMI SIVANANDA SARASWATI
(1887-1963)

Bhajeham jagatkāranam satswarūpam,
Bhajeham jagadvyāpakam chitswarūpam
Bhajeham nijānandamānandarūpam,
Sivānanda yogindramānandamūrtim

I worship the One who is causal energy of the universe,
The embodiment of truth,
I worship the One who is omnipresent,
The embodiment of consciousness,
I worship the One who is the embodiment of bliss,
Who is blissfully engaged in contemplation of the self,
(He is) Sivananda! King amongst Yogis! The Image of Bliss!

Swami Sivananda Saraswati

It was a bright day in August 1963. In Munger, in the eastern Indian state of Bihar, Swami Sivananda Saraswati opened the door and strode into the room of his young disciple, Swami Satyananda Saraswati. He explained to Swami Satyananda, in detail, the mission he wanted the latter to fulfil. Swami Satyananda asked a few questions, which the elder swami explained comprehensively. After this long chat with the young swami, Swami Sivananda walked out and shut the door behind him.

Swami Satyananda sat deep in thought for a long time. What he had just experienced would have been, for an ordinary man, both thrilling and unnerving. For, barely ten days ago, Swami Sivananda had passed away and his mortal remains had been buried in his ashram in Rishikesh in the presence of hundreds of onlookers.

ॐ ॐ

This was Swami Sivananda; a six-foot tall sannyasi with a beaming visage and a booming voice that attracted thousands of disciples from all over the world. He was an *ajanabahu* saint, not bound by body, mind, time or space.

This question of who he was is beautifully expressed in the enquiry of Swami Omkarananda, 'Who is this Sivananda, on the banks of the Ganga, in the heart of the foothills of the Himalayas, whose "voice" is heard by a few continental European devotees in Germany and Denmark, day after day? This sage, in whom the divine nature is so fully manifest and active, this Sivananda who has been granting sight of his physical form, at the same time to two persons – one in the isle of Ceylon and the other in Santiago, South America – who is he?'

Many people from all over the world were drawn to him by visions in their dreams; those who had never seen or heard of him and lived in foreign lands with no possible connection to him. Some heard his name and some even received lessons in yoga and mantra.

N. Ananthanarayanan writes about Swami Sivananda thus, '[He]… was indeed a strange Hindu monk. He shaved his head, but wore an English overcoat in winter. An Indian to the core, he wrote in English. He came from an orthodox Brahmin stock, but his catholicity embraced even the [so-called] untouchable in its sweep. He himself underwent the harshest austerities but advised his disciples to care for the body. He stayed with his guru fleetingly only for a day or two but realised God unerringly. He ran an ashram without a budget and trained students by the thousands without a set syllabus. He stuck to the Ganga bank like a leech for over three decades, but his name was heard and respected in every continent in his own lifetime. He displayed no miracles in public, but his devotees all over the world affirmed and reaffirmed that he had wrought miracles in their lives.'

Birth and Youth

Swami Sivananda was born in the village of Pattamadai in Tamil Nadu in the year 1887. His parents, Vengu Iyer and Parvathi Ammal, were simple-hearted souls. His father was a great devotee of Lord Siva and would, sometimes, lose himself in his deep devotion to the Lord, tears streaming down his face as he chanted His name.

The child was named Kuppuswamy. He was full of fun and mischief, and in the eyes of the casual observer, there was nothing to indicate the great soul he harboured within. However, Kuppuswamy was selfless and large-hearted and if his mother gave him a piece of cake or sweetmeat, he would, at once, rush to find friends to share the delicacy with. 'He rejoiced in giving. He distributed snacks to servants, to cats and dogs, crows and sparrows. Kuppuswamy took beggars into the house and fed them.' In fact, he would make his father also share food with beggars. Kuppuswamy would serve his father by collecting *bael*[1] leaves for worshipping Lord Siva. He would attentively listen to his father's devotional incantations. He would also participate wholeheartedly in the family prayers and kirtans, but the activity he really enjoyed getting involved in, was serving sadhus, sannyasis and other holy men.

The child's father descended from the great saint Sri Appayya Dikshitar. Other saints and scholars such as Sundara Swamigal and Nilkantha Dikshitar were also his ancestors, but Appayya Dikshitar was the greatest of them all. Appayya, who lived in the sixteenth century AD, was born in Adaipalam in what is today the state of Tamil Nadu in India. Many people considered him to be an incarnation of Lord Siva. Once, on a visit to the famous Vishnu temple in Tirupati, he was refused admission by the priests on account of his being a devotee of Siva and the next morning, the Vishnu idol was found to have changed into the form of Siva. The priests immediately begged forgiveness from Sri Appayya and beseeched him to restore the form of Vishnu in the idol. The saint agreed and carried out their wishes. Kuppuswamy's parents believed that he was a reincarnation of this great saint, as they had witnessed many good omens prior to the child's birth.

Traditionally, Brahmins are supposed to focus on knowledge. As the child grew up, he became fond of exercise. He would sneak out of home – hiding from his parents, who were not happy with this inclination – for his daily workout. Kuppuswamy learned fencing from an adept who belonged to a so-called 'low caste'. The hold of tradition in those days was strong. Some people tried to explain to Kuppuswamy that, according to customs, as a Brahmin, he should not mix with such people. The young man reflected on this for some time but intuitively felt oneness between his family guru and the fencing instructor. He realised that the stature of a guide was beyond the confines of the caste system, so, he went and prayed to the man as a guru. With this incident, he mentally did away with the caste distinctions that plagued traditional Hindu society.

As he grew older, Kuppuswamy would, sometimes, wander away from home for a few days. Once, he walked all the way to see the Subrahmanya temple at Kazhugumalai and did not eat anything at all for three days. In fact, he started to disappear so often that if he did not return at night, his mother would assume he had gone off to a religious place.

But it was in educational pursuit that he stood out. He consistently topped his class, whether in school or in college. In college, Kuppuswamy lapped up all the material he could get on spirituality, particularly that which related to Biblical teachings and the lives and philosophies of Christian mystics.

In 1905, he entered the Tanjore Medical Institute to learn medicine. He was so passionate about his studies that by the second year, he knew as much of the subject as a fifth-year student. He utilised all his spare time in reading books and journals and, in his vacations, spent his time studying in the college rather than going home. His professors recognised both his brilliance and his perseverance and was allowed to freely enter the operation theatre and dissection room where he could witness dissections and surgical procedures. His professors appointed him as their assistant, and he utilised this opportunity to further his knowledge of surgery. As a result, he soon knew more than most 'doctors with covetable degrees'. He had the highest scores in all his subjects and, in the course of time, graduated with a medical degree.

The Ambrosia

Kuppuswamy was not only an ardent student but also believed in sharing and dissemination of knowledge. Halfway through his college programme, he started a monthly journal in English called *The Ambrosia*. Another motivation for launching the journal was to raise money for his education, as his father had passed away and his mother was unwell. The family was going through financial difficulties. Kuppuswamy borrowed ₹100 — a large sum of money in those days — from his mother to start the journal. In addition to being the initial financier, he also worked as the editor and a contributor of articles to the journal — he wrote under many pseudonyms. The journal focussed more on health, hygiene, dietetics, and preventive aspects of medicine rather than on the curative aspects. It also included various articles on Ayurveda. Some articles in the journal were also in Tamil — Kuppuswamy's native language.

The journal, though popular, did not become a financial success. There were only a few literate readers in those times and even fewer advertisers. Moreover, Kuppuswamy would shy away from asking people for money and would instead distribute the journal free to many. But it was enough for him to support his education and once, when his mother required money, he managed to give her ₹150.

As a Doctor

After getting his medical degree, Kuppuswamy became a practicing doctor at Tiruchi (Tiruchirapalli). He continued with the publication work of the journal. In 1913, he received an invitation to work as a doctor in the rubber plantations in Malaya and he readily accepted. In those days, Indian labourers lived and worked in horrible conditions, ridden with disease and poverty, and to Kuppuswamy, this was more of an opportunity to serve the needy than merely an offer of employment. He told his friends that, for him, service was a sure way of 'thinning out the ego', and so began to look forward to the assignment.

He said, 'Book knowledge will not take us far. I studied anatomy. I dissected the human body. But I could not find the atman within.' He was sure that selfless service was the best way to erase the ego, so decided to do a charitable deed everyday and to remember God with a yearning heart.

Dr Kuppuswamy sailed to the Malayan peninsula on the *SS Tara*. Being an orthodox Brahmin by upbringing, he was also a strict vegetarian. He, therefore, avoided food on the ship and depended on the sweets prepared by his mother. As a result, 'when he reached Singapore, he was almost half-dead'.

Once there, he was introduced to A.G. Robbins, manager of a rubber estate in Seramban, who needed a doctor to manage the estate hospital. He was a large man with an intimidating figure and was reputed to have a horrible temper. He asked Dr Kuppuswamy if he could manage a hospital all by himself. The young doctor boldly replied that he could manage three hospitals, leave alone one. He was immediately hired at a salary of ₹150 a month.

Work was difficult. Dr Kuppuswamy single-handedly tended to patients, dispensed medicine, kept accounts and maintained documents, including medical history sheets, temperature charts and admission cards. He did everything with meticulous perfection and exhorted the hospital staff to maintain cleanliness.

Like many other doctors, Dr Kuppuswamy also ran a private practice. However, unlike most doctors, he did not target a rich clientele and attended to poor patients. He did not even charge poor patients a consulting fee and, sometimes, also gave them money for medicines and other treatment. He would often wait the entire night at a patient's cottage and would leave only when recovery was in sight. In addition to his dedication to the health, cure and recovery of his patients, he was full of encouragement and good humour. Patients responded to his treatment. He prayed while tending to them. In the hospital, he held a weekly prayer each Friday, after which, he distributed prasad to all who attended and personally gave it to those who were too unwell to have come. Needy people who came to the doctor for charity never returned empty-handed.

Dr Kuppuswamy did not let orthodox Hindu caste prejudices come in the way of his service to patients. He treated people from the so-called lower castes with uncommon love and diligence. Labourers in the plantations held him in high esteem and he, sometimes, even represented their case before the management.

Dr Kuppuswamy wrote articles on health and hygiene, which he contributed to the *Malaya Tribune,* and also wrote several books on these subjects. He became a member of the Royal Institute of Public Health and the Royal Asiatic Society, and an Associate of the Royal Sanitary Institute, all based in London.

He would never waste time in idle gossip and usually wished his friends 'good morning' only from a distance, hurrying along his way, lest he got entangled in unproductive activities. The only topics he loved to discuss were spiritual. He had built up a large library of books on spiritual subjects — he would be engrossed in reading them and discussing the contents with like-minded individuals. He would carry several copies of the list of his books in his library and hand them to booksellers, asking them to supply any spiritual books not on the list.

His spirit of service is exemplified in the following tale: 'Once, a poor man, drenched to the skin, came to the doctor at night. His wife was in birth pangs. The doctor went there at once to her aid and, after attending to her, stayed outside the hut in spite of the heavy rain. Only after the child was safely delivered, did he return home the next morning.'

Though he worked very hard, many difficulties cropped up. At times, he would feel like resigning but Mr Robbins would not let him go.

Seeds of Renunciation

Dr Kuppuswamy always had a religious disposition, but gradually the seeds of renunciation and deep spirituality began to take a stronghold. He would serve monks and yogis eagerly. If he ever heard of a sadhu or yogi travelling in a train, he would search them out on the station and insist they stay with him for a few days, at the end of which, he would give them a first-class train ticket for the onward journey.

Once, a sannyasi whom he nursed back to good health, gave him the book *Jiva Brahma Aikyam Vedanta Rahasyam* written by Swami Satchidananda, a spiritual luminary. This book roused Dr Kuppuswamy's dormant spirituality. He then immersed himself in spiritual literature. He collected a large number of spiritual books and would sit up late nights poring over them. He regularly went through religious scriptures such as the *Bhagwad Gita*, the *Ramayana*, the *Bhagwata* and the *Mahabharata*. He was visibly influenced by the works of Swami Vivekananda, Rama Tirtha and Adi Shankaracharya, and also by the literature of the Theosophical Society, and the *Holy Bible* and *The Imitation of Christ*.

Regularity of practice is the key to spiritual advancement and that is what took Dr Kuppuswamy ahead on his spiritual quest. He was extremely regular in his daily prayers and his practices of Hatha Yoga. He also practised Anahata Laya Yoga and Swara Sadhana. He loved singing bhajans and kirtans and conducting devotional music sessions.

The spirit of continuous service in Dr Kuppuswamy was beginning to result in the purification of the senses. In addition, seeing sickness, misery, pain, death and despair at close quarters in the plantation hospital had begun to have a profound impact on his psyche. His gentle heart broke each time he was unsuccessful at saving a patient. He began to wonder about the mystery of death and the true purpose of life and became increasingly introspective.

He wrote at that time, 'Is there not a higher mission in life than the daily round of official duties, eating and drinking? Is there not any higher form of eternal happiness than these transitory and illusory pleasures? How uncertain is life here! How insecure is existence on the earth plane – with various kinds of diseases, anxieties, worries, fears and disappointments! The world of names and forms is constantly changing. Time is fleeting. All hopes of happiness in this world terminate in pain, despair and sorrow.'

The state of detachment emerges from transcending attachments, which is often done by suppressing minor attachments and experiencing major attachments till they become minor enough to suppress. Dr Kuppuswamy was very fond of fancy clothes, rings, trinkets and other items of gold, silver and sandalwood. He would enter a shop and collect a few articles, pay for them and leave. At times, he would wear ten rings on his ten fingers. He was obviously playing out his karmic attachments in this way.

Renunciation: The Flowering of the Seed

Finally, *vairagya,* or the fire of complete renunciation, consumed his consciousness. *Vairagya* blossomed as a result of selfless service, prayer and charity, knowledge and regular yogic practice, devotion and determination. His mind rose above mundane considerations of wealth, position and honour. In 1923, Dr Kuppuswamy left his job, donated his belongings and returned to Madras.

On the journey back home, a stranger who was a palmist read his palm and exclaimed that Dr Kuppuswamy had the *bhikshu rekha* (line of beggars) on his hand. The palmist predicted that he would someday need to beg to meet his needs. Once, in Madras, Dr Kuppuswamy left the little luggage he had with a friend and without letting anyone know of his plans, went on a pilgrimage. He visited holy cities and various temples and met many holy men, saints and yogis.

Dr Kuppuswamy walked barefoot from village to village. Being completely inexperienced in begging, he was extremely shy in asking people for food. As a result, he would often go hungry for days. Sometimes, he would eat fruits from trees and sleep under them. When forced by hunger, he would shyly approach people — whisper to them that he was a Brahmin from Madras and was hungry[2]. Some people, recognising him as an extraordinary God-intoxicated individual, would feed him well. But, he would never return to beg again at the house that had fed him once. Even if a family requested him to stay on, he would continue on his travels. He was increasingly becoming indifferent to pleasure and pain.

At Kashi[3], he had the blissful darshan of Lord Viswanath and, as a result, he felt his accumulated karma melt away. He continued his itinerant ways and met a postmaster in the Dhalaj village. He stayed with him and served him as his cook. Finally, the postmaster directed him to go to Rishikesh, a place suitable for solitary meditation. Rishikesh, a small town in the foothills of the Himalayas, was—in those days—frequented only by those consumed with a true desire for self-realisation. Dr Kuppuswamy was also thirsting for spiritual initiation and the desire for a guru was foremost in his mind. Hence, he proceeded to Rishikesh in search of a guru.

Meeting the Guru

Within a month of his arrival in Rishikesh, Dr Kuppuswamy met Swami Viswananda Saraswati. He recognised Viswananda as his guru and the latter recognised Dr Kuppuswamy as a disciple[4].

The Guru

Not much is known about the guru. Swami Viswananda was a great ascetic and a yogi. He lived mostly in the Himalayas and spent most of his time sitting in a state of samadhi, sometimes for weeks on end. Though details of his birth are not available, it is known that he was born in Punjab. He was fluent in the Punjabi language, and often gave examples in it, when explaining spiritual concepts. He was an advanced adept of yoga and wore nothing but a *kaupeen*. He remained a celibate all his life. At the age of 115, around the year 1945, he voluntarily gave up his body, sitting in the lotus pose. Even at this advanced age, he appeared to be merely forty-five years old.

Swami Viswananda would maintain equanimity with all of the Lord's creation. It is said that Swamiji had a bull and a tiger living in harmony with each other in his mountain hermitage. Some consider Swami Viswananda as an incarnation of Lord Siva. He accepted only three disciples in his life—Swami Sivananda, Swami Vidyananda and Swami Vishudhananda. When leaving his disciples, he told them that their meeting him had been preordained and that they would never meet him again.

Initiation and Sadhana

Dr Kuppuswamy began to live in his guru's hut. The same day, he decided to visit Kali Kamliwala Kshetra[5] in Rishikesh, where food was distributed to monks, but he returned empty-handed. Dr Kuppuswamy was not aware that the food was distributed only to initiate sannyasis. This prompted Swami Viswananda to give his disciple sannyas initiation, which, it is believed, was a transmission of wisdom and knowledge by the guru. Dr Kuppuswamy was renamed Swami Sivananda Saraswati. He was taught the esoteric doctrines of *kaivalya* and other practices of the spiritual order. Subsequently, he was formally initiated into the Dashnami Sampradaya[6]. Swami Vishnu Devananda in the Kailash Ashram in Rishikesh performed this initiation.

Swami Sivananda Saraswati shifted to Swargashram, a locality in Rishikesh. He began to live in a small, dilapidated hut, in an area infested with scorpions and other insects. He immersed himself in intense spiritual practices and would meditate for over twelve hours a day. Often, he would do *japam,* from early morning to sunrise, standing waist deep in the icy-cold water of the Ganga. He would observe silence for days on end or would fast for long periods, sometimes, for several days at a stretch—lost to the world outside. He would keep a stock of chapattis in his hut and eat them with water from the sacred Ganga—all this to avoid having to move around and interact with people. He went deeper in the state of samadhi and lengthened the experience. All this while, Swamiji would also maintain his Hatha Yoga routines to keep himself physically fit, and sometimes supplemented these practices with jogging and sprinting; daily pranayama gave him tremendous strength too. In course of time, this conferred upon him the power of psychic healing, while also giving him a razor-sharp memory.

Sadhana and Service

However, even amid these austerities, Swami Sivananda did not lose the spirit of service. Swamiji was always on the lookout for opportunities to serve. He once said, 'On rare occasions, you must even be aggressive in your service. Sometimes, helpless persons in need of aid will foolishly refuse it. In such cases, do the required service in spite of their hesitation.'

He would nurse sadhus and sannyasis in times of their ill health and beg on their behalf. Whether it was common cold or lethal diseases of those times, such as smallpox and cholera, he never restrained from helping people. He would clean their huts, fill their water pots, wash their clothes and feed them.

Meanwhile, Swamiji's insurance policy had matured and a lawyer friend helped him salvage ₹5,000 of the matured amount, in those days a healthy sum. Swamiji refused to use the money for personal benefit and deposited it in the post office with the objective of using it for service. With this money he, along with Swami Kalikananda, started a charitable dispensary in Lakshmana Jhula (Rishikesh) in 1927, called the Satya Sewashram Dispensary. The dispensary was located right on the path taken by various pilgrims on their journey further into the Himalayas, and so they thought it would be a good location to render service to pilgrims.

Swamiji also kept up with his literary pursuits. He would often get some spiritual books from the Rama Ashram library in Muni-ki-Reti and study them. Some of his favourite books were the *Avadhoot Gita, Vivek Chudamani* and the Upanishads. Though he did maintain the company of saints, he seldom engaged in idle talk. Even while walking, he would be immersed in *japam* or some form of pranayama. He considered interacting with people as interruptions in his sadhana, which had now become intense. He would go away for long spells to pursue his sadhana on the rocky ledges on the Ganga's banks or bushy regions in the hills nearby. 'A favourite spot was a rock almost midstream (in the Ganga) where the current was strong. On many an evening, he would go there for his meditation. He used to hide himself in the hollow angular cut of the rock. In course of time, he increased his meditation to eight hours a day, further increasing it to twelve to sixteen hours in winters. At times, he would be closeted for days in his hut, deep in his meditation. '

He was vigilant to ensure that in this critical stage of his sadhana, temptations did not lure him away. Like so many devotees who visited Rishikesh and were awed by this dynamic sadhu, the queen of Singai also developed reverence for him. She would send him sweets and fruits everyday, but he distributed them to others. One day, she invited Swamiji to a ceremonial meal for sadhus, but he refused to participate and to even partake of the food sent by her through a servant. He quietly locked himself in his hut for three days, staying inside until he was certain she was gone. He spent this time without food or water, deep in meditation.

Finally, his austerities bore fruit, and he attained the ultimate superconscious state. Now he had nothing more to achieve for himself in this life. He had never lived for himself anyway; now he dedicated his life to serving spiritual aspirants who visited him for direction and succour.

Swamiji never disclosed the date or place of his self-realisation. With regard to lesser spiritual experiences, by chance, some disciples did get to know that during the master's periods of deep meditation, he had been blessed by living visions of Lord Krishna and the Upanishadic sages.

The Saint and the Teacher

Writings of Sivananda

Swamiji had a habit of jotting down his thoughts and, over a period of time, he began to write them down as practical advice to spiritual aspirants. His dedication to writing was so intense that by the end of his life, he had written over 300 books on spiritual subjects—all of them in the last twenty-five years of his life. While churning out such a large body of work, he never compromised on quality, making his books some of the best on the subjects covered. He would write multiple books on several subjects at the same time and allot some hours daily to each book.

He wrote relentlessly and passionately and proclaimed that he would continue to write thus even if he went blind. He said that even if he did lose his vision, he would dictate to his disciples to ensure that till the end of his life, his efforts to disseminate spiritual knowledge to the world continued.

In one of his poems, it becomes evident that Swami Sivananda had received the mandate from God to don the mantle of a guru. The master wrote:

> *I heard a voice from within: Siva wake up*
> *And fill the cup of your life with this nectar,*
> *Share it with all, I shall give you strength, energy, power and wisdom;*
> *I obeyed his command, He did fill the cup,*
> *And I shared it with all.*

He had a missionary zeal to reach out to thousands of seekers through his writings and adopted the strangest of ways to achieve this objective. Swamiji, once, began to contribute regular articles to a popular but morally questionable publication, which carried pieces on romance and advertisements on sexual themes, something considered unfit for a saint. However, Swamiji took this as a way to reach a wide circle of readers who needed spiritual guidance. Within a short span of time, hundreds of aspirants who were subscribers of the magazine began to write to him for guidance.

Sometimes, Swamiji would send a copy of his writings to a postmaster, and request him to print and distribute free as much of the literature as he could.

The writings were only a means for spreading spiritual teachings and aid in human transformation. The gentle saint had no attachment to his own works. An author, once, sent some flashy and expensive books on spirituality to him, and he directed a disciple to write a review of the same in the *Divine Life* magazine. The disciple realised that the author had plagiarised the content, word by word, from Swamiji's own writings. When he brought this to Swamiji's notice, Swamiji was not displeased at all. He praised the way the author had represented his own teachings and insisted that no action be taken against him as he was, after all, in a way distributing knowledge.

Essentials of His Teachings

Swamji believed that self-realisation was the ideal to be worked for by all devotees, and that achieving it was very easy. It was the preparation for that state — the purification and the stabilisation — that, he claimed, was difficult.

Swamiji considered 'idleness, aimlessness and procrastination' as the thieves who stole the spiritual merit of aspirants. One of Swamiji's key principles was D.I.N — Do It Now. He would never procrastinate and would be tirelessly attached to service and action. In addition, whatever he did, he would do with all his heart and soul. He would continue to do the same till his task was complete. He laid stress on maintaining a spiritual diary as a tool for continuous introspection on the quality and commitment towards spiritual practices.

Integrated yoga was also central to Swamiji's teachings. He laid stress on a good diet and a routine of asanas and pranayama to maintain health and energy. He emphasised on meditation and *japam* for spiritual progress — reading of holy books for spiritual knowledge was equally important. In fact, he recommended continuous repetition of a mantra or the name of God while doing one's daily activities. But most of all, he prescribed service or hard selfless work for playing out the karma. In his view, all of these supplemented each other. In general, he prescribed six hours of meditation, six hours of selfless service and six hours of study to his disciples.

Swamiji believed that any form of attachment was detrimental to spiritual progress. He, once, told a devotee that even 'attachment to *vairagya* [detachment]' was a bar to spiritual growth. A balance in the pursuit of spirituality was critical to Swamiji's teachings. He would restrain disciples from excessive austerities that could harm the body.

The core of his teachings lay in his message, 'Serve, Love, Give, Meditate, Realise'. He encouraged his disciples to strive on the path, irrespective of negativity and difficulty.

Humility, Simplicity and Tolerance

Swami Sivananda was extremely humble in his interactions. He considered even the act of being a master of his disciples and guiding them as a service. He would often end letters to his disciples with the signature 'Thy Humble Servant, Sivananda!'

Swamiji did not don any ornamental robes, neither did he sport marks of religious distinction[7]. He would interact with ashram visitors with such simplicity that people who did not recognise him were not able to realise—until told—that this ordinary man was Sivananda himself. The thousands who flocked to his ashram found a simple, unassuming saint, who seemed more delighted to meet them than they were to meet him. When he travelled by train, he would not engage a porter or allow his disciples to carry his luggage. Instead, he would come out of the compartment with the luggage on his head and carry it to the destination.

Whenever a disciple, troubled by some material difficulty, begged him for his grace, Swamiji would promise to pray for the aspirant. If the disciple's troubles came to an end miraculously, he would never accept credit for it but attribute it to the grace of God.

Swamiji was a model of humility and simplicity, but his meekness was not a sign of weakness. One of the world's most prominent spiritual leaders once came to meet him in Rishikesh. Swamiji was unwell and in bed. In spite of being in pain, Swamiji got up and greeted the man reverentially. Unfortunately, the man had not come to meet Swamiji out of the spiritual attraction to a holy man's company. He accused Swamiji of publicly criticising him. Very humbly, Swamiji defended himself saying he did not believe in criticising others. This was not enough for that spiritual leader. He repeated the accusations and threatened to ruin Swamiji's reputation through his network of global disciples. Swamiji's face hardened and his response was swift. 'Do whatever you want,' was all he said, abruptly closing the meeting. He had no time for critics and scandal mongers, or people spreading negativity.

Glory of Sannyasa

Swami Sivananda attached great importance to the institution of *sannyasa* and initiated men and women, young and old alike into it. Some questioned his indiscriminate granting of *sannyasa*. Swamiji responded by emphatically declaring that even the sannyasis who had gone astray or had renounced *sannyasa* were worthy of veneration. He praised them that 'for at least one day' they had boldly challenged the forces and temptations inherent in Nature.

Swamiji would often encounter people who behaved strangely, but he maintained his simple and straightforward behaviour. He was once approached by an individual who insisted that Swamiji accept initiation into *sannyasa* by him. He claimed, his own guru had appeared in a dream and had commanded him to initiate Swamiji. The saint gently told the man that he had already been initiated. A couple of days later, the man was back. This time he was, for himself, seeking initiation into *sannyasa* from Swamiji. Swamiji did not belittle him, nor did he taunt him. He gave him the initiation as sought. The man, however, was emboldened and there was more to come. He asked Swamiji to also give him the title of 'Lion of Vedanta', as he claimed his knowledge of the subject was unmatched. Swamiji agreed and asked his disciples to address the man by this title. After a few days, the man began asking Swamiji's disciples to desert Swamiji and accept him as their guru. He said Swamiji did not know much about Vedanta and he could guide them better on the Vedantic path. For some disciples, this was too much to bear, but for Swamiji, the emotion of love for the man superseded all; he insisted that his disciples continue addressing the man as the 'Lion of Vedanta'.

Tirelessness

One remarkable thing about Swamiji was his constant cheerfulness and energy. He might have worked extremely hard and late the previous night, yet would be up at four o'clock the next morning, chanting *Om* and waking up other spiritual aspirants for the morning prayers. In health or in sickness, whenever anyone asked him how he was, he would reply 'most wonderful'. His face would seldom reveal the trouble the body was enduring. During his all-India tours or while attending Parliament of Religions, he would be involved in very exhausting routines with very little sleep. Yet throughout, he was always fresh, cheerful and energetic. His boyish enthusiasm was almost a miracle.

Where did he get such energy from? Swamiji attributed it to his practice of pranayama and the repetition of the Lord's name or the result of an awakened kundalini.

If a disciple was not active and energetic, Swamiji would gently reprimand him. He did not want anyone to confuse spirituality with indolence. One particular disciple in the ashram got into the habit of maintaining a lost frame of mind, believing that to be an expression of spiritual tranquillity. One day, Swamiji interrogated him. He asked him whether his diet was insufficient or whether he was not doing enough exercise. Thereafter, he was sent jogging around the bhajan hall to energise himself.

Vision of Universal God

Swamiji saw God in all creatures, including scorpions, ailing dogs, ants, in sadhus or in criminals. This was a vibrant, living belief, not an intellectual concept. He, once, even scolded a disciple who was about to crush a scorpion. He would nurse the orphaned litter of a rat with the same devotion with which he served sick people in his dispensary. 'The Master fed ants with sugar, birds with rice, monkeys with gram, fish with bread. He kept water in pots for birds.' He refused to let disciples spray kerosene and kill the bed bugs on his cot.

The ashram, like Swamiji's heart, was open to all and he made continuous efforts not to hurt anyone, especially people from other (non-Hindu) communities. He, once, instructed his disciples to take special care of an orthodox Muslim who stayed at the ashram, ensuring that his feelings were not hurt and that he could follow the practices he was used to. The Christians who came to the ashram found their faith respected and, in fact, discovered a deeper meaning to Christianity. Swamiji would glorify the teachings of all religions. While most of the ashram inmates were from the southern part of India, people from other parts of the country — or the world — received a special treatment to make them feel more at home.

The Will of God

Swamiji's belief in God was unshakeable. Once, when a young swami complained of shortage of money for managing the ashram, Swamiji told him to have faith. However, the young swami was not completely satisfied. It was probably the questioning attitude of the disciple that triggered an 'instant miracle'. In a short while, an affluent lady arrived and insisted on meeting Swami Sivananda. She handed over ₹10,000 to him, saying it was her late husband's last wish.

The Ashram and the Travels

Swamiji, once, confessed that when he had set out on the spiritual path, all he wanted to do was spend his time in chanting and meditation, begging for food and not caring for a roof, but the Lord had different plans. He had destined a life of spiritual service for Swamiji. In 1934, Swamiji received a grant of land from the king of Tehri Garhwal in Rishikesh. He set up an ashram and a dispensary there. He named it Ananda Kutir — the house of bliss — though the ashram was also called Sivananda Ashram. He established the Divine Life Trust in 1936 and the Divine Life Society in 1939, to spread the spiritual culture he had envisioned. Hundreds of people flocked to him for solace.

But every now and then, the need for solitude would overwhelm Swamiji, and he would leave the place quietly for an unknown destination to meditate in peace. In 1941, he disappeared for ten days and eventually was located at a farm in Jagdishpur, miles away from the ashram. His disciples realised the need for the master to get away from time to time. So, they decided to construct an underground cave for him, where he could meditate in solitude. The cave was called Kaivalya Guha[8] by the master.

Swami Sivananda travelled widely across the country, conducting kirtans and spreading the message of yoga and Vedanta. Though his disciples were spread all over the world, he never travelled outside the Indian sub-continent. In 1950, he organised an India-Ceylon tour, in which he visited many places in both the countries. In 1953, he organised the World Parliament of Religions in the Sivananda Ashram itself.

Hordes of people would flock to his programmes. The master was an inexhaustible source of energy as he exhorted people to transform their lives. Swamiji would give mantra initiation to aspirants. Often, he would recommend a mantra for assisting the disciple in material difficulties. For instance, he would give the Katyayani Mantra for getting a good husband, the Santana Gopala Mantra for giving birth to a child, the Maha Mrityunjaya Mantra for warding off evil and difficulties and the Aditya Hridaya Stotra for good eyesight.

Sivam *Leela*

When Swami Sivananda took responsibility for a spiritual aspirant, he took it holistically for his welfare – spiritual, material or physical. The master would come to the rescue of his devotees and disciples in mysterious ways. Many disciples mentioned how Swamiji appeared before them and gave them words of guidance and blessing, or rescued them from grave danger. However, Swamiji attributed all such miracles to the grace of God.

Even the seemingly ordinary actions of Swamiji worked in mysterious ways. Once, a disciple who was addicted to smoking was upset. He couldn't find a cigarette to control his craving. Swami Sivananda gave some money to another disciple and asked him to arrange for cigarettes for the swami – much to others' discomfort, as cigarette smoking was considered a breach of ashram rules. However, the cigarettes had the desired effect. The swami probably reflected on the episode deeply and decided to completely quit smoking thereafter.

The Divine Pull

Swamiji attracted disciples from world over in mysterious ways. A lady from Canada wrote, 'I came to know Swami Sivananda through a dream. It was a strange dream. I saw his name and learnt how to get in touch with him. Swami Sivananda has got the power to cause his disciples and devotees to have visions of himself while one is awake though living at a great distance from him.' Another aspirant who prayed for a mentor had a vision of his own family guru in his dream. The saint directed him to Swami Sivananda and revealed the way to find him.

Once, a disciple of Swamiji came to the ashram in the earnest hope of meeting his guru. He travelled for seven days to reach the ashram only to find that Swamiji was not there. He could not hold back his tears and began crying silently. Suddenly, he saw a flash of lightning and Swamiji came out of his hut. He bowed before Swamiji but before he could say anything or call anyone, Swamiji disappeared.

Swami Sivananda Sarada, a devotee from Germany, had never met Swamiji and neither had she seen his photograph. One day, she heard his voice in her room and in the Christmas of 1951, she received a living vision of the master. Strangely, a few days later, her husband gave her a book with a picture of the master on the cover. She went on to establish contact with Swamiji and became a disciple.

The Autograph

In 1953, Swamiji sent an autographed booklet titled *Pilgrimage to Badri & Kailas*[9] to his disciple, Dr Kutty, with his blessings. Four years later, she went on a pilgrimage to Badri and Kailas and looked up the booklet for guidance. On finding the book, she was surprised to see that four years ago, Swamiji had written the date below his signature as '6.5.57' (6 May 1957), the exact date she was to commence her pilgrimage. She considered the pilgrimage blessed by Swamiji.

The Devotee and the Dacoit

Saints are often the targets of attacks. While Swamiji was always engaged in serving the world, he was indifferent to verbal or physical attacks. Once, a mentally deranged man called Govindan attacked him with an axe, aiming three blows at Swamiji's head. Fortunately, the room was dimly lit and the axe hit a door and only the handle hit Swamiji's turbaned head. The assailant was nabbed, but Swamiji would not allow the police to prosecute him, claiming that nothing but divine will could have motivated the attack and nothing but divine will had spared his own life. He concluded that his physical body had been saved as, perhaps, there was still more service left for him to perform. He blessed the man, initiated him and sent him back to his hometown with gifts of books and fruit. The master added him to the list of free recipients of Divine Life Society literature. Swamiji's persistent kindness bore fruit and Govindan eventually became a transformed man. He treated himself as a disciple of the master and besought Swamiji to remedy his shortcomings.

Visions and Remote Manifestations

Swamiji's devotees saw him before them at different places while he would still be in the ashram itself at that point of time. Some saw him when they were meditating, while others saw him during kirtans. He appeared before some and accepted their offerings of prasad.

One devotee had a beautiful vision at his home, where Swamiji appeared in an orb of blue light. Even as he saw the vision, he was wondering if it was a play of his mind. However, his mother corroborated his vision; she also saw the orb of light but could not see Swamiji within it.

During the partition of India, a time ridden with violence and rioting, Swamiji appeared in a devotee's dream. He asked him to move with his family immediately from their home in Sialkot in Pakistan and go to Haridwar in India. They left as directed and, in hindsight, realised that the timely move had saved their lives.

The visions were not limited to Indian devotees. Frau Walinski of Germany insisted that Swamiji woke her up everyday and she had frequent visions of Swamiji. In some of those, he instructed her spiritually. Another lady received a photograph of his, which tallied exactly with the vision of Swamiji she had had a few days earlier.

A doctor-disciple was in a state of worry due to personal and professional difficulties when she heard Swamiji calling out to her from outside her door. She opened the door and saw him standing before her, stick in hand and a smile on his face. She was delighted to see Swamiji there and prostrated before him, only to find he had vanished when she looked up. She realised that the master was always with her and she overcame her worries.

In a similar vein, another disciple, A.K. Sinha, recounted how his son despaired during an examination, where he could not answer any of the questions. He was about to hand over a blank answer sheet to the invigilator when suddenly he saw Swamiji before him — forcing him to sit down. The boy sat down and attempted all the questions and came out with flying colours.

Swamiji would often suggest that his disciples keep his photographs and concentrate on them. He would assure them that his photos could communicate with them. For this reason, he would also insist that his picture should appear in prominent places in books and magazines. Swamiji would insist on the same without a touch of ego or pride. And, devotees would write their experiences, discussing how Swamiji's photo came alive, how he spoke to them through the photographs and how miracles were achieved through them.

The Cure

In his early life as a doctor, Swamiji had helped many by curing them of their physical ailments. He now cured defects of the spirit and yet, when required, he still cured the defects of the body. He was truly a doctor of doctors. Swamiji's ability to cure people was unique — for now, he needed no medicine and did not even need to be physically present. Hundreds of people got cured even with Swamiji not being present.

Paramhansa Satyananda, a disciple in the ashram, once suffered from jaundice. Swami Sivananda told him he needed no medicine and would be fine on his own. This would be difficult for a medical man to accept but the body actually recovered in a short while.

Another disciple, Swami Krishnananda was suffering from a liver problem. He had fever for a prolonged time and therefore became extremely weak. He tried all remedies, including medicine and fasting, but to no avail. Just when he was giving up on his health, he witnessed a miracle. He felt a surge of energy and his illness seemed to wane all by itself. He saw Swami Sivananda everywhere around him in the room — on his bed, on the walls, in the walking stick. In a moment, Swami Krishnananda was completely healthy again.

Once, a lady was suffering from third degree burns that had become septic and her relatives were worried for her life. She received an invitation by mail from Swamiji for a Sadhana Week programme. The family realised that if the master had invited her, she would certainly recover before the event. She did indeed experience a miraculous recovery in a short while.

Another devotee meditated upon the master, calling out for his grace for his son who was critically ill. He vividly saw the master walk into his house and take the ailing child on his lap, assuring the devotee that his son would recover. The vision ended and, in a little while, the child's health was restored.

Manifestation of the Divine Mother

One of the master's neighbours in Rishikesh, Rajarajeshwarananda, was a devotee of the Divine Mother. He had been worshipping Her for the last twelve years, but She didn't appear to him in a vision. A desire crept into his mind to offer silk cloth and ornaments at an auspicious time to the goddess. Unfortunately, he didn't have the adequate means to carry out his wishes. One day, a group of girls appeared at his door and gave him money and material for the worship, claiming to have been sent by Swami Sivananda. Rajarajeshwarananda felt indebted to Swami Sivananda, but was mystified at the generous gift from a saint who lived on donations, and he went to thank Swamiji. The saint denied any knowledge of sending the girls and Rajarajeshwarananda, despite his best efforts, could not find a trace of them at Ananda Kutir. He then realised that it was probably the grace of the Divine Mother acting at Swamiji's request.

The Disciples

Swamiji had a large following that consisted of many inspired and gifted individuals, the lives of each of whom can fill several volumes. I cover the lives of only a few of his disciples in the following paragraphs.

Swami Satyananda

Swami Satyananda was born in Almora, in the foothills of the Himalayas, in December 1923. In the early years of his life, he had the opportunity to interact with various pilgrims and saints. As a youth, he had several spiritual experiences that drove him to the path of self-realisation. At some point of time, he encountered obstacles in his spiritual journey and could not overcome them. This led him to seek a realised master. He met many saints, including Anandamayi Ma, one of the greatest saints of the twentieth century, but his quest for a guru continued. When Swami Satyananda finally met Swami Sivananda, he recognised the latter as his guru. He felt complete tranquillity and a cessation of all intellectual analysis. When the young aspirant asked Swami Sivananda how to overcome spiritual obstacles, the saint advised him to busy himself in service in the ashram. Swami Satyananda so completely immersed himself in service that he ignored ailments and difficulties. Finally, he managed to transcend the spiritual obstacles and attain complete enlightenment. In course of time, Swami Sivananda initiated him into *sannyasa* as a Paramhansa Sannyasi[10]. The master referred to Swami Satyananda as a 'versatile genius' and said that Satyananda was full of the highest form of renunciation.

Once, Swamiji was busy in giving spiritual initiation to a lady in his ashram. All of a sudden, she saw Swami Satyananda sitting in place of the master, Swami Sivananda. In a short while, she again saw the form of Swami Sivananda before her, smilingly telling her that he would himself come to her home and initiate her. In that vision, she saw the unity between Swami Sivananda and Swami Satyananda, and also realised that the latter was destined to be her guru. In course of time, Swami Satyananda initiated her.

Swami Satyananda completely identified himself with his master. Swami Sivananda one day called him and asked him what sadhana he practised, and whether he had the knowledge of Kriya Yoga. When Swami Satyananda replied in the negative, Swamiji transmitted the entire knowledge of Kriya Yoga to him in a matter of a few minutes.

Swamiji gave Swami Satyananda ₹108 and asked him to spread yoga 'from door to door and shore to shore'. Swami Satyananda went on to establish a vast global network of ashrams and affiliated yoga institutions. After successfully carrying out his guru's command, he finally appointed Swami Niranjanananda as his successor and renounced his mission. He handed over management of the ashrams and institutions to Swami Niranjanananda and left on a pilgrimage in 1988. For a long time, none of his disciples knew of his whereabouts. He finally reappeared before the world and settled in the remote village of Rikhia in present-day Jharkhand, where he immersed himself in the Vedic Panchagni Sadhana and other esoteric spiritual practices. On the night of 5 December 2009, he called a disciple and informed her that the time had come for him to take samadhi. He sat in the lotus pose and immersed himself in a meditative state. In a short while, he voluntarily left his body in the state of *mahasamadhi*.

Swami Chidananda

Sridhar Rao was born in Mangalore, in 1916, in an affluent family. He was deeply devoted to religious pursuits since childhood. He was influenced by various saints, the first being Papa Ramdas of Kanhagad. The lives of Ramana Maharshi and Ramakrishna Paramhansa also influenced him. He participated wholeheartedly in the activities of the Ramakrishna Mission in Madras. Though a brilliant student, over a period of time, he developed a desire to renounce everything and devote himself purely to God. Sridhar Rao left the worldly life but his parents tracked him down and convinced him to return home. However, he, once again, left home and eventually reached the ashram of Swami Sivananda in 1943. He recognised Swamiji as his mentor and surrendered himself at the master's feet. Swamiji also announced Sridhar Rao as his successor in this very first meeting between the guru and the disciple.

In 1949, Swami Sivananda initiated Sridhar into *sannyasa* and named him Swami Chidananda. After that, Swami Chidananda wrote *Light Fountain*, one of the earliest biographies of Swami Sivananda. This devotee-turned-swami spent over a decade in the ashram. He then travelled widely for another decade, preaching yoga and Vedanta on behalf of his master. After that, he sank into a mood of deep detachment and began to live a life of seclusion, or was travelling like an itinerant monk. Swami Chidananda returned to the ashram three weeks before Swami Sivananda left his body. After the saint passed away, Swami Chidananda was elected president of the Divine Life Society. He held this post as long as he retained the body, guiding thousands of spiritual aspirants with the message of Sivananda — the immortal sage.

On 31 August 2008, Swami Chidananda passed away. This gentle unassuming saint had left instructions to give his body *jal samadhi*, by immersion in the holy Ganga, with minimal fanfare, and without even once chanting the name Chidananda.

Swami Krishnananda

Subbaraya was born in 1922, to a family of devout Vaishnavas in what was then South Kanara district — currently Dakshin Kannada in the state of Karnataka. Very early in life, he developed an interest in the Hindu scriptures, both Vaishnava as well as those of the Adwaita doctrine. He knew the *Gita* by heart. However, his mind was plagued by philosophical questions, which he felt could not be answered in material settings. Though he joined government service in 1943, towards the end of that year, he set off in search of a spiritual guide. After visiting various holy places, he finally reached Ananda Kutir in the summer of 1944. Swami Sivananda did not speak to him for three days, during which, Subbaraya faced difficulties in finding food. He was uncertain whether he would even be allowed to stay in the ashram. At the end of the period, Swamiji called him, whereupon Subbaraya prostrated himself before the saint. Swamiji asked him to stay in the ashram until death and prophesied that kings and ministers would bow before Subbaraya. Swamiji encouraged the disciple to assist him in his spiritual writing. Eventually, he initiated Subbaraya into *sannyasa* and named him Swami Krishnananda. Swami Krishnananda was possessed with the fire of renunciation. In 1961, he was appointed the general secretary of the Divine Life Society, a post he held till his *mahasamadhi* in 2001.

Swami Chinmayananda

Balakrishna Menon was born in Ernakulam, in what is today the Indian state of Kerala, in May 1916. His parents were devout souls and orthodox. Balan, as he was called by his near and dear ones, imbibed deep religiosity from them. In addition, he was influenced by his family gurus and saints, many of who predicted a bright future for him. Balan grew up to be a brilliant student, but with a rational and critical attitude towards everything.

While he was still a student, Balan got involved in the Indian freedom movement and was, therefore, imprisoned for several months. Living in terrible conditions changed his perspective on life (and death) and he resumed his studies. After graduating, he took to journalism. He was a voracious reader and had read the works of Swami

Vivekananda, Mahayogi Aurobindo, Ramana Maharshi, Swami Rama Tirtha and Swami Sivananda.

In 1947, as a journalist, he went to interview Swami Sivananda, who advised the young man to stay in the ashram for a while, and only then would he get to interview the saint. Balan took the advice, but when the time came for the interview, the journalist in him had receded, and he had mentally become part of the ashram. He returned to Delhi, but kept coming back until he permanently became a member of the ashram. In course of time, Swami Sivananda initiated him into *sannyasa* and named him Swami Chinmayananda. Swamiji advised the young sannyasi to go high in the Himalayas and seek out Tapovan Muni, a learned saint, for further instruction in Hindu scriptures.

Swami Chinmayananda stayed with, studied under and served Tapovan Muni for many years. After that, he travelled all over the world, spreading the message of Vedanta. After more than forty years of untiring effort, Swami Chinmayananda attained *mahasamadhi* in San Diego, California, in August 1993.

Swami Vishnudevananda, the 'Flying Swami'

Kuttan Nair was born in December 1927 in the present-day state of Kerala. He finished his studies and went onto become a teacher. However, after some time, he joined the army — this was motivated by a difficulty in financial circumstances and a desire for scientific education. One day, he found a pamphlet containing Swami Sivananda's instructions. The teachings impressed him so much that he decided to meet Swamiji at once. The first meeting left a visible impact on him and created a desire to come back for more. On his second visit, Swami Sivananda gave him an insightful cosmic vision and some spiritual instructions by personal example. Swamiji then asked the young aspirant if he would stay on in the ashram and Kuttan agreed. Kuttan immersed himself in service of the ashram, and learning and practising different aspects of yoga, his favourite being Hatha Yoga. In course of time, he became an adept in it. Swami Sivananda initiated him into *sannyasa* and named him Swami Vishnudevananda. One day, Swami Sivananda gave ₹10 to Swami Vishnudevananda, and instructed him to travel the world and spread the message of Vedanta.

After this, Swami Vishnudevananda travelled tirelessly around the world, preaching yoga and Vedanta. He even learnt to fly and would pilot a small plane over strife-torn areas, dropping pamphlets with messages of peace — this earned him the epithet of 'Flying Swami'. He spoke and taught in many parts of the world, where his centres of instruction were established. He established the International Sivananda Yoga Vedanta Centre (ISYVC), headquartered in Quebec (Canada), with centres around the world, for imparting instruction in yoga. He breathed his last in November 1993.

The End and the Signs

It was the end of 1962. Swami Sivananda's health began to decline. He had now not only achieved the mission the body was intended to support, but in fact had also guided innumerable spiritual aspirants along the path. While he had not started a religion or a cult or a sect, he had built a superstructure in the shape of the Divine Life Society to perpetuate his immortal message of service, love and spirituality. He had also 'given birth' to many swamis who were now qualified to guide humanity along the path, or rather along various spiritual paths. It appeared a good time to leave the body, to merge into the Absolute.

Towards the end, Swami Sivananda had begun to give hints about his eventual *mahasamadhi*, perhaps preparing his disciples for the infinite departure. The year he passed away, he encouraged his disciples to seek initiation on Sivaratri, an auspicious day, adding ominously, 'Who knows, what may happen next Sivaratri?'

Another indication of Swamiji's intent was an episode related to the monthly magazine of Divine Life Society. The magazine would always carry an inspirational letter from him, which he would write in December in advance for all twelve issues of the following year. However, in December 1962, he merely wrote for eight issues.

When asked by a disciple, he brushed off the enquiry, and insisted that only what he had written should be published. The disciple, unfortunately, could not gauge the reason behind Swamiji's action.

Swamiji's health was now fast deteriorating, but the spirit was untouched. Whenever he was asked how he was, he would brightly and emphatically say he was fine.

Swamiji was also seen by several disciples browsing through the calendar frequently, but he gently brushed them off if they asked him about it. He was probably looking for an auspicious day to give up his body. According to Indian astrology, 14 July 1963, was the favourable day. On that day, Swamiji's condition worsened. He was unable to swallow even a little amount of water. When the disciples tried to give him barley water, as was the usual practice in the ashram, he refused, and insisted on consuming only the water from the holy Ganga. Strangely, he was now able to swallow half a glass of the Ganges' water[11]. Shortly after that, he left his body. Disciples were shocked at the abruptness of the saint's departure. Some cried, and others watched stunned. Some disciples placed the saint's body in lotus pose with his hands on his legs and fingers interlocked. The body was bathed, clothed and garlanded.

Devotees and disciples had begun to crowd the ashram for a last glimpse of the saint's body. The next day, ceremonial rites continued for many hours and finally, the saint was given a befitting burial. Over time, a *sivalingam* was installed above the burial site and, eventually, a shrine was built around the spot. Till this day, devotees from around the globe experience spiritual energy and peace radiating from this shrine.

The end of the body was not the end of the saint. From time to time, Swami Sivananda would appear before his disciples and devotees. He would appear before Swami Satyananda and guide him on his mission and Swami Satyananda would note the guidance in his diary. Though Swami Satyananda struggled for many years in fulfilling the mission, he realised that he never experienced any obstacles in the fulfilment of the guidance given by Swami Sivananda. More importantly, when Swami Sivananda would appear before Swami Satyananda, the latter would, sometimes, hold his feet and realise these were not ordinary visions. The timeless saint was appearing in flesh and blood.

The master, they say, lives on.

ॐ

Endnotes

1. Leaves of the *bael* (*Aegle marmelos*) tree are used by Hindus for the worship of Lord Siva.
2. In those days in the Hindu society, it was considered a virtuous act to feed a hungry Brahmin.
3. Kashi is one of the holiest cities for Hindus, as it is the location of one of the twelve *jyotirlinga*s of Lord Siva, and the centre of countless *mutts* and ashrams. Other names for Kashi are Benaras and Varanasi.
4. Recognising the guru and disciple here indicates recognition of the psychic connection between the guru and the disciple that goes beyond the confines of this life. Otherwise, there were many great saints who the doctor may have met during his wanderings. It demonstrates that Dr Kuppuswamy had developed a very high level of consciousness to recognise the guru predestined for him.
5. The Kali Kamliwala Kshetra in Swarashram, Rishikesh, is named after a saint known as the Kali Kamli Wale Baba (Swami Vishudhanand). It is a charitable trust that serves pilgrims and daily provides food to monks.
6. The Dashnami Sampradaya is a consolidation of ten monastic orders in India, including Saraswati, Giri, Puri, Bharti, Tirtha, Van, Aranya, Parwat, Ashram and Sagar. The great medieval saint, Adi Shankaracharya, formalised the rules of initiation and spiritual life in this order. Many great saints and yogis have been initiates of the Dashnami Sampradaya.
7. Many Hindu saints and religious leaders sport marks on their forehead, denoting affiliation to a spiritual group; often, the mark also has other spiritual connotations. This point merely illustrates the simplicity of Swami Sivananda; it is not intended to question the sanctity of the practice of sporting such marks, as many great and genuine saints have sported such marks.
8. *Guha* refers to a cave.
9. Badri and Kailas are two of the holiest pilgrimage places in the Himalayas for Hindus. Badri, or Badrinath Dham, has a famous Vishnu Temple and, according to Hindu mythology, Mount Kailas is the abode of Lord Siva and his consort, Parvati.
10. Initiation into Paramhansa Sannyasa is a higher form of initiation than the normal *sannyasa* initiation.
11. It is a custom in Hinduism to offer the water from the sacred Ganga to a dying person; it is believed that this ensures the emancipation of the soul from the cycle of birth and death.

ANANDAMAYI MA

(1896-1982)

Yā dévi sarvabhūteshu, dayārupéna sansthitā
Namastasyai, namastasyai, namastasyai, namô namah
Yā dévi sarvabhūteshu, matrirupéna sansthitā
Namastasyai, namastasyai, namastasyai, namô namah

O Great Goddess, the One Who permeates all existence
Who is the embodiment of compassion,
I bow to thee, I bow to thee, I bow to thee, I bow repeatedly.
O Great Goddess, the One Who permeates all existence
Who is the embodiment of maternal love,
I bow to thee, I bow to thee, I bow to thee, I bow repeatedly.

Anandamayi Ma: Blissful Mother

Dharmendra's parents were worried about the young boy. Nobody in the small town of Almora could understand their child's ailment. He would experience a complete loss of consciousness and feelings of disembodiment. He had dreams and visions of world travels and of buildings and ashrams. His parents concluded that there was something seriously wrong with him and took him to doctors and traditional healers, but they drew a blank with even the most-qualified and experienced individuals. Some yogis hinted that the young boy was a highly developed spiritual soul and there was nothing they could do to 'cure' him. This, though, did not satisfy the anxious parents. One day, they got to know that a lady-saint had come to their town and they decided to take the child to her.

The saint could see that the young boy was an elevated soul. She also realised how easily the world could brand this divine youth as a madman or a possessed soul and subject him to inhuman tortures. She assured Dharmendra's father that the boy was not suffering from any kind of possession or mental aberration, but due to his positive karma, his spirit had begun to awaken spontaneously.

She placed her hand on Dharmendra's back and blessed him saying, 'Sing the praises of the Lord, become a saint.' The moment she touched the boy, he experienced transcendental bliss, a feeling that stayed with him for many days. That blissful state of awakening receded over the next few months but the memory lived with Dharmendra forever. Later in life, Dharmendra went on to become the renowned yogi, Swami Satyananda Saraswati. Often, he would recount that magical event to his disciples.

CR ☙

B.K. Guha was a content man. He had secured a job as the caretaker of a house and a small orchard in Kashi. It left him with enough time to pursue his studies in Ayurveda and live in relative comfort. In his spare time, he would visit various temples in the holy town.

One day, he was surprised to see a dark, young girl of striking appearance in the orchard. She was around fifteen years old, wore a simple red-bordered white sari and white glass bangles on her wrists. She walked barefoot and had wonderful long black hair, flowing down to her waist, hanging loose. Oddly, Guha found himself developing a sense of reverence for this young girl.

'Sir', she asked, 'won't you give me some mangoes from the orchard?'

Guha tried to refuse, claiming that the mangoes were not yet ripe, but the girl persisted, pointedly asking him if he had any lying in his room. Guha remembered that he did indeed have some fresh, ripe pieces and found it strange that the girl should be so sure when speaking of them. He ran and got them for her, but the girl now had a new request. She insisted he also give her some roses from the garden. After getting the roses, the girl was delighted. Guha asked her several questions about herself.

'I live in the Bhadaini Kali temple,' was all she said with a sparkle in her eyes before she was gone.

Guha stared after her for a few moments and then ran to the gate to see where she went. He looked left and right but could not see her. Nobody outside the gate could remember seeing any girl coming out — she seemed to have disappeared. There was something mystifying in her appearance—Guha wanted to meet her again. He was satisfied that at least he knew where to find her.

In the following weeks, Guha found that there was no prominent Kali temple in the locality of Bhadaini. Nor did the girl come again for more mangoes or roses, and he gave up hope of ever meeting her again. Then one day, when he had gone to take a dip in the holy Ganga in Bhadaini, and was emerging from the river, he saw a lady at a distance inside a temple. She was waving her hands and apparently beckoning him from the window. Guha could clearly see large, white bangles on her wrists. He decided to enter the temple, which he found was the Annapoorna temple in the premises of Anandamayi Ashram, an ashram of the famous lady-saint Anandamayi Ma. Unfortunately, the saint was not in town then, so he could not meet her.

However, when he went inside he found a wonderful idol of Kali, the Divine Mother. Convinced that the Annapoorna temple was the Bhadaini Kali temple the little girl had referred to earlier, he asked the ashram inmates about her. But, once again, his efforts met with disappointment, as nobody had seen such a girl. The other mystery that flummoxed Guha now was the identity of the lady with white bangles who had beckoned him. He failed to trace her in the temple and the inmates could not tell him about any such person who fitted the description.

Guha intuitively felt the answer to both the mysteries lay in the Anandamayi Ashram. A week later, he solved the riddle. Anandamayi Ma was visiting the ashram and many devotees had congregated there for darshan. Guha joined them, eagerly waiting to meet this lady who was worshipped the world over.

Sometime later, he saw the lady-saint. She was nearly sixty years old and had a definite air of divinity around her. When Guha saw the saint's white-bangled wrists, he understood who had beckoned him from within the temple. And when he looked into her eyes, he realised it was she who had visited him in the form of the young girl.

ᎧᏍ ᏦᏛ

The lady-saint who first awakened Dharmendra was the same who Guha believed appeared before him as a young girl. She was Anandamayi Ma, literally, 'the bliss permeated mother', a saint who was considered by thousands of her devotees as a perfect incarnation of the Divine Mother or the Supreme Soul.

Her perfection was apparent from the fact that she did not perform any sadhanas, though many yogic *kriya*s spontaneously manifested themselves in her. Often, she would describe incidents that had taken place when she was but a small child in her mother's lap. Her mother would corroborate the incident but would be surprised as to how Anandamayi Ma could remember such details pertaining to a time when she was a mere child. Her strong memory convinced many that she was and had always been eternally conscious.

Anandamayi Ma confirmed what devotees felt in her words, 'My consciousness has never associated itself with this temporary body. Before I came on this earth…I was the same. As a little girl, I was the same. I grew into womanhood, but still I was the same…and…now, I am the same. Ever afterwards, though the dance of creation changes around me in the hall of Eternity, I shall be the same.'

Birth and Childhood

Anandamayi Ma was born in a small village, Kheora, in the present-day district of Brahmanbaria in Bangladesh, on 30 April 1896. She was born during *brahma muhurta*, the pre-dawn period that yogis devote to meditation and to the contemplation of the Absolute. Her father, Bipin Behari Bhattacharya, and mother, Mokshada Sundari Devi, were devout souls. Before the birth, the mother-to-be had visions of divine beings in her dreams and these continued even after the girl's birth. The father also experienced an extraordinary sense of renunciation before the delivery and left the house for a period of ten months — donning the robes of a monk, spending his time chanting the name of God. The mother felt no pain during labour and neither did the newborn cry. The child was named Nirmala Sundari, or 'the pure beauty'.

Hindu culture in the late nineteenth century considered the birth of a male child as extremely auspicious. A few months before the delivery, Bipin's mother had gone to a temple to pray for a grandson. Strangely, once at the temple, she was overpowered by a desire for a female grandchild and so prayed accordingly.

There were various incidents that identified Nirmala's divinity even when she was a child. When she was ten months old, a luminous being dressed as a sannyasi appeared before her. The little girl seemed to recognise him as someone dear to her and crawled up to him. He fondled her with loving care and then made a gesture of obeisance to her. He then turned to her grandmother and said, 'This is the Mother — beyond all bonds. No one can confine Her to a home.' And then, as suddenly as he had appeared, he was gone.

The Brahmanical Hindu society in that age was very orthodox and believed in the concept of ritual purity. They held that this purity could be lost if one interacted with those of other faiths, such as Islam and Christianity. But, Nirmala was fated to rise above such narrow boundaries and, as a child, she played in the laps of many Muslim neighbours. Once, when she was young, Christian missionaries paid a visit to Kheora. She was so moved by their devotional singing that she compelled her mother to buy a small book of hymns in Bengali.

As she grew up, she developed into a wonderful girl with a pure and sweet disposition. Often, minor incidents took place that indicated she was not an ordinary mortal but the girl's relatives were oblivious to her exalted spiritual state. Her aunt, once, asked Nirmala to clean the hearth. When she had finished, her aunt was surprised to see a grown-up woman's handprints instead of a child's.

As a result of her simplicity, Nirmala was, sometimes, considered dull but when she began her schooling, she amazed everyone with her quick learning skills. She learned the entire Bengali alphabet in a single day. Her success in tests could also be attributed to a little bit of 'luck' — oddly, the tests conducted covered the limited material Nirmala had studied. When she applied herself to learning, she effortlessly learnt what she had set out to learn, but bookish learning did not motivate her.

Few realised Nirmala was a born adept at the science of the spirit. A very interesting incident took place when Nirmala was a small child. Her grandmother had the habit of chanting mantras everyday in secrecy. One day, the little girl surprised her grandmother by repeating the mantra, word to word. The old lady wondered how her granddaughter could ever know what she had kept only to herself[1].

What also set Nirmala apart was her relationship with plants and animals. She communicated animatedly with all life forms, it appeared to many, that these beings—dogs, trees, cows and the rest too—responded in the same vein. They undoubtedly loved her and became restless without her.

Marriage: A New Chapter

When Nirmala turned twelve, her father started looking for a suitable match for her. She appeared to know what the future held in store for her and predicted that she 'saw' a policeman in the house. Very soon, a match was fixed with Ramani Mohan Chakravarti, who worked in the police department. Ramani was a simple man and Nirmala used to call him Bholanath, the Lord of Simple People[2]. They got married in 1909, a couple of months prior to Nirmala's thirteenth birthday.

Initially, Nirmala lived in the house of Rebati, Bholanath's elder brother, as his wife was unwell, and they needed someone to take care of the household, including the children. Here, Nirmala immersed herself in caring for the family. She would clean the house, wash clothes, do the dishes, cook for everyone and tend to the children. This meant spending hours in a cramped, tin-roofed kitchen that radiated heat and was uncomfortably hot. This continued day after day, for months on end, without a single word of complaint from Nirmala. She was a perfectionist. Often, someone else was praised for an act she had performed, or she was criticised for someone else's fault, but she never complained—choosing instead to remain in a cheerful state.

Yogis of India

As a result of overworking in such difficult circumstances, Nirmala lost her health. She spent some time with her parents to regain her strength and then immediately returned to her in-laws' home. Gradually, she began to experience trance-like states. When she was sixteen years old, her brother-in-law passed away due to ill health and she began to live with her husband.

Bholanath had realised very early in the relationship that his wife was of an exceptionally pure disposition. In accordance with tradition, Nirmala would faithfully serve her husband and obey him as she had been instructed by her mother. However, their marriage was never consummated from a worldly perspective. Once, when Bholanath approached and touched Nirmala with the intention of physical interaction, he felt a strong electric shock. Other times when he approached her, her body began to take on the attributes of a dead person. Bholanath, himself of deeply spiritual temperament, eventually decided to live the life of a married celibate. Years later, Nirmala would speak highly of Bholanath's pure temperament, which enabled him to live a life of *brahmacharya* without unnatural mental suppression.

Unfolding the Bliss

In 1913, Bholanath left the police department and was employed by the Nawab, erstwhile ruler/administrator of Dhaka, as a Law Clerk in the Settlements Department. He was stationed in the small town of Ashtagram. There, Nirmala made a small circle of friends.

Harakumar, an acquaintance of Bholanath, would treat Nirmala with utmost reverence. He was the first person to address her as 'Ma', or mother, and he prophesied a time would come when the whole world would recognise her as such. Harakumar would seek her blessings daily and request Bholanath to persuade Nirmala to bless him. Nirmala seldom interacted with men and even then, only in the traditional, shy fashion of a simple rural housewife—from behind a veil. She would bless Harakumar on Bholanath's insistence.

Harakumar began to organise kirtan sessions, knowing Nirmala's love for them. She would, sometimes, appear to be possessed by godliness and, at other times, spontaneously chant unknown mantras, but nobody realised the significance of these occurrences. Nirmala herself perceived extraordinary divine manifestations in her body when she chanted the name of God, or even heard someone else doing it. Often, they would cause a deep current of unimaginable devotional fervour. She tried her utmost to hide these manifestations. The same situation would arise when she tried to read a religious book. It did not matter what the contents of the book were like — the mere knowledge that it dealt with the subject of God was enough to ensure that a profound spiritual mood would overpower her.

Around this time, Nirmala again experienced a bout of ill health and spent some time in her parental home. The divine manifestations on her body grew more pronounced. Much later, speaking of that period, Nirmala said, 'I felt a glow surrounding this body. As the body moved, the glow moved along with it.' Nirmala also found that she felt a total state of bliss in the presence of holy people.

When the family moved to the small town of Bajitpur in 1918, people began to notice the drastic manifestations of divinity on her body during kirtans. Sometimes, her face would become flushed with tears streaming down continuously, and she would apparently lose consciousness. At other times, she would find herself automatically in meditational yogic postures. She would also get varied visions. Sometimes, her body exuded a luminous glow. Bholanath would often return home from work to find his wife lying unconscious on the kitchen floor, with the food overcooked. All efforts to revive her would prove fruitless and she would gradually regain consciousness on her own.

A strange incident took place in Bajitpur. In those days, Nirmala would wake up early morning and begin housework. One day, Shashi — a servant of questionable character — approached her with evil intentions and caught hold of an end of her sari. The minute he did so, he began to scream and fell on the floor senseless. Nirmala called out for Bholanath. After some time, Shashi regained his senses, but for the rest of his life remained mentally imbalanced.

Apparent Sadhana

Nirmala began to experience a period of intense sadhana. Many devotees contemplated on the question whether this was sadhana at all — was it even required for the one who was endowed with universal consciousness from the time she was born. Yet, the spontaneous immersion in sadhana would occur every evening and often also at different times of the day. Nirmala herself described later on, how it had started. 'One day in Bajitpur…while pouring water on my head, the *kheyal* [spontaneous divine inspiration] came to me, "how would it be to play the role of a *sadhaka*?" And so the *leela* began.'

After completing the domestic chores, Nirmala would sit in her room, while many yogic asanas, mudras, *bandha*s and *kriya*s manifested themselves one after another on her body — she did not wilfully perform them. In fact, if she tried to do so consciously or interfered with their performance in any way, she experienced negative results. Sounds and mantras would pour forth from her lips. For those people, who had knowledge of the correct techniques of yogic and tantric sadhana and also had the good fortune to see her performing these *kriya*s, she appeared to be an adept. Engaged in this 'sadhana', Nirmala would appear lost and detached from everything, including her body. Sometimes, this bodily detachment resulted in injuries or burns but she remained indifferent to them.

Years later, Nirmala mentioned to a devotee, Gurupriya Didi, that she did not need to perform these sadhanas. When queried why she practised so many yogic *kriya*s, she replied that each had a role in opening the *granthi*s (inner psychic knots). Nirmala also told her that she needed to observe the *kriya*s for a few seconds only to get the benefit that other aspirants received when they practised these for years on end, sometimes for a lifetime. Again, she repeated that she did not need to perform these sadhanas, but did so to experience the obstacles that aspirants came across in the course of their own practice. This also enabled her to explain the keys to overcome such encumbrances.

Nirmala did not receive initiation in the traditional sense. She mentioned that she would perceive divine beings emerging from her body, guiding her, initiating her and again merging into it.

Bholanath would often watch in wonderment at this stream of yogic activities. Her body appeared to be made of boneless rubber and would undergo various contortions — unmanageable for ordinary aspirants. He would respectfully allow her sadhana to continue. At some point during all this, however, the family became convinced that Nirmala was possessed by spirits, and they employed various means to exorcise her. Eventually, a physician advised Bholanath that Nirmala was in a very exalted spiritual state. The physician also said she must not be exposed to examinations by just anyone, and that was where the matter ended. No more exorcists were called in. After this, her sadhana gained momentum and she experienced a continuous stream of visions and revelations. She would frequently be lost in moods of intense spiritual absorption.

During one such mood of hers, Bholanath asked her who she was. Nirmala replied that she was *purna brahma narayan* or the ultimate cosmic reality. When asked to give evidence, she placed her hand on her husband's head. Apparently, the vibrations from a mantra were rumbling through her inner body and as Bholanath uttered the word *Om*, his body became still like a lifeless doll. Unknowingly and mechanically, he sat down in a special posture of meditation, his eyes half closed and looking upwards, the body motionless like a statue and devoid of all outward senses. He remained in that position for hours, until Nirmala brought him back to normalcy.

Nirmala also predicted the day and time that her husband would receive initiation into spiritual practices. On the nominated day, Nirmala herself initiated him into the mantra and the secrets of sadhana. A few days after this, Nirmala realised that she had completed her sadhana phase. At times though, her body would still assume yogic postures. She would now be perpetually lost in bliss, even while involved in mundane household work.

Emergence of Anandamayi Ma

In 1924, Bholanath lost his job and the couple moved to Dhaka, searching for a livelihood. Despite his best efforts, he was unable to secure a suitable job, and thus, wanted to send his wife to live with his relatives, as it was difficult making ends meet. However, Nirmala requested him to wait for three more days and, on the third day, he suddenly managed to find work. He was employed as the supervisor of the extensive Shahbag gardens belonging to the daughter of the Nawab of Dhaka. The couple shifted to a comfortable residence in Shahbag in the Ramna area of Dhaka.

It was here that Nirmala eventually emerged from her assumed role of a traditional Indian housewife into the role that destiny had marked out for her. She, gradually, became a spiritual guide to thousands of seekers across the world.

While in Shahbag, Nirmala would spend hours at the Kali temple in Ramna. Though her sadhana phase was complete, from time to time, she assumed various vows motivated by some inner direction. Initially, she had taken a vow of silence and had maintained it for three full years. For hours, and sometimes days at a stretch, she would be in a state of ecstatic divine absorption. She would eat very little; for many days, she took a vow to eat only four grains of rice. In the meantime, her fame began to spread and hordes of devotees would line up at her doorstep. She still lived, in accordance with tradition, behind the veil, pulling one end of her sari to completely cover her head and face.

The fortunate few who received a glance despite the veil would find themselves experiencing 'heavenly delight'. Rarely could someone touch her feet, but those who did, lost external consciousness for some time. Sometimes, the place where she lay or sat would become unnaturally warm.

Kirtans were organised in the Shahbag hall twice a week, and many came to attend these programmes, knowing Nirmala would be present. Gradually, the frequency of these programmes increased till they were conducted daily. Nirmala would encounter various trance-like states during kirtans such as *Bhava Samadhi* and *Mahabhava*. Before her, adepts such as Ramakrishna Paramhansa and Chaitanya Mahaprabhu had experienced such states and become famous in that region. As the crowds grew, Nirmala slowly began to emerge from the veil. Initially, devotees would only be able to catch glimpses of her face when the veil slipped off in spells of divine intoxication. Her face would radiate spiritual bliss. However, it took several years for her face to completely appear from behind the veil.

Once, she began to recite the namaz at the tomb of a Sufi saint. People were surprised to see her familiarity with Muslim practices. She would spontaneously chant *sura*s of the *Koran*. This was something she had never learnt but the knowledge surfaced on its own. All of these added to the mystique that surrounded her.

Some of her great devotees came to her during this period. One of them was Jyotish Chandra Roy, affectionately called Bhaiji (brother), who was considered the greatest of her devotees. Another was Adarini (pronounced Adorini) Devi, who went on to eventually become the permanent companion and caretaker of Nirmala. Adarini Devi was addressed as Gurupriya Didi[3] or just Didi by others. Brahmachari Yogesh and Swami Akhandananda also became devotees during this phase.

Bhaiji obviously had a karmic connection with Nirmala. He was a devotee of the Divine Mother and considered Nirmala to be Her embodiment. Nirmala had visited the Siddheshwari Kali temple, on the outskirts of Dhaka, a few times. This was an ancient holy site that had been rediscovered by Nirmala. One day, she requested Bhaiji and Bholanath to accompany her to the Siddheshwari Kali temple. Nirmala was in a blissful state and full of radiance. Bhaiji bowed reverentially to Nirmala and declared her to be Anandamayi Ma.

From that day onwards, she began to be known as Anandamayi Ma, the name that devotees from all around the world eventually came to address her by.

The Fame of Anandamayi Ma

Worshipping the Supreme as the Divine Mother is very popular in Bengal. Anandamayi Ma's fame first spread in Bengal, with many believing her to be an incarnation of the Divine Mother.

It became known that Ma would experience stages of deep absorption in the Divine. It would often take hours to revive her. People thronged to see her in these states of samadhi. Till 1926, she was attracting lay devotees by the hundreds but remained largely undiscovered by the saints and spiritual institutions of India. That was to change over the next couple of years.

In 1926, at the request of a devotee and his guru, Balananda Brahmachari, Ma visited their ashram at Deoghar. The guru was widely regarded as a perfect master by contemporary spiritual adepts in India. He was a great yogi. Many believed that he was more than 100 years old. While visiting his ashram, Ma experienced elevated spiritual states, and during one such trip, she blessed Balananda. The elderly yogi was deeply influenced by her and went on to say, 'She is not a seeker of Truth – she is...complete in herself. Such souls come to earth to serve specific purposes.' Balananda also revealed that she had appeared in his ashram in her subtle body, prior to coming in her human form.

Another spiritual luminary who was enamoured by her was Sri Gopinath Kaviraj. A householder, Sri Kaviraj was one of the most celebrated scholars of yoga and tantra in India and a disciple of the Himalayan yogi Swami Vishudhananda Paramhansa. Those were the days when householders, no matter how spiritually advanced, were not accorded the same recognition in the spiritual hierarchy as sannyasis. Gopinath, though, was an exception; he was also considered a great master and practitioner of spiritual sciences. In 1928, Gopinath first met Ma at a function organised by her devotees in Kashi. This meeting changed him. He became a lifelong devotee of hers and stayed in her Kashi ashram during the last years of his life. Gopinath declared that the divine manifestations in Ma were described in the yogic scriptures as denoting the highest spiritual attainments.

The meeting between Gopinath and Ma is also historic in another sense – it marked a change in the manner in which she used to interact with the world. Throughout the meeting, she behaved like a child and also exhibited signs of divinity. After that session, she progressively increased her interaction with the general public, while simultaneously, the public spells of deep spiritual intoxication receded.

Many spiritual masters began approaching Anandamayi Ma after Sri Balananda Brahmachari and Sri Gopinath Kaviraj spoke so highly of her. This process was accelerated after Prabhudutt Brahmachari, a Vaishnava[4] saint, invited her to join a council of sadhus in Jhunsi in the state of Uttar Pradesh. Erudite scholars of philosophy would direct complex metaphysical questions at her, and this semi-educated lady responded in simple words on the basis of her spiritual experiences. Aspirants and masters, yogis and *bhaktas*, all began to approach her for holy company—often seeking guidance on the spiritual path. Another great saint, Baba Sitaramdas Omkarnath, considered her a complete embodiment of Bhavatarini Ma, the Goddess worshipped by Ramakrishna Paramhansa. When Mahayogi Sri Aurobindo saw her photograph, he declared that she was in the highest state of *sat chit ananda*[5].

In 1929, the Indian Philosophical Congress held its session in Dhaka. Spiritual luminaries, philosophers and writers had come together in the city. Though Ma did not attend the Congress, many participants were drawn to her, influenced by her growing reputation. They came in large numbers to meet her and address their queries to her. Once, they kept her engaged in a three-hour long discussion. The beauty of the discussion lay in the simplicity with which she explained the most intricate metaphysical doctrines and esoteric concepts. Many onlookers were also surprised to note the spontaneity of the responses and the complete lack of nervousness in her. They had heard of her mystical experiences but were unprepared for her span of knowledge and her communication abilities.

Ma's Travels

From 1928 onwards, a period of almost continuous travel began and she covered the length and breadth of the country, going to towns, villages — visiting almost all the key religious centres. She used to return for brief stays in Dhaka but these became fewer with time. Though her trips focussed more on northern India, she also went to various key urban and religious centres in southern India. For more than half a century, Ma toured relentlessly, in health and in sickness, in good weather and bad, in peace and in turmoil, often neglecting her own bodily comforts.

Bholanath had, meanwhile, himself begun intense sadhana in Siddheswari Kali temple. After he received some divine visions, Ma advised him to continue *tapasya* at Tarapith — now in West Bengal — one of the most prominent centres of Shakti worship in India[6]. Bholanath moved to Tarapith and performed rigorous penance there. He would sleep in the open veranda of the temple, disregarding insects, various kinds of discomfort and was constantly absorbed in divine contemplation. He spent many days without leaving his asana[7], completely immersed in sadhana. Finally, he achieved a very high state of spiritual consciousness. When Ma moved to Raipur in northern India, Bholanath continued his sadhana there and also undertook a prolonged spell of intense *tapasya* in Uttarkashi. Between Bholanath's periods of sadhana, he would come along with Ma on her travels. Other companions who often went along with her were Ma's parents, Bhaiji, Gurupriya Didi and Dr Shashank Mohan. Bhaiji passed away in 1937 and Bholanath in 1938, but Ma remained unmoved and, in fact, after these events, her tours only increased.

Wherever she went, devotees, disciples and curious souls swarmed around her for a glimpse, or a word, or a moment. Her devotees included members across generations from Kamala Nehru, Jawaharlal Nehru and Indira Gandhi—all of whom held her in great esteem. She was visited by heads of states, ambassadors, senior bureaucrats, kings, queens and prominent politicians. Ma remained the picture of untainted and indescribable bliss.

Though Ma considered the whole universe as an ashram, many ashrams dedicated to her sprang up in different parts of the country, though Ramna and Siddheswari—both in and around Dhaka—were the early ones. Other prominent ashrams included the ones at Kankhal, Almora, Kashi, Delhi, Pune, Vrindavan, Vindhyachal, Dehradun, Kishanpur, Raipur, Varanasi and Calcutta.

Anandamayi *Leela*

Siddha yogis or yoginis are perfect beings[8], accomplishing this state over many lives. Ma was born a perfect yogini. Miracles are the natural companions of yogis, though they do not give them importance; Ma's devotees too saw her life as a continuous stream of miracles. The states of *bhava* and samadhi that manifested in her body before hundreds of followers were in themselves miraculous. Ma's *leela*s lay more in the intense love with which she interacted with her devotees and the transformations she effected rather than the miracles they experienced. However, her miraculous charisma was an integral part of her *leela*. Here, we share some special expressions of her supernormal personality and the mysterious and blissful manner in which she interacted with her devotees.

Omniscience

Ma's omniscience was well known, but she made efforts to hide her capabilities from those who were not very close to her. However, those who knew her had innumerable experiences.

Once, a curious individual asked her if she could always read the mind of all her devotees. Ma replied, 'No, not always. But, whichever direction I look towards, I clearly see the thoughts and minds of devotees.' She would often be speaking to one devotee but would indirectly respond to the mental queries of others who were around her and would do so very subtly. She probably did not want people to expect constant miracles from her. Once, a seeker came to her and said, 'Tell me, why I have come here…I have asked you mentally, answer me.' Ma smiled and said, 'You asked me mentally. I responded mentally. Understand it.'

Another interesting incident in Delhi underlines her power of intuition. One day, Ma was sitting in a blissful mood in silence in her Delhi ashram giving darshan to devotees. Suddenly, she asked her helpers to arrange for items that are normally used in first aid, particularly fractures. Soon after, a lady arrived who was apparently in terrible pain. Devotees learnt that she had set out to meet Ma when her car had met with an accident and she had injured her knee. The lady, however, insisted on coming to Ma, instead of going to a doctor or hospital for appropriate medical attention. There was no way apart from her omniscience by which Ma could have known of the accident. Ma gently nursed the lady and bandaged the wound and then sent for a doctor.

Swami Virajananda recounted an incident when he came across a tiger while walking along a forest road. He froze in fright and kept praying mentally to Ma to save him. Fortunately, just then, a truck appeared from nowhere and he was saved. He did not mention the incident to anyone. A year later, he was travelling with Ma on the same road in a car. Suddenly, she asked the driver to stop, got down and walked around for some time. Then she stopped at the very spot Swamiji had seen the tiger and asked him whether she was standing at the correct spot. Swamiji nodded. The devotee realised Ma had indeed been with him on that day of need.

Lack of Bodily Association

Ma identified her consciousness with the universal consciousness and had an impersonal relationship with her body. She referred to her body in the third person, calling it 'the body' or 'this body', avoiding terms such as 'I', 'me' and 'my body'. Sometimes, she referred to her relatives as 'father of this body' or 'brother of this body'.

Bhaiji was once curious about her bodily detachment and asked if she could keep a burning coal upon her foot. As if in response, a few days later, she smilingly took a burning piece of coal upon her foot and watched it. She mentioned that as it burned, she did not perceive any change in her consciousness, or in her state of bliss. The wound itself remained for a month and then it rapidly healed. Bhaiji, though, experienced intense remorse for having caused the burn.

Ma felt no need to either eat or drink and spent months on little or no food, and it would surprise those who saw the level of activity she was engaged in. She, once, abstained from food and drink for twenty-three days at a stretch. On the other extreme, once, she was coaxed into eating more than her desire to; she effortlessly ate what would have been enough for almost ten people.

Curing the Sick

Ma's life is full of instances when she cured people of incurable diseases—sometimes, a word was enough to effect a cure, sometimes a thought, while at other times, it was her mere presence. Her reluctance to cure some of those who approached her could be misinterpreted as part of her desire to steer clear of miracle seekers, looking for short-cut options to surmount accumulated karma. In reality, she said, she would cure any person if a *kheyal* arose within her. However, the *kheyal* was often triggered by the suffering or the intense prayer of a devotee. Once, it arose in her mind, the cure was instant. Sometimes, she would take upon herself the affliction of her follower or even create a wound on her body and the devotee would experience relief.

A devotee had been suffering from asthma for many years. In 1942, he got a chance to spend some days with Ma and other devotees in Bhimtal, in the Himalayas. One day, she left the group as she had other engagements in far off places. In her absence, the devotee had a severe asthmatic attack. For several nights, he could not sleep and was in a miserable condition. When she returned, she assured him he would be completely fine once he slept, but could not believe her. Moreover, he had been unsuccessfully trying to sleep for the last few nights and so could not see how it would be possible. Strangely, that night, he had the soundest sleep of his life, and he awoke completely cured. The next night, he again had slept well and the following day, he asked Ma how she had cured him. When he found her evading a clear answer, he asked her what he needed to do if the trouble recurred. Ma said, 'Why should the disease recur? It is already gone.' And it was. The problem never resurfaced for the rest of his life.

A lady, once, approached Ma requesting her to cure her ailing husband. He was suffering from a dreadful disease and all kinds of treatments had been unsuccessful in curing him. When she met Ma, she became speechless and went into a state of thoughtless bliss. She had to make an effort to regain her composure and repeated her request. Ma told her to pray sincerely to God, something the lady had been doing for long. It was Ma's sweet insistence that made the lady happy and hopeful. In a short while, her husband was up on his feet.

Ma herself considered ailments and sicknesses as guests in her home, her body and welcomed them with complete dispassion. She would suffer silently and happily. Often when devotees could not withstand her suffering, they would beseech her to cure herself, and she would shake off the long-running and deep ailment in a short while. Bhaiji, once, begged her to cure herself from a long-standing ailment. Ma was probably moved by the intensity of his emotion and promised, she would be perfectly fine the next day. And so she was!

Annapoorna, Provider of Food

Many seekers flocked to meet Ma. In such times, the devotees or ashram inmates took upon themselves the task of feeding them. Apart from the regular requirements of cooking for the visitors, sometimes ritual feasts were also held in honour of Ma's presence. There were innumerable incidents when food should have run out, but did not. Ma always ensured that food did not fall short, particularly if it was brought to her notice.

Bhaiji recounted an incident in Dhaka when food was prepared for fifty to sixty people only while close to 120 arrived. Everyone ate to their heart's content, yet it was left over. Similarly, in 1942, devotees in Dehradun planned a public feast in honour of Ma. They prepared for a little over 300 people, but had to feed more than 500. Ma had instructed her devotees to feed everyone lavishly and there had been no miserliness. Yet, plenty of food was left over.

Bound by Devotees

When followers asked her who she was, she would respond with a characteristic, 'I am who you think I am.' She was bound by her devotees' desires if they were motivated by faith and devotion.

Ma had once gone to meet Bhaiji and his family at his home. In a short while, a car came to pick her up and take her back to her home. Bhaiji was disappointed to have Ma's company for such a short spell, and he came to see her off in a very unhappy state of mind. Ma could read his thoughts and looked at him, smiling meaningfully. The car refused to start despite several attempts. Ultimately, a carriage was arranged for her, which was not a comfortable mode of travel. Bhaiji now felt sad that Ma would have to travel in such discomfort, and he wished she could go in the car. Just as he wished it, the car started and Ma left in it. A few days later, while discussing some other incident, the yogini said with a smile, 'The other day, you threw out of gear the car in which I was to leave.' Apparently, Ma did not let the car start until Bhaiji was mentally comfortable in letting her go.

Ma's Different Avatars

While Ma remained detached from her body, many of her devotees had visions of her in different forms. Bhaiji once went to Shahbag to meet her but she was not in her room, and he had to wait alone in the hall. All of a sudden, he saw her, not in her usual form but as a 'divinely beautiful goddess as genially bright as the sun at dawn, illuminating the whole room'. Before he could react, she withdrew the light into her body and once again resumed her normal smiling form.

Once, when Ma was in Vrindavan, a *brahmachari* felt uncomfortable following a 'lady-saint', and he decided to spend the entire night at a Krishna temple. The next day while Ma was sitting on a cot, he approached her and suddenly saw her in the form of the Krishna idol at the temple. Then she said very softly, 'People don't believe until they see.'

Many saw a divine aura around her, often so bright that it eclipsed her form itself. Narayan Chaudhary, a devotee, recounted his first experience of meeting Ma thus, 'I observed at first only a mass of lustrous brilliance in the sitting posture on a cot, a mass that looked like a human form completely covered with a cloud of whiteness.' He was unable to understand the phenomenon but after a few moments, the aura receded and he was able to see Ma clearly.

During one puja and kirtan session in Shahbag, Ma went into a deep spiritual mood and requested everyone to shut their eyes and chant the name of God. The atmosphere in the hall was surcharged with divinity and people lost sense of time. When they opened their eyes, they found one of them, Basak, lying unconscious on the floor. After he regained his senses, he recounted that he had opened his eyes in the middle of the puja and looked at Ma. He had seen a powerful glow of light radiating from her face. He had fallen unconscious, overcome by the intense light.

Raja Durga Singh, the erstwhile ruler of the princely state of Solan, thought of Ma as Goddess Kali. During a public function in her honour, he realised that she was of extremely fair complexion, but Kali was dark. Just then, she let out a peal of laughter and her complexion became dark. Durga Singh was wonderstruck but also a little frightened and he prayed to Ma to regain her normal appearance. The next instant, she was back to her normal self.

Initiation

Bholanath was the first person to whom Ma gave mantra initiation. Later, she bestowed the task to initiate seekers to Bholanath and after he expired, she passed on the duty to her mother, Mokshada Sundari Devi (Didima). However, Ma continued to play an active role in this entire process of initiation. An individual, once, recounted how Ma intervened and asked Didima to give the Krishna mantra to an aspirant, instead of the Narayana mantra that the latter was planning to give. At that point, neither Didima nor Ma was aware that the seeker was a devotee of Lord Krishna.

Some aspirants did report initiation by Ma in dream-states. Others received flowers along with mantras in their dreams and when they awoke, they found the flowers near their beds. Ma also gave *sannyasa* initiation to very close devotees.

Ma strongly recommended the regular practice of chanting the name of God or a mantra as a sure means of attaining liberation. The name she said was enough, but she mentioned that the *bija* (mantra seed) was given to aspirants by a guru, in line with the disciple's *sanskaras*. The *bija* accelerated the process of liberation. Ma also gave *shaktipat* (transmission of spiritual power) to whoever she deemed capable of receiving it. Adolphe Weintrob better known as Swami Vijayananda received initiation by this process. When he came to see her, he had already visited various saints and had spent many hours in meditation. He had come to India looking for a guru and had narrowly missed meeting great saints such as Maharshi Ramana and Mahayogi Sri Aurobindo as they had passed away shortly before he visited their ashrams. A Canadian lady advised him to meet Ma in Kashi, though he was not keen as he was not looking for a female guru and definitely not someone he considered traditional. When he saw her, his consciousness was completely captivated by her and when he returned to his hotel, he experienced 'an explosion of waves of bliss'.

Gradually Transcending Customs

Anandamayi Ma, in her own way, tried to challenge the established order of the day. For instance, animal sacrifice was considered a fundamental facet to most Hindus in Bengal, where she hailed from.

She gradually discouraged her disciples from performing such sacrifices, without directly opposing it in the early days.

In one of the initial public Kali pujas that was done in her presence, devotees were insisting on sacrificing a goat. Ma gave them permission but first she kept the goat in her lap and caressed it tenderly, while she herself was in tears. Then she chanted some mantras while touching different parts of the goat's body and whispered something in its ear. The animal went into a trance. Ma placed the butcher's knife on her own neck. To everyone's surprise, the sound of goat's bleating emanated from her lips. When the goat was sacrificed, it did not move, let alone struggle, and there was not a single drop of blood on the severed head. Later, she would avoid the sacrifice, or it was observed that for some reason, the exercise could not take place.

She allowed her ashrams to continue enforcing orthodox Hindu caste-based rules, though she herself did not scrupulously observe them. This process often caused inconveniences to many foreigners, but her loving compassion held them to her.

Also, in terms of giving *sannyasa* to women, Ma sought the opinion of some scholars to confirm that this could be done before sanctioning it.

Established in Adwaita

Ma had attained the stage of universal identification. During her sadhana period, many deities had manifested from within her body. When a particular deity manifested, she would worship it with a sense of identification. Then, the deity would merge with her and another one would emerge. Ma later clarified that the sadhana phase was itself possible only with the superimposition of some *ajnana* (ignorance) over *jnana* (perfect knowledge). After her sadhana phase, she had stopped bowing before deities and idols. She experienced complete identification with God, with Truth, and with any of their aspects.

Once, Ma was engaged in a very serious discussion with Sri Balananda Brahmachari. He suggested that there were two entities,

God and his worshipper. Ma insisted there was only one. She was clear that when there is God, there is only him. The individual then loses his identity. Balananda realised that Ma was permanently established in that state.

Her sense of close identification with different deities was often noticed. Once, the Kali temple in Ramna became a target of robbers and Ma was far away in Cox Bazar—now in Bangladesh. The thieves broke the hand of the Kali idol to get the ornamental bangles. At that very moment, Ma began to twist her hand exactly at the point where the thieves had broken the idol's hand, saying, 'I am going to break it', and asking, 'tell me, is it broken?'

Another time, she was on a tour to Vrindavan and was staying in her ashram. Some *sivalingam*s had been procured for a ritual to be held in her presence. However, pandits in Vrindavan for some reason, suggested to her that these *lingam*s should be immersed in the Ganga; Lord Siva has a natural affinity with the holy river. But, since the river was far from Vrindavan, the *lingam*s were immersed in the nearby Yamuna River. From the moment the *sivalingam*s were immersed, Ma began to shiver and in a short while, she was completely immobilised in bed. She felt Lord Siva was being drowned and asked the pandits to locate the *sivalingam*s and had them retrieved from the river and sent to Kashi for immersion in the Ganga.

Yogic Siddhis

Ma possessed yogic siddhis or supernormal powers[9], which left onlookers and her devotees in awe. Gurupriya Didi, once, experienced Ma's body as weightless when pulling her up on a train. In another episode, Ma was in an elevated spiritual mood and she climbed on top of a disciple's shoulders, but he did not feel her weight at all. In Siddheshwari Kali temple, she once lay on a flat stone slab, covering her body with a cloth. After some time, the devotees saw her body shrink until it appeared there was nobody under the cloth. Later, her body again began to grow until she assumed her normal size.

There are innumerable incidents of her being seen in more than one place at the same time. Somewhere between 1929 and 1931, she saw the Hindu-Muslim riot in Dhaka a few days before the incident actually took place. Similarly, when there was a stampede at the Kumbha Mela, where many people were crushed to death, Ma was far away but she could hear the shrieks and cries of the affected people.

Ma also had the capability of tasting food offered to her remotely. She could also transfer that taste to others. Once, Bhaiji and Ma were travelling in the mountains and were very thirsty. Suddenly, their thirst disappeared. Ma and Bhaiji later explained that Atal, a disciple, had offered a melon drink to her photograph, which caused their thirst to disappear.

She had complete knowledge of yogic and tantric concepts, without having read about them in books. One day, she drew on the floor the detailed psycho-physiological structures relating to the psychic channels and the chakras, and it was found to be accurate when compared to reputed texts.

In terms of exceptional human capabilities, Ma had a photographic memory. Richard Lannoy has mentioned that Ma '...Possesses an extraordinary gift of remembering people she has met despite the ceaseless and numberless parade of faces which passes daily in front of her eyes.'

The Devotees

When a great soul incarnates in the form of a spiritual guide, other evolved souls are born along with it. Many advanced souls are said to wait for long periods before taking birth again, as they actively seek such opportunities. Some are followers from previous births, who are seeking completion of their spiritual journey, while others are perfect disciples who wish to accompany the guru in his divine quest. The mentor seeks these souls out and draws them to himself, and the spiritual romance of the teacher and disciple continues in the current lives as well. Many of Ma's disciples were such perfect souls in their past lives.

Once, she mentioned that the seers and sages of yore existed even in the present day, and she pointed out three of her devotees – Atulda, Yogeshda and Kamalakantada.

Her own mother and husband, Bholanath, were considered as perfect saints by Ma. Her mother was named Muktananda Giri after initiation as a sannyasi, though Ma's devotees continued to call her Didima (grandma) as a term of endearment. Indian saints such as Gurupriya Didi, Bhaiji, Swami Akhandananda and Haribaba, and foreigners such as Atmananda, Swami Vijayananda, Richard Lannoy and Arnaud Desjardins were jewels amongst her devotees. Her list of disciples spanned great leaders and poor farmers, and included Hindus, Muslims, Buddhists, Jains, Christians and Zoroastrians.

Outlines of just a few of these devotees' lives are given here.

Jyotish Chandra Roy (Bhaiji)

Jyotish Chandra Roy was born in July 1880 in Bengal. At a very young age, he lost his mother. He would feel a deep sense of loss when he saw other children calling out to their mothers and would let a silent tear console him in solitude. When he was twenty-eight years old, he was initiated by the family guru into the Shakti mantra, a mantra used to worship the Divine Mother. In his prayers, he would repeatedly call out to Her with all his heart. His desire was to meet a living mother who was an embodiment of the Divine Mother, who would accept him and transform him. He visited many spiritual centres and met many saints in connection with his quest but his desire was not fulfilled. Jyotish moved to Dhaka in 1918, in connection with his work and, in 1924, heard of Anandamayi Ma. He heard of her activities in the Shahbag garden, and the fact that she had been maintaining a vow of silence for many days.

One morning, with Bholanath's help, Jyotish managed to meet Ma. His entire being was filled with joy and he felt that he had finally met his guru. However, Ma was aloof to him and continued this behaviour for many days. Jyotish returned after the first meeting with a storm in his heart and his devotion kept increasing in leaps and bounds. He wrote many wonderful poems expressing outpourings of the emotions of his heart, including the very special *A Madman's Song* (*Pagaler Gan*). Ma was obviously testing Jyotish's devotion, and with time, she began to treat him with great affection and revealed to him some facts of his previous birth, in which he apparently had led a life of monkhood. In 1927, he was diagnosed with tuberculosis and doctors had no hope of recovery. During his illness, Ma had a vision that Jyotish was in her lap. She shared her thoughts on this dream with her husband who was very concerned about Jyotish's health. When his condition further deteriorated, Bholanath took Jyotish to Ma and requested her to cure him, as he was her spiritual son as indicated in the vision. Jyotish miraculously recovered. From that day, Ma's devotees who considered her as their mother started addressing Jyotish as Bhaiji, their brother.

Once, Bhaiji repeatedly asked Ma who she really was, and she kept evading the queries with intellectual and rational responses. This went on for some time, until Bhaiji lost his patience and told her, 'These words of yours…do not satisfy my yearning.' Ma responded with slight vehemence, 'Tell me, tell me, what more you desire?' There was a 'dazzling flood of heavenly light [that] shone forth from her face. All doubts were laid to rest.' He had visions and experienced a continuous stream of miracles during his life, accompanied with complete transformation of his consciousness.

For Bhaiji, the centre of consciousness was always Anandamayi Ma and he dedicated his life to serving her, her family members and her devotees, and spreading her glory. It gave him great pleasure to silently and continuously gaze at her transcendental form. Once, someone photographed Ma alone, but when the print was developed, Bhaiji appeared standing behind her. Towards the end of his life, he experienced very high states of consciousness and wanted to become an *avadhut* sannyasi. When he passed away in 1937, in Almora, Ma disclosed that she had given Bhaiji *sannyasa*, and named him Mounananda Parvat.

A samadhi was built in his memory in Almora, which now stands within an ashram of the Shree Shree Anandamayee Sangh.

Gurupriya Didi

Adarini Devi was born on 14/15 February 1899 in Dhaka, in a prominent and affluent family. Though of a pure disposition, she was not a very social child and would not generally interact with others. She was married at an early age, but refused to live with her husband, probably owing to deep karmic impressions of celibacy. In 1926, Dr Shashank Mohan Mukherjee, Adarini's father, went to meet Anandamayi Ma. When Adarini heard about Ma, she felt as if her heart was wrenched, and she longed to meet her so badly that she wept in private. She could not understand her own reactions, for she had never had any particular desire to meet any saint. Though Adarini did not disclose this wish to anyone, on the second meeting itself, Ma asked Dr Shashank Mohan to bring his daughter to her.

The first meeting left a lifelong impression on Adarini, who decided she had encountered the aim of her life. Ma was then in a deep state of spiritual absorption and was finding it difficult to retain her consciousness on the physical plane. After some time, she took Adarini into a room for private interaction and one of the first things she asked was, 'Why did you take so long to come?' Then, Ma told her that 'she was going' and fell on the floor lifeless. Adarini, who had heard of similar states experienced by Sri Ramakrishna Paramhansa, realised it was a state akin to samadhi.

The vibrant image of Ma grew deeper within Adarini's consciousness and with each passing day, she felt the need to meet the lady-saint more frequently. In those days, Ma was going through a tough phase. There were times when she was lost in elevated states of consciousness and could not perform even mundane tasks. Adarini would take care of her and also help in the household chores. In 1931, she left her home and permanently shifted to Ma's residence.

Adarini spent a life of single-minded devotion to Ma. Ma treated her with so much of affection that she began to be addressed as Didi by her devotees. So deep was Didi's absorption with her that Ma did not need to verbally communicate with her, as the devotee could deduce what she wanted. Mrs Talyarkhan, a Parsi devotee of Ramana Maharshi, was directed to Anandamayi Ma by the Maharshi himself in his last days. When she once accompanied Ma to a temple in Rameshwaram, she saw the lady-saint as Goddess Durga. In the same vision, she had seen Didi in the form of Nandi[10]. Didi was unquestioning in her obedience of Ma's commands. She was uncompromising in her objective of protecting Ma against any disturbance from the large crowds of devotees that began to gather around the yogini. While Didi was a bundle of affection for Ma's devotees, she maintained a rough exterior and was often feared or resented by those who did not understand her true nature. Towards the end of her life, Ma herself initiated Didi into *sannyasa*, and named her Gurupriyananda Giri.

Didi passed away on 16 September 1980 in Kashi, gazing peacefully at Ma's portrait by her bedside. At that moment, Ma was attending a religious ceremony in Vrindavan. She had no means of knowing the time of Didi's death, but Ma spontaneously said, 'Didi has left.' Ma had already alerted some devotees in Kashi that she would not be present with Didi in the latter's last moments. She had also instructed them not to follow the usual cremation process as Didi was a liberated soul. Hence, a befitting funeral was arranged and her body was immersed in Manikarnika ghat, in the waters of the sacred Ganga.

Swami Paramananda

Swami Paramananda was born in October 1900, in village Lakshmipur, in Bengal. As a young boy, he came into contact with a lady-saint, Brahmajna Ma, and was deeply influenced by her and she, in turn, was fond of him. As he grew up, an intense feeling of renunciation developed in him, which deepened with time. In 1921, while still in college, he set out in search of a life of asceticism in the foothills of the Himalayas.

Over the course of the next few years, he visited various religious centres, particularly in the Himalayas. He befriended Haribaba, the great saint devotee of Anandamayi Ma during these years. He was closely associated with the Ramakrishna Mission, though he also interacted with and had profound knowledge of many other spiritual institutions. He remained devoted to his first guru and cared for her, until her passing away in 1934. He rendered whatever service he could to Nirvana Math, the institution started by Brahmajna Ma and maintained contact with it till the end of his life. When he was in the Ramakrishna Ashram in Dehradun, he met Bholanath and decided to see Anandamayi Ma.

Meanwhile, prior to Bhaiji's passing away in 1937, Anandamayi Ma had a vision of him being replaced—in terms of his role in the Anandamayi *leela*—by another saint, who she later identified as Swami Paramananda. She was waiting for him when, a few weeks later, he came for a short visit to the Dehradun ashram.

The minute Anandamayi Ma saw him she exclaimed excitedly, 'Oh, you have come!' She treated him with great affection, insisting he return the next day for a meal. The next day, Ma herself cooked and served food to Swami Paramananda.

Swami Paramananda's association with Ma strengthened and in 1938, he became a member of the Shree Shree Anandamayee Sangha. She miraculously saved Swamiji's life several times, including once, from a poisonous snake bite and, once, from falling off a cliff. Swamiji spent the rest of his life serving Anandamayi Ma. He became the 'main architect and builder of most of the ashrams' and worked tirelessly, even at the cost of his health. However, his will to persist with life in the face of health problems seemed to weaken after Anandamayi Ma passed away in 1982. He, however, consoled other devotees and spent his energy in looking after Ma's ashrams across various cities over the next year or so. Towards the end of his life, his philosophical adherence to *adwaita* Vedanta (unqualified monism), gave way to devotional fervour. He passed away in Kankhal, a holy town close to Haridwar in March 1983.

Swami Paramananda's importance in the spiritual tradition of Anandamayi Ma could be understood from the quote of Swami Janamananda, who once said, 'Swami Paramananda was "practically the successor". Ma did not need to say it.' Anandamayi Ma always trusted his judgment implicitly and, in times of doubt, would refer devotees to him.

Swami Chinmayananda

Mrinmoy Chowdhury was born in 1919, in a well-to-do family. His father was a senior official in the Government of India. His mother was deeply religious and would invite various saints for discourse or kirtans to their home.

Though he was extremely brilliant in studies, Mrinmoy was influenced by the Independence movement of India at that time. He was suspected of being a revolutionary and was pursued by the police but he managed to evade arrest and finally escaped to Calcutta and then Dehradun. There, he stayed with an acquaintance who was an accomplished yogi. Mrinmoy became so impressed with him that he requested initiation into the spiritual path. The yogi politely refused to be Mrinmoy's guru but explained to the latter that he was destined to be the disciple of a great lady-saint, who was, 'staying in a Siva temple, situated at a solitary place, adjacent to the hills'.

A few days later, Mrinmoy was again on the run from the police, and he took refuge in a Siva temple. Anandamayi Ma also happened to be there with a group of devotees and when the police entered the temple, they began to quiz her. Later, Anandamayi Ma gave them permission to search the premises. To Mrinmoy's surprise, despite searching thoroughly, the police could not find him, though he should have been easily identified. He then remembered the yogi's prediction, and from that point onwards, became a lifelong devotee of Ma. Till the end of his life, he considered himself her child.

He was subsequently initiated into *brahmacharya* by Didima and *sannyasa* by Sri Mangal Giri and named Chinmayananda. An uncompromising idealist, he was compassionate and extremely soft at heart, but was often externally harsh. Sometimes, his sharp words would create a drastic change in the behaviour of those at whom they were directed. He spent most of his last years in the Anandamayi ashram in Agarpara, on the outskirts of Calcutta, on the banks of the River Ganga. Towards the end of his life, he was perpetually in a transcendental state. On 13 October 1996, Chinmayananda gave up his body at the Agarpara ashram.

Swami Omkarananda

Abani Shankar Bhattacharya was born in Pattan village in Tripura district of East Bengal in 1908. He hailed from a clan that boasted saints, philosophers and yogis in their lineage. His father became an ascetic when Abani was merely four years old.

Abani was a multitalented individual—an excellent student, a prolific writer, a dramatist, an active sportsman and a lyricist of devotional songs. He was also involved in the revolutionary activities of an organisation called the Anushilan Samiti, for which he incurred the wrath of the British government.

In accordance with his family profession, Abani would give spiritual initiation to hundreds of seekers, though he himself was one. He came into contact with numerous spiritual personalities in his quest for attaining the ultimate objective of human existence. This pursuit intensified after the untimely demise of his wife and, finally, in 1979, he met Anandamayi Ma. After meeting her, his life 'attained a strange and inexplicable level of spiritual visualisation'. Though he had met Ma towards the end of her bodily existence in this world, he was deeply affected by her. After Ma's passing away he spent the time meditating on her, or studying and chanting the scriptures, under the guidance of Swami Chinmayananda.

Eventually, Abani was initiated into *sannyasa* and given the name

Yogis of India

Omkarananda Giri. The *sannyasa* initiation was the beginning of another phase of intense sadhana. In 1987, Swami Omkarananda experienced the state of samadhi for the first time. With time, his behaviour underwent a lot of change. Sometimes, he appeared like a madman, and at times like a sloven individual. There were times when he looked like child or a lifeless corpse.

Towards the end of his life, one day, he requested his son to give him a copy of the traditional Hindu calendar and pointed out an auspicious date. That was the date he had selected for his own final departure. On 22 January 1996, he kept looking at Anandamayi Ma's photograph for a long time and then left his body amid devotional singing.

Swami Swarupananda

Swami Swarupananda was born in Bengal, in 1919, to a family of wealthy landlords and his parents were spiritual souls. Though he himself was deeply spiritual, the turning point in his life came when his mother passed away. He cut off all bonds and renounced the material world in search of Truth. He spent many years meeting different saints and yogis and experimenting with various paths, until, at the age of fifty, he happened to meet Anandamayi Ma. This meeting in Kashi was a short one but he realised his search had come to an end. He devoted himself to sadhana under Ma's guidance and dedicated his life in the service of her mission.

After meeting Anandamayi Ma, he immediately shifted to the ashram in Kashi and in a few days, he sought and received *sannyasa* initiation, a rare phenomenon for someone so new to the ashram. Later, he went to the Himalayas and also visited the banks of the Narmada to perform rigorous sadhana. Once his sadhana was complete, he spent his time preaching the message of Ma and in setting up and managing the infrastructure across the Shree Shree Anandamayee Sangh ashrams across the country. In 1984, he was appointed the general secretary of the Shree Shree Anandamayee Sangh.

With advancing age, Swamiji's health suffered and he was diagnosed with throat cancer. Throughout the period of hospitalisation, he was in immense pain but he always appeared to be in a constant state of meditation, until he passed away on 14 September 2002. According to the Hindu calendar, this was the same day that Anandamayi Ma had given up her body, exactly two decades earlier.

The Mother Moves On

In the late 1970s, Anandamayi Ma had begun to withdraw herself from active public interaction increasingly for longer spells. Visitors were told that she was unwell, though she looked the picture of serenity and beauty. She was probably preparing her devotees for the final departure. Previously, whenever she was unwell, she would, sometimes, perform yogic *kriya*s to cure herself. However, in the final years of her life, she refused to interfere with illness.

The last great public interaction was in Kankhal during the Ati Rudra Maha yagna that was organised in April and May 1981 under her guidance. Mrs Indira Gandhi, the then Prime Minister of India, also came there to seek Ma's blessings.

In June 1982, she gently turned down the request of the Shankaracharya of Sringeri to cure herself, saying, 'This body has no illness, Pitaji [father], it is being recalled to the Unmanifest.' Once, Baba Sitaramdas Omkarnath came to see Ma, feeling apprehensive about her health. He repeatedly prayed to her to cure herself but she remained unmoved. Doctors, however, could not diagnose her illness. Ma Yogashakti, a lady-saint, had a dream that Anandamayi Ma was unwell and flew down from the United States to meet her. A few days later, Swami Krishnananda, a disciple of Swami Sivananda Saraswati, had a spontaneous urge to worship Ma in the form of Radha, the Hindu Goddess, and the mythical consort of Lord Krishna.

On 27 August 1982, Ma gave up her body at eight o'clock in the evening, in the Kishanpur ashram in Dehradun. The loving mother had consciously ended her bodily existence.

The next day, leaders of different monastic orders gathered in grief and a consensus emerged that they would jointly take charge of her body. A massive crowd of devotees took her body to Kankhal, with saints of different orders paying homage to the departed soul. Two days after Ma's departure, a befitting funeral was organised in the Kankhal ashram in the presence of Mrs Indira Gandhi. Ma's body was buried near an ancient tree, under which she used to sit on many occasions and gave darshan to the visitors. Saints of the Mahanirvani akhara performed the last rites amid kirtans and Vedic chanting. Later, a white marble shrine was built over this spot.

Anandamayi Ma: Eternal Consciousness

Ma had once said, 'What more can you say when one continues to exist even after death.' These words became living experiences for many of her disciples. Many others who had never met her saw her only after she passed away. She is now in an undefinable state, though she does sometimes, manifest herself in the form of the body she had lived in.

A young devotee had received mantra initiation but had forgotten the mantra. After Ma's *mahasamadhi,* the youth fervently prayed to the yogini to receive the mantra again. He had a vision of Ma showing him a cloth, on which it was written. In another episode, she appeared before a worshipper at her samadhi and asked him to stop a certain sadhu from going overseas, since the latter's life would be in danger. The sadhu unfortunately did not believe that Ma had actually appeared before the worshipper, but when he was leaving, he found his limbs had become immobilised. He realised it was Ma's grace and changed his plan.

Even today, she showers her grace on the faithful who call out to her.

ॐ ॐ

Endnotes

1. In accordance with tradition, the efficacy of sadhana, including mantra chanting, is multiplied when it is kept secret. The shastras repeatedly urge the aspirant not to disclose the sadhana—*na kathitavyam, na kathitavyam, na kathitavyam kadāchana*. The elderly lady was, therefore, justifiably surprised.
2. Bholanath is also a name for Lord Siva.
3. Literally, 'the sister who is the beloved of the guru'.
4. Vaishnavas are devotees of Vishnu or his incarnations, such as Krishna or Rama. The Vaishnava Sampradayas are the spiritual sects that focus on such worship and devotees of these sects are also considered Vaishnavas. The well-known Vaishanava sects are those that follow lineages from saints such as Sri Ramanujacharya, Sri Madhawacharya, Sri Ramanandacharya, Sri Nimbarkacharya and Sri Vallabhacharya.
5. Being in the state of *sat chit ananda* or *satchidananda* means to be permanently established in the ultimate state of truth or purity, consciousness and bliss.
6. Tara is one of the Dasa Mahavidyas (Ten Great Sciences or, alternatively, forms of the Divine Mother), along with Kali, Tripura Sundari, Bhuvaneshwari, Bhairavi, Dhumavati, Bagulamukhi, Chhinnamasta, Matangi, Kamala. Worship of these sciences or deities is at the core of many tantric cults.
7. Asana normally means yogic pose, also including meditational yogic poses such as the *siddhasana* (the perfect yogi's pose) and *padmasana* (lotus pose). Asana also colloquially refers to the mat that meditators sit on during their meditation. Here, I refer to him sitting on the mat and probably in the *padmasana* (as he has been photographed in that pose) for long stretches.
8. Here, the reference is not to the popular siddha yoga path; siddha yogis and yoginis are those who have attained perfection on the path of yoga, in other words, those who have taken their sadhana to the ultimate point of siddhi (perfection in sadhana).
9. There are some variants of the legendary *ashta* siddhis or eight major (categories of) supernatural powers, but commonly these are *anima* (ability to reduce one's size), *mahima* (ability to increase one's size infinitely), *laghima* (ability to reduce one's weight), *garima* (ability to increase one's weight infinitely), *prapti* (ability for supernatural powers such as clairvoyance, clairaudience), *prakamya* (fulfilment of desires), *vashitva* (control over living beings) and *ishititva* (supremacy over Nature). For a lay man, exercise of these powers is a major obstacle in the path of yoga, self-realisation or God realisation.
10. Nandi is the mythological devotee of Lord Siva in the form of a bull. His devotion is considered to be unparalleled. In almost every Siva temple, Nandi's small statue faces the *sivalingam*. Didi was also like a bull in her devotion to Ma, protecting her from the streams of devotees coming to meet the lady-saint.

PARAMHANSA RAM MANGAL DAS
(1893-1984)

Srī paramhansa paramārthi ram mangal das mahan hain
Āwey jété dīna dukhī traya tāpa tapāvé
Jôga siddhi bala tinhé tôsha pôshat sati bhavé
Anubhava gūdha rahasya alaukika kahey navīnau
Gyāna virāga nidhāna bhagati dasadhā mey bhīnau
Pragat déva darsan karéin, ina sam kau na āna hai
Srī Paramhansa paramārthi Ram Mangal Das mahan hain

Great is Paramhansa Ram Mangal Das,
The guide on the path of the ultimate aim of existence
Of those who are afflicted by the threefold problems,
Whoever approaches him with humility
He uses the power of Yoga to make them complete and satisfied

He is the knower of great secrets,
And he describes many untold truths
The resting place of knowledge and detachment,
He is immersed in the ten-fold forms of devotion
He has *darsan* of the Gods, there is none other like him
Great is Paramhansa Ram Mangal Das.

Paramhansa Ram Mangal Das: The Ajanabahu Sage

It was the year 1952. Shankar Dayal's family was hopeful that morning. A famous saint had arrived in the town of Sitapur, Uttar Pradesh, and Karunashankar Dixit, the neighbour, had assured them that the saint's grace could cure their only son. The suffering youth was eighteen years old and, for years, had been enduring an arthritic problem that left his joints swollen and his limbs twisted, rendering him immobile. His parents had cared for him lovingly all these years, bathing him, feeding him and doing all they could to reduce his discomfort. They had consulted numerous doctors, both traditional and allopathic, sadhus and occult practitioners, but nothing had worked so far. But, as hope lurks eternal in the human heart, the family remained hopeful. Their neighbour had promised to bring the saint to their house to see their child, optimistic of the yogi's power to cure him.

When the saint came to their house, he merely looked at the boy and softly exclaimed, 'His *bhoga* [karma] is so severe that it was meant to last this lifetime.' Saying this, he turned and walked away with his disciples, not entertaining any further discussion on the matter. The parents were deeply disheartened and perplexed.

However, as the day progressed, they found to their amazement, that their son's limbs and joints were improving and by evening, he could walk unassisted, though by using a bamboo stick for support. Within a few days, he was completely cured and the parents became lifelong devotees of the yogi.

As was his habit, the saint did not entertain questions about the cure, but when he returned to his ashram in Ayodhya (one of the holy cities of India), a disciple noticed that his feet were swollen. On enquiry, the yogi told him that he had taken the youth's ailment upon himself. Soon, his entire body was in the same painful and contorted condition as the boy's had been. His disciples served him relentlessly but were depressed at his condition. He reassured them that his health would improve after the day of Sharad Poornima — a holy full moon night in the beginning of Indian winter. True to his prophecy, on the day of the full moon, his condition began to ease and he was completely healthy in a few days.

This was not the first or the last time that he had taken upon himself the suffering of his followers, though he could easily extinguish the karma of the disciple. His teaching to his disciples was to play out their karma and if he saw that it was unbearable for them, he would take the karma upon himself. He pointed out that he would need to suffer only a small percentage of what the disciple would, and his action would set an example to strengthen his followers to bear the burden of their karma.

The saint was Paramhansa Ram Mangal Das, the *ajanabahu* sage, who liked to remain hidden from the public eye. Another wonderful physical quality was that his feet were soft and rosy like a child's, even though he had never worn a shoe all his life and had always walked barefoot no matter how rough the ground was. While he was a picture of simplicity and humility, great saints would be motivated to bow before him and drink the spiritual nectar exuded by his silence.

Unlike many contemporary yogis, he discouraged his disciples from spreading his name. He, once, cautioned Ganesh Prasad Mathur,

a dedicated devotee, against popularising him by saying, *'Tumhari hani hoyegi'* (harm will come your way if you try to popularise me). Yet, when he walked the streets of Lucknow or Kanpur, a sea of followers would run after him.

Birth and Infancy

His birth, like his life, was miraculous. His mother would tell his disciples how she never had difficulties or felt any pain during pregnancy. One day, around the time when the baby was due, she saw a divine light in the sky in the east and that light approached her and eventually engulfed her. In a semi-aware state, she gave birth painlessly to a male child. The wise men of the village who studied the newborn's horoscope proclaimed he would be a great yogi. He would serve as a catalyst for the liberation of many souls.

He was born in the village of Ishvarvara, in Sitapur district of the present-day Uttar Pradesh, on 12 February 1893. The child's parents were very pure-hearted souls. His mother, Maharani Devi, was a pious, tender-hearted lady who could not bear to see anyone in distress and would reach out to help him. His father, Shivdarshan Lal, was a great devotee of Lord Siva.

The child was of an agreeable disposition and seldom cried. The pandits named him Yogeshwar, based on his horoscope; his parents named him Arjun Lal, and many years later, his guru gave him the name of Ram Mangal Das. The last name was what he eventually became known by.

The parents experienced many strange phenomena as the child grew up. One particular incident happened when a mentally-challenged woman approached Arjun's mother and requested her to allow her to play with the child. Though known to have fits of insanity, the woman insisted that she would be cured if she played with the boy. His mother, against the opinion of her friends, gave her consent to the lady. The woman took Arjun to a secluded room and played with him for half an hour and brought the boy back to the mother.

She thanked her and declared that she would be cured now. She blessed the boy, 'Balakjug, jug jiye' (may the child live long) and left. To everyone's surprise, after the incident, the woman's condition began to improve rapidly and in a few days, she was completely cured.

Another incident occurred when Arjun turned eleven. A religious ceremony was scheduled to take place in his house and there was a lot of activity. All of a sudden, a saint of striking appearance appeared at the doorstep. Shivdarshan Lal immediately welcomed the yogi and asked him what he would like to eat or drink. The saint initially refused every thing but on being pressed, he agreed to have some milk. He then said, 'I normally do not eat or drink anything at anyone's home, but I am accepting this milk as it is being offered out of love. I have come to see your son Arjun. He will one day be a great yogi.'

The parents were taken aback at the words of the saint, but they were happy to hear his prophecy. They called in Arjun, who the yogi blessed, and then immediately left. Shivdarshan Lal became busy in the ceremony at home, but later regretted not finding out who the wonderful saint was. In his dreams that night, he perceived that the pious individual was none other than Lord Siva, the eternal yogi, who had come to bless the child.

Growing Up, Prayer and Contemplation

Shivdarshan Lal got the child enrolled in the local school, but Arjun studied till the second grade only as by then, he had lost interest in studies. His childhood was mostly spent in playing and immersing himself in prayers. He and his friends would swim all night in the village pond and would play all kinds of games. Arjun also learnt the use of weapons, including stick fighting, sword fighting and even handling traditional Indian weapons such as *gatkas*, *pharis* and *dhals*.

Whatever Arjun took up, he worked on it with all his spirit, and he ensured that the object was achieved and this is what defined him as a yogi. It is said in the *Bhagwad Gita*:

Yôgah Karmasu Kaushalam
Yoga lies in perfection in whatever work is taken up.

Arjun loved devotional and classical music and would participate in singing sessions with wandering mendicants and sadhus in the village. He gained great proficiency in classical music. Many years later, a professor in the Department of Music at Faizabad University, would recount how, even when he made a minor error in rendering a particular raga, Paramhansa Ram Mangal Das (Arjun) would immediately point it out to him.

Unlike people of his age, Arjun was also fond of immersing himself in prayer and would go on for hours, in deep concentration. Sometimes, he would burrow into a haystack and spend hours meditating on the Lord. He had some favourite prayers, such as the *Sukhmani Sahib*, the *Surya Stotra*, the *Hanuman Chalisa* and the *Hanuman Gyarahi*, that he would repeat with faith over and over again, until the prayer transformed itself into an energised and purifying chant. There were instances when he would pick one of them and repeat it religiously many times for a few days. For example, he would chant the *Hanuman Chalisa* a hundred times every day before eating anything, and this would take him over four hours. In those days, he received visions of Lord Hanuman, Lord Siva and the Sun God.

Sometimes, Arjun's behaviour was unorthodox, and it led to some friction in the family. When he was ten years old, he created a small platform for his daily prayers in the neighbourhood and kept various *Sivalingams* there. He would insist on sweeping and cleaning that area personally. In those days, Brahmins were not expected to even touch a broom for fear of ritual pollution, let alone use it for sweeping. This, however, did not discourage Arjun from waking up in the wee hours of morning and cleaning the platform. The family would scold him, but to no avail. One day, his mother followed him to try and again dissuade him. It was still dark as night had not yet receded, but she found the area around the platform lit up with a divine luminescence — she had a vision of the gods. 'Tell me Mother, now that you have had this vision, how do you expect me not to clean this platform?' He also cautioned her

from discussing her vision with others. His mother decided that from then onwards, she would never interfere in any of his practices.

He was also fond of serving the sick and the needy and would spend days nursing them back to health. He learnt traditional medicine from Hakim Bhudhar Das, who was also an accomplished mystic. He also learnt medicine from Ayodhya Prasad, another traditional healer. Arjun's popularity as a great devotee and as an accomplished vaidya grew in the neighbouring villages. While people approached him for his ability to cure even the most incurable of diseases, they would also call him in their last hours to receive spiritual succour.

Arjun would spend hours in physical labour—cleaning places, helping on farms and, in general, assisting people. He possessed exceptional physical strength and a mental dedication to serve. Once, he went to his uncle's farm and pointed towards the land that had to be ploughed and asked him, 'How long would it take your bullocks to plough the entire land?' His uncle estimated and replied, 'Roughly, two days.' Arjun released the bullocks, and picked up the plough himself and ploughed the entire farm in a matter of a few hours. His uncle was awed and he remarked suspiciously, *'Tumne kaun bhoot sidhha kiya hai, rey?'* (Have you gained control over some spirits, using occult practices?) To which, Arjun replied, 'It's the grace of the Lord.'

Sometimes, Arjun would get completely immersed in contemplation—in a spirit of total detachment. Once, in the rainy season, he was walking in the fields in a deep, contemplative mood. He saw a bullock-cart stuck in a mud-hole. The bullocks were unable to pull the cart and themselves out of the hole. Some passersby also lent a hand, but to no avail. Arjun saw this and, without a word, plunged neck deep into the mud and pushed the cart out. He then walked away, still silent and deep in contemplation, completely oblivious of the expressions of gratitude and unmindful of his dirty clothes.

Arjun would prefer praying and meditating in lonely areas such as the forest close to his village. Years later, a disciple—Ram Das—described

an incident when Arjun was discovered by the local shepherds at a solitary spot in the forest. He was sitting in deep meditation, while a cobra was resting on his body with its hood providing shade to Arjun's head. They spread this story to the villagers who began to gather to witness the event. By that time, the snake had slithered away. Local astrologers interpreted this event as a good sign. They again emphasised their earlier prediction—the youth was on his way to spiritual success, of becoming a king among monks.

Marriage and the Intensification of *Vairagya*

By 1908, Arjun had progressed considerably in his spiritual practices. Though still a child, he had entirely given up attachment to material objects—so deep was his love and devotion for the Supreme. His parents had always recognised his spiritual bent of mind, but wanted him to get married. Arjun, however, wanted to lead a life of *brahmacharya* and was not willing to marry.

At that time, child marriages were a common practice in India. Marriages were arranged by parents or close relatives only, and the groom and bride usually did not even get a chance to speak or see each other prior to the wedding rituals being completed. Arjun's parents were determined to fix his marriage despite his protests, and they finally found a good match for him in the daughter of Lallu Tiwari.

As the day of the wedding drew near and preparations began, Arjun grew increasingly detached and, one day, he ran away from home and escaped to the nearby city of Lucknow. There, he settled at Bandariya Bagh, a public park, and immersed himself in meditation. For sometime, there was no news of his whereabouts and his parents became frantic and worried.

Coincidentally, one of his elder cousins happened to pass by and spotted Arjun. He caught hold of the young boy and scolded him, saying that his mother was crying continuously for him. At the mention of his mother's sorrow, Arjun relented and returned home. The parents were overjoyed and preparations for the wedding resumed.

Unfortunately, when the marriage procession arrived from the bride's village, they somehow found out that the boy had run away and also learnt of his preference for a monk's life. Lallu Tiwari decided to call off the wedding. Arjun was overjoyed, but his parents were deeply affected. They became desperate to find a suitable match for him. Finally, at the age of fifteen, Arjun was married to Chandrani Devi of Natthapur, a village in the same district.

Arjun was unaffected by the marriage and continued his devotional way of life, roaming in the wilderness and praying intensely, and serving the sick and needy whenever he could. Somewhere during this period, his father passed away. Arjun was only sixteen at that time. His detachment for all material things only appeared to intensify, and his yearning for a spiritual guide was now gathering momentum.

Alongside meditational practices, Arjun's spirit of universal service kept growing. In his wanderings, he, once, entered a small village that had been affected by plague. The entire settlement appeared to have been wiped out, with the inhabitants either dead or infected and dying. The stench of dead human bodies and rats was unbearable, but Arjun found this a perfect avenue for service. He went from house to house on his mission. He would burn the bodies of the dead rats far away from the village and clean the dwellings. He would then nurse the living inhabitants and cremate the dead. In this manner, he spent many days without food or sleep. Arjun also realised that the grace of the Lord had kept him alive, despite his spending so much time in that village, and touching so many plague-infected bodies.

During this period, Arjun met a great Sufi saint, Bhulan Shah Sahib, who had come to Ishvarvara to meet one of his disciples, Kanhai Teli. Arjun had already heard about Bhulan Shah from Ilahi, another follower of the saint. He eagerly went to meet the great soul. Bhulan Shah took an instant liking to Arjun and he recited some prayers composed by him, included some *Alifnamas*. He handed over the *Alifnamas* to Arjun before leaving. The interaction with Bhulan Shah deepened Arjun's understanding of *adhyatma*, and he was motivated to renew his efforts for self-realisation.

It is said, 'When the time is ripe, the guru appears before the spiritual aspirant.' While Arjun's life was full of spiritual effulgence, the spiritual romance was incomplete without a mentor, but now the time was ripe for the teacher to appear.

The Guru Appears

Arjun's cousin, Ambika Prasad, had gone to Ayodhya, seeking initiation from a saint. Some urgent work came up in the village for Ambika and Arjun was sent to bring him back. Arjun went to Ayodhya and located his cousin, but Ambika refused to return. He claimed he had come for initiation from Paramhansa Beni Madhav Das, a great yogi of the Ramanandi Sampradaya[1]. Unfortunately, the saint had been delaying the initiation. Ambika promised to return after the fulfilment of his aim and he excitedly told Arjun many tales about Paramhansa Beni Madhav Das. Arjun now decided that he would also request the saint for initiation. He beseeched Ambika to take him along for his next meeting with the yogi. This time, the saint complied with Ambika's wishes, but he told him that he would initiate Arjun first. Paramhansa Beni Madhav Das initiated Arjun with a mantra, introduced him to the path of Raja Yoga and guided him into practices he would need to adopt in his daily life. He also gave Arjun the name Ram Mangal Das. The saint then gave initiation to Ambika, but only with a mantra. The two brothers returned to Ishvarvara happily.

Paramhansa Beni Madhav Das

Arjun's guru, Paramhansa Beni Madhav Das, was a noble saint and yogi. During his childhood, he was influenced by the life of another famous yogi, Baba Raghunath Das (Bade Maharaj) of Ayodhya. Encouraged by his saintly parents, Beni Madhav had followed a deeply spiritual life since childhood and had had many mystical experiences in his early life itself. It was said he had twice experienced the grace of Lord Rama and, on both occasions, the Lord had asked him what he wanted.

On the first occasion, he expressed the desire that the Lord be always with him and, on the second, he requested that he should always be with the Lord. After these two experiences, his life became spiritually complete, but he also realised that he would still need formal initiation — to uphold the sanctity of the yogic path, which is traditionally based on an unbroken lineage of spiritually realised masters. When his parents expired, he gave away all the family property to a needy soul and left the house in search of a guru. In Ayodhya, he came to Baba Raghunath Das's ashram and found that the Baba had passed away; his successor, Baba Jagannath Das, was managing the hermitage. He chose a corner in the premises and settled down into deep meditation, without moving for eight days. On the eighth day, Baba Jagannath Das came to him, blessed him and asked him to eat and drink something light. He then initiated him into the science of mantra and Raja Yoga.

Paramhansa Beni Madhav Das performed his sadhana for the next thirty-six years, breaking his meditation only for daily ablutions, bathing thrice a day and hurriedly eating a small meal of simple food. In course of time, he was successful in spiritual attainments. Some of his disciples considered him to be an incarnation of Guru Nanak, the first guru of the Sikhs.

Serving the Guru

Ram Mangal Das, once, took his wife to meet his guru. The guru blessed her by saying, 'putravati bhava' (may you give birth to a male child). The disciple was stunned, for he did not wish to engage in any physical entanglement but bowed before the guru's wish. In a short while, a boy was born—Ram Mangal Das was then twenty-five years old. The boy, affectionately called Putan, was apparently an exalted soul, for he would hardly ever cry and sit silently in a meditative pose even as a baby. But, this situation was not meant to last. Six months after delivering the child, the mother expired and two years later, the child also passed away.

Ram Mangal Das was unaffected by these happenings and he plunged deeper into his spiritual practices. He would roam the neighbouring villages, losing himself completely in meditation. Sometimes, he would go so deep into it that he would lose bodily consciousness for days. Many years later, he would show some close disciples the deep wounds that had developed on his hips as a result of sitting motionless on burning rocks for days. Ram Mangal Das also spent a considerable amount of time serving inmates and visitors in the ashram of Baba Tikadas, a saint from the Udasina Sampradaya[2].

Baba Tikadas had a beautiful hermitage on the banks of River Gomti, close to Sitapur. It was in harmony with Nature—animals and birds lived in peace with humans and each other. On a couple of nights, Ram Mangal Das had seen Baba absorbed in deep meditation and experiencing divine visions. Ram Mangal Das, therefore, had developed a reverential attitude towards the saint. Baba was also very fond of him and addressed him as Brahmachari and had allotted him various duties, including feeding the rats. These were no ordinary rats—they were very particular about the timing of their food and if Ram Mangal Das delayed the feeding, the rats would climb up on Baba Tikadas, who would then call out to the young yogi, reminding him to feed the creatures.

Baba Tikadas, once, asked Ram Mangal Das to practise chanting of certain prayers every day and through dedication, the latter perfected these. As a result, one day, he had a vision of Guru Nanak. During this period, Ram Mangal Das also saw the legendary yogi, Bhartrihari. He recognised Bhartrihari from some signs on his body, described by his guru. He also met Shukadeva and though he could not recognise him, he knew that he was a great yogi. He was told much later by his guru who Shukadeva[3] was.

Somewhere around this time, Paramhansa Beni Madhav Das required a disciple to serve him, as he spent all his time in spiritual pursuits. He appeared before Baba Tikadas in his subtle bodily form and requested him to send his disciple back to Ayodhya. Baba Tikadas immediately complied with his wishes and ordered Ram Mangal Das to join his guru. On his way to Ayodhya, the young yogi stopped at his home to meet his mother. He informed her about his future plans and she gave her blessings to her dear son to achieve success on his path. Ram Mangal Das was twenty-seven years old when he finally left the material world to live with his mentor. Paramhansa Beni Madhav Das had also renounced the material world at the same age.

It was during this long stay with his guru that Ram Mangal Das learnt many spiritual practices, and devoted himself to serving the saint and his disciples. Sometime during this period, the British government allotted a plot of land to Paramhansa Beni Madhav Das for a hermitage in Ayodhya. Gokul Bhawan, the ashram, was built on this land and the yogi with his key disciples shifted there.

Ram Mangal Das served his guru with extraordinary dedication. He managed all the work of the ashram himself—performing all tasks, menial as well as those involving the ritual worship of the gods.

Paramhansa Beni Madhav Das consumed only fresh cow milk once a day, directly after the animal was milked, while the drink was yet warm[4]. He would not eat anything else during the day. His disciples would ensure that their guru received a regular supply of fresh milk. For this, they used to depend on cattle near the ashram. Once, during a period of drought, they could only manage to make the arrangements in a village that was two miles away from the ashram. It was not an easy task to collect the milk in the wee hours of dawn for the guru, but Ram Mangal Das took it up as a challenge and, every morning, used to milk the cow himself. He would then sprint over two miles—carrying the container of the freshly extracted milk, ensuring that its freshness and natural warmth was not lost.

When Paramhansa Beni Madhav Das was eighty-seven, he fell ill and Ram Mangal Das devoted himself completely to nursing and caring for his mentor, who had left himself to the will of God and refused to take any medicines. The guru was unwell for close to six years and, during this period, serving him became Ram Mangal Das's constant preoccupation. He was so immersed in serving his master that he would not sleep more than a few winks and hardly slept at all for the entire duration of six years. Consequently, his own health deteriorated, but he refused to stop serving the guru. During these days, he found that immersing himself in service was taking him to unimaginable spiritual heights.

At the age of ninety-three, Paramhansa Beni Madhav Das decided to leave his body. He declared that the way his disciple, Ram Mangal Das, now himself a Paramhansa, had served him was unmatched in history. He handed over the mantle of guru to Paramhansa Ram Mangal Das and consciously took *mahasamadhi* in front of the disciples.

Paramhansa Ram Mangal Das as a Guru

In 1934, Paramhansa Ram Mangal Das became the guru and remained so for fifty years, till he left his body. Some sources considered him the reincarnation of the medieval saint, Nabhadas, while others believed he was an avatar of Mansukha, one of the childhood companions of Lord Krishna. To the Paramhansa, it did not matter who he had been; he dedicated himself to his task in the present life — guiding spiritual aspirants along the path of perfection. The Paramhansa obviously had the mandate of the Lord to play the role of a guru. Many devotees came to him after visions of the Lord or similar experiences, where they were directed to his guidance.

Egoless and Desire-free

Despite being a renowned saint and guru, the Paramhansa did not show any trace of ego. He began writing letters to his disciples with an untraditional '*dandawat pranam*' (reverential bow). He would also not make a move to bless people who touched his feet[5]. The reason was his exceptional humility and he did not want to make it appear that he had the capability to bless anyone. To some devotees, he explained that he was nobody to give blessings; to others, he mentioned that they flow directly from the heart.

Once, one of the richest families of India offered to refurbish the ashram with marble and modern amenities. The Paramhansa refused, suggesting instead that they line their own house with marble and leave his ashram as it was.

He wore no ornaments or garlands or sported any marks denoting religious affiliation. The Paramhansa would initially sit on a piece of sack cloth on the floor. After a lot of insistence by the devotees, he reluctantly began to sit on a plain wooden platform, slightly raised above the ground.

The Paramhansa had no desire to make any discrimination, and he welcomed saints and sinners alike with love and compassion. Once, a prostitute approached him and begged to be accepted as his follower. The Paramhansa's disciples were sure he would not accede to her request, but he insisted that such people required a spiritual guide the most. He took her under his wing without any qualms.

There were many incidents in his life where the Paramhansa displayed fearlessness as well as compassion in rescuing people's lives. He, once, jumped on a crocodile in the Saryu River to protect a pilgrim from being attacked. He had also on numerous occasions saved people from drowning. But, his compassion was not just limited to the human race; it extended to the animal kingdom as well — he had saved the lives of bulls, snakes and birds too.

Mantra Initiation

Initially, the Paramhansa would initiate disciples on holy days, in accordance with the Hindu calendar. Subsequently, on divine inspiration, he began to initiate disciples at any time on any day, though he did not like it if the recipient received the mantra empty stomach.

Great saints and gurus consider initiating disciples as a primary duty. Once, Malti, a great devotee of the Paramhansa, insisted that her husband, Kalidhal, take initiation from the Paramhansa. Kalidhal, many years ago, had already been secretly initiated by a saint into a Durga Mantra and though his mentor was no more, he was unwilling to take initiation again. To add to his discomfiture was the fact that the Durga Mantra normally given by the Paramhansa was different from the one he had received from his guru. In line with his teacher's instruction, he had kept this mantra secret from everyone, including his own wife, and was very attached to it. However, he did not want to upset his wife and so he consented to her request. To his surprise, the Paramhansa initiated him into the same Durga Mantra that his guru had given him. This incident reflected both the psychic insight of the Paramhansa and his spirit of maintaining single-minded devotion to one's mentor and dedication towards a mantra.

Initiation into a mantra is a great day for spiritual aspirants and miracles, sometimes, accompany the act. Once, an elderly lady, who was over ninety and very sick, approached the Paramhansa for initiation. He normally whispered the mantra into the right ear of an individual. The lady and her relatives who were aware of this process kept trying to explain to the Paramhansa that he should whisper the mantra into her left ear, as she was suffering from an infection in her other ear. A regular discharge of pus from the infected ear had made life miserable for her, the cotton towels on her pillow had to be changed several times during the day. To the dismay of her family, the Paramhansa pulled the lady and whispered the mantra into her infected ear. However, the woman was surprised to find that she had clearly heard the mantra, and was even more surprised when she found that the pus discharge had permanently stopped!

Sometimes, the Paramhansa would recommend his disciples to chant particular mantras for specific objectives; some were to save them from distress and difficulties. A lady whose husband had gone abroad and was out of contact for many years approached the Paramhansa. She had received information from other sources that her husband had re-married overseas and was not planning to return. Travel and communication were expensive and difficult in those days and she was feeling despondent and helpless. The Paramhansa gave her a mantra and instructed her to chant it religiously for a few days. Soon, she received a letter from her husband, who had not contacted her for several years. In a few months, he came back to India and their marital bliss returned.

Unorthodox Approach

The Paramhansa's methods in spiritual direction were, sometimes, quite non-traditional. Once, he was approached by Colonel Grewal of the Sikh Regiment, who wanted to know if he could get any spiritual experience. The colonel was very fond of praying and would chant various kinds of prayers all day, but nothing gave the desired result. The Paramhansa questioned Colonel Grewal about his daily spiritual routine. Finally, he asked the military man to considerably reduce the time he prayed daily. The emphasis was on quality and not on quantity, and the Paramhansa explained that there was a natural trade off between them. The colonel agreed and, within a few days, he began to have spiritual experiences.

On another occasion, the Paramhansa was approached by a poor man who had been told to feed a hundred souls by an astrologer.

'I cannot afford to properly feed my family, how do I feed a hundred souls?' he asked. The Paramhansa asked him to place some food close to an anthill and promised him the same spiritual benefit as he would get from feeding humans.

Communal Amity

In those days, Gokul Bhawan was the only place where non-Hindus were allowed to stay. In the Hindu-Muslim riots of 1936, the ashram gave shelter to Muslims, and Hindu rioters did not have the courage to attack it. The Paramhansa would also instruct Muslim spiritual aspirants with meditative practices belonging to their own religion. The Sufi saints, Abu Muhammad Siddiqi of Bahraich and Manzoor Alam Sahib of Kanpur, were regular visitors at his ashram—both considered the Paramhansa as one of the rarest yogis in humanity.

Manzoor Alam Sahib gave the Paramhansa the title of *Santon Ke Gavarnar* (Governor of Saints). Muslims, Sikhs, Jains and Buddhists came to him in large numbers and he welcomed them all, instructing each in a unique way — in line with his own respective religion.

Once, a Muslim beggar spread his hands before Shambhu Ratna Tripathi, an author and a spiritual soul. Shambhu was then going to meet the Paramhansa and thought of giving alms to the beggar. However, Shambhu, a devout Hindu, changed his mind when he realised that the beggar was a Muslim. When he met the Paramhansa, the latter broke his customary silence and said, 'One must not discriminate on the basis of religion when doing charity.' Though these words were apparently spoken to nobody in particular, the Paramhansa was looking directly at Shambhu when he spoke.

Spirit of Service

Even as a guru, he would take care of sick people, cleaning their wounds, bathing them, serving them — no matter how sick or unclean they were, or what the nature of their illness was, or what it was that he would be required to do to nurse them. Once, a dying man came to Ayodhya, and nobody was tending to him, as a foul smell emanated from his whole body due to illness. The Paramhansa agreed to serve the man and he did so uncomplainingly until the man's death. But, he was very particular about hygiene and would spend a lot of time ensuring that the ashram was spotless.

He also encouraged the devotees to keep the holy city of Ayodhya clean. During religious festivals, thousands of people would come to Ayodhya but the city did not have the necessary sewage facilities to handle such mammoth crowd. Consequently, people would relieve themselves in open fields and grounds. Many areas would become horribly dirty and stink. Even the municipal workers assigned with the task of cleaning up the mess would find it difficult to enter these areas. In such times, the Paramhansa would spend several days clad in his *kaupeen*, cleaning up the dirt.

Vakil Sahib was a realised saint, who was also initiated into spiritual disciplines by Paramhansa Beni Madhav Das and he, thus, came in contact with Paramhansa Ram Mangal Das. He was a great admirer of the Paramhansa's spirit of service. He was, once, a prominent lawyer, but after attaining self-realisation, he began to lead a life of meditative solitude in Ayodhya. Many people flocked to him for emancipation. Once, Shivmurti Tripathi, one of Vakil Sahib's disciples, came to meet his guru but Vakil Sahib, in a semi-meditative state, asked him to immediately go and see the Paramhansa. Shivmurti found the Paramhansa in a field, half-naked in his *kaupeen*, dispassionately cleaning up a stinking mess that had been created by pilgrims. Shivmurti realised that his own mentor wanted him to witness the Paramhansa's exceptional spirit of service.

Acharya of Shabda Yoga

The Paramhansa was a teacher of Surat Shabda Yoga and he had achieved the highest level of yogic attainment. Ancient saints who had left their bodies would appear before him and discuss concepts relating to yoga and *bhakti* and bless him. The Paramhansa compiled all the teachings of these saints verbatim into a series of volumes that have been posthumously published. During his lifetime, he also wrote *Bhakta Bhagwanta Charitavali Evam Charitamrita*[6], a series of short biographies of saints, many of whom were illiterate.

Once, an advanced mantra practitioner came to Gokul Bhawan to seek initiation into Shabda Yoga. He was determined not to disclose the purpose of his visit to anyone and wanted to see whether the Paramhansa would understand the reason on his own. The Paramhansa ignored the aspirant for five days and, each day, the man would come early in the morning and leave late in the evening. He would speak to no one in the ashram. On the fifth day, the Paramhansa walked straight to him, grasped his hand and led him to the terrace of Gokul Bhawan and initiated him in the practices of Raja Yoga. The moment he was initiated, he entered into a state of samadhi and remained in that state for a long time. Finally, when he came back to his normal state, the Paramhansa advised him to leave Ayodhya and continue his meditations in Vrindavan. He also told the aspirant that he would never see his (the Paramhansa's) physical body again.

The Giver and Taker of Experience

The Paramhansa's capability as an acharya was unique, and the following incident illustrates but one facet of his capabilities. He had a disciple, Maharaj Bahadur Asthana, who had achieved a very advanced stage of practice in Surat Shabda Yoga and would often be lost in the bliss of samadhi. Maharaj Bahadur was, once, recovering from a surgery following an illness. However, his yogic experiences had become so pronounced that he could not withstand them, and they had started to interfere with his recovery. It was a time when he needed to divert all his energies towards recovery. After a few days, he approached the Paramhansa and narrated his plight. The Paramhansa blessed Maharaj Bahadur and for the next two months, the latter's yogic experiences receded. Once, his physical recovery was complete, his yogic abilities came back in full force.

There were many similar incidents, where due to a mistake in their sadhana, disciples found their spiritual attainments withdrawn. They would approach the Paramhansa. He would guide them and their spiritual attainments would be restored rapidly.

A disciple, Gangaram Das, once, approached him and lay prostrate before him, with his head at the Paramhansa's feet. As his forehead touched the yogi's feet, Gangaram Das went into a superconscious state and remained prone for a long time. The Paramhansa had obviously transmitted his spiritual force into Gangaram, which resulted in the latter experiencing the state of samadhi. The Paramhansa, however, brushed off any credit for the incident and instead praised Gangaram's spiritual development, telling everyone, 'See Gangaram's spiritual state! He bowed before me and went into the state of samadhi.' But, Gangaram realised it was a result of the guru's grace.

Mangal *Leela*

The ways of a *sadguru* are beyond the understanding of ordinary people. Sometimes, they deflate the disciple's ego and, at other times, give so much love that the person is enthralled.

Bagheshwari Narayan Srivastava, a retired senior government official, was one of the many followers of the Paramhansa. He, sometimes, wondered whether the Paramhansa knew who he was in the vast crowd of devotees that came to him. On one such visit to Ayodhya, he was mentally yearning for some sign of recognition from the yogi. Though the Paramhansa did speak to him that day (which itself was rare as he hardly did so), he behaved in a manner completely contrary to Bagheshwari's expectations and spontaneously asked, 'Are you a teacher?' This hurt Bagheshwari, since he had never been a teacher in his life and the seemingly naive question demonstrated what appeared to be the guru's ignorance about him. He returned, disheartened, to his hometown, Lucknow. Though he did not share this incident with anyone, it kept playing on his mind and he was sad for the next few days. He tried to mentally rationalise that saints could not keep track of thousands of individuals, but the sadness would not leave him.

A few days later, early in the morning an unknown visitor rang the doorbell.

The stranger was delighted to meet Bagheshwari and explained that he had just returned from Ayodhya where he had met the Paramhansa. The master had given him some spiritual advice and had then asked him where he was from. When the person said Lucknow, the Paramhansa again asked which part of the town he lived in.

'When he heard I came from Nirala Nagar in Lucknow, the Paramhansa brightened up and told me that a dear disciple of his stayed in Nirala Nagar. He then told me your name and address and I could not resist coming and meeting you personally.'

With silent tears, Bagheshwari realised that the guru had given a clear signal that he did indeed know each and every one of his disciples.

Languages

The Paramhansa spoke the language of the common man. He spoke a dialect of Hindi called Awadhi. Unlike many saints, he would seldom embellish his speech with complex words from Sanskrit.

Maharshi Patanjali, the author of the *Yoga Sutras*, has written that at a point in the spiritual path, the unknown becomes miniscule, or in other words, the capability of the practitioner to know the unknown becomes limitless. Neither subject, nor language, or script will be a barrier to knowledge. A small incident illustrates a related faculty developed by the Paramhansa.

Once, a spiritual seeker from South America travelled to India, a place he believed where his search for a guide could end. Despite visiting various holy places, he could not find a single soul that satisfied his thirst. Finally, a saint named Advaitacharya[7] took him to Gokul Bhawan and introduced him to the Paramhansa. Advaitacharya, himself a spiritual adept, was not a disciple of the saint, but he considered the master to be the greatest living yogi. In spite of the fact that the Paramhansa was educated in a village school and that too only till the second grade, he could explain complex metaphysical concepts to seekers.

But, there was a problem: the first being that the Paramhansa seldom spoke and spent most of his time in silent meditation — very infrequently communicating by writing on a black slate with chalk. The second was that Paramhansa declared that he could not converse with the visitor, since he could only speak Awadhi and the South American could only speak English. Advaitacharya knew that the Paramhansa was hardly educated and in his long years, the yogi had never been heard to speak in any other language but Awadhi. Advaitacharya, therefore, immediately offered his services as an interpreter.

The Paramhansa refused saying an interpreter could never intervene in a spiritual dialogue between a guru and a seeker. He then closed his eyes and lapsed into his usual silent meditative state. Advaitacharya was saddened that he had brought the foreigner so far only to be disappointed.

Suddenly, the Paramhansa opened his eyes and looked at both of them with compassion, grasped the foreigner's hand and took him to a room, where the two remained closeted for more than half an hour. When they emerged, the young seeker was beaming and he claimed that all his spiritual questions had been answered. He also added that the conversation had taken place in English, which the Paramhansa spoke fluently.

That was the only documented instance in his life where someone mentioned that the Paramhansa had spoken in English; his life had been well researched, but nobody ever came across any evidence of him having learnt or spoken any language but simple Hindi or Awadhi. It baffled devotees as to how he could have spoken in English; but as his life was full of mystery, they simply let the question remain unanswered.

Another incident revolved around a book called *Prasanga Parijata*, the biography of Jagadguru Ramanandacharya. The book was written in verse consisting 108 esoteric *Ashtapadi*s (sets of eight stanzas), in the Paishachi language. The language was used during medieval times by devotees to shield esoteric knowledge from the unworthy, but the usage of the language had died and nobody could translate the original book. A scholar-saint called Sri Balakram Vinayak, who had somehow partially learnt the language, translated the book. He received help in this exercise from the Paramhansa, who he found could understand the script and the language.

Helping the Disciple

There are many incidents of the Paramhansa's supra-normal capability to help disciples who called out to him when in distress.

276   *Yogis of India*

Once, Ram Das, a close disciple, was returning to Ayodhya in a crowded train from Bihar. He had stepped out at the platform to fill his water bottle. While filling water, he suddenly realised that the train had started to move again. Ram Das ran back, but the train had already gathered speed, and only the last coach was reachable. He jumped, bottle in hand, and grasped a door handle, but lost his grip and fell heavily on the platform. The last thing he remembered before losing consciousness was hitting his head on the ground—at that instant, he mentally called out to his spiritual master. After a long time, he woke up and, to his amazement, found that he was sitting in the same compartment he had got off from. The water bottle in his hand was now full. On reaching the ashram at Ayodhya, he went to his guru both mystified and overjoyed and told him what had happened. The Paramhansa smiled sweetly when Ram Das narrated his tale and then he closed his eyes, and, once again, relapsed into his silent meditative state.

On another occasion, Ram Das and the Paramhansa were sleeping in a room, when the former was bitten by a snake. He woke up to see the snake slithering away. He began to shout in fright and in pain, but the Paramhansa quietened him down and told him to go to sleep. In that instant, he forgot that the guru is all-knowing and all-powerful. He felt that the master had not fully understood what had happened. He repeated that he had been bitten by a snake. The saint asked him to show the snakebite and when he saw it, rubbed the spot with his fingers and directed Ram Das to go to sleep. Normally, victims of snakebite are asked to stay awake and Ram Das was initially too shaken to sleep, but after staying awake for some time, he gradually lapsed into sleep. He woke up the next morning with a burning sensation in his eyes and a hot feeling in his head. The Paramhansa asked someone to give him a drink made of honey to cool down the body. The heat in his eyes and head subsided gradually over a period of a year, but Ram Das always remained grateful to the guru for the gift of life.

Freedom from Imprisonment

There were several incidents where devotees of the Paramhansa would pray to him for release from prison. In one case, relatives of an arrested man approached the yogi, begging him for help. The Paramhansa asked for the background and learned that the man had had a labourer crushed to death by an elephant. The master refused to help and instead scolded the family. The family said the prisoner was deeply repentant, and they promised to make amends for the man's mistakes. The Paramhansa gave the family a mantra and asked them to guide the prisoner in practising it in the prison cell. Soon, the person was set free. The Paramhansa made the released man compensate the dead labourer's family and also distribute money to the poor.

Intuition

The power of intuition marked every action of the Paramhansa. Once, he announced on the day before Guru Purnima[8] — in that particular year — that celebrations should be completed by eight o'clock in the morning. The disciples were mystified because Guru Purnima celebrations normally continued well into the afternoon, but the Paramhansa did not entertain any discussions on the subject. The next day, at eight o'clock, when the celebrations were over, two men came to see the Paramhansa in the ashram and informed him of the passing away of Vakil Sahib, the saint. The yogi was a very close friend of the Paramhansa and, thus, the master left immediately to join the funeral procession. The disciples now realised that the Paramhansa had known the previous night itself that Vakil Sahib would pass away the next day early in the morning, and that they would receive intimation of the event at eight o'clock.

On another occasion, the Paramhansa was staying in a disciple's house in Allahabad. The disciple's younger brother was then searching for a job and on that particular day, he was going for an interview to a prestigious organisation. As the youth was leaving, he sought the Paramhansa's blessings. The master gave his blessings and asked the elder brother to test the interviewee. The disciple posed two difficult questions, neither of which his brother could answer. The Paramhansa then asked the elder brother to give a detailed answer to both the questions. Later that day, the man was amazed to hear the chairman of the interview board asking him one of the questions. His detailed response impressed the interviewer and the young man eventually got the job. He attributed his success to the Paramhansa's power of intuition.

The Sick and the Ailing

As a traditional healer in his younger days, the Paramhansa had acquired quite a reputation. In his life as a guru, he, sometimes, healed sick people using his knowledge of traditional medicine. He would ask disciples to suffer the malady and play out the accumulated karma. However, his compassionate nature would often get the better of him and he would offer to take the ailment on his own body. The Paramhansa himself used to avoid taking any medicine and would happily suffer the ailment that afflicted him. He would usually know how long the illness would last and when the predicted time arrived, he would be his normal self again. In later years, he would suggest some occult practices to cure the ailments, but it was almost always his word that would result in the cure.

Ramchandra Srivastava, a devotee, once wrote to the Paramhansa about a carbuncle that had become poisonous. The family feared for his life, but when the letter reached the Paramhansa, Ramchandra began to recover automatically. However, at the same time, the Paramhansa developed a horrible boil on his back and it appeared to other devotees that only the master could bear the boil with such fortitude and calm. After some time, the boil subsided.

Devotee Nand Kumar's brother, Ravindra, had developed an acute ailment in his eye and he thought he would lose his eye sight. Nand Kumar decided to seek his master's help in saving his brother's eye. With that objective, he quietly locked himself in a room and began to repeatedly chant the *Hanuman Chalisa*, simultaneously calling out for the grace of the master. Around midnight, Ravindra called him out of the room excitedly. 'Did you see the Master?' he asked and then continued, 'he appeared before me and told me my eye would be all right soon, and then he went to your room.' The patient indeed recovered in a short while.

In a similar incident, Brij Behari Lal was suffering from weeping eczema. When he could not stand it any longer, he approached the Paramhansa, who suggested applying *amritdhara,* an Ayurvedic lotion on the infected parts. The Paramhansa assured him that the eczema would be gone in three days. After three days, when Brij Behari Lal recovered, he decided to distribute *amritdhara* to people who were facing the same problem, but the cure did not work for anyone else. He was mystified and then realised that more than the medicine, it was the yogi's grace that had been the cure.

Yogesh Bajpai's son had a bad accident and he received a grave injury on his leg. With no cure in sight, doctors decided to amputate it. Yogesh prayed mentally to the Paramhansa to save his child's leg. That night, he dreamt that the saint was sitting in an awkward position. In the dream, he told Yogesh to straighten his leg, which he did, and the Paramhansa gave him a meaningful smile. The next day, the doctors were surprised to see a miraculous recovery in the boy's leg, and they decided to put off the amputation for a few days. In the next few days, the recovery was complete.

Photographs of the Saint

In the initial years as a guru, the Paramhansa did not allow people to photograph him. Once, when he was at a disciple's house in Lucknow, some people got a professional photographer, who tried to take the saint's photo while he was washing his hands. The photographer clicked when someone was handing over a towel to the master. The Paramhansa angrily exclaimed, 'No matter how you play around with that camera, nothing will happen.' Strangely, when the film was developed, all shots were fine except the one of the saint—that frame was blank. The photographer apologised to the Paramhansa for taking his photograph without his permission.

However, many years later, some of his disciples insisted on taking his photograph. They tried to convince him that many of them lived far away and he should either appear before them in visions or at least allow them to take a photograph. Only then did he, very reluctantly, permit them to go ahead. Subsequently, he became completely indifferent to photography and would often ignore photographers and behave as if nothing was happening.

The first photograph, however, will always be special for his devotees. One devotee, Dr Nigam of Kanpur, wanted to replicate it in a life-size portrait of the master. But, he had a condition, the artist should be a pure-hearted individual, of spiritual temperament *and* a great portrait painter. Dr Nigam eventually located a Muslim painter, who fitted those requirements, but the painter was very old and infirm. He told the doctor that he had given up his vocation. No inducement would make him agree. The doctor returned disappointed, but to his surprise, he found the painter at his doorstep the next day. The painter claimed that he had seen a divine vision the previous night, where the photograph of the Holy Kaaba[9] instructed him to make this last painting. The painter had, therefore, come to take the photograph from the doctor, and he went on to make a beautiful portrait from it. Soon after the painting was complete, the old man passed away.

Power of the Command

It is believed that if a guru gives a command, it should be obeyed uncompromisingly and immediately. Fulfilling the master's command leads to spiritual and temporal welfare, while ignoring it leads to difficulties. That is why many times a guru avoids giving commands and instead gives indirect hints. The Paramhansa also would only give a command to the devotee who had the mental readiness to fulfil it and those who complied with his order invariably benefitted.

Another aspect of the Paramhansa's *leela* was that if someone requested permission for some planned act, the master would give it instantly and happily. In such cases, following the course of action always resulted in success. But, if the Paramhansa did not approve of the request, he would, sometimes, avoid giving a direct answer and if the devotees persisted, he gave permission. In these cases, even if the yogi changed his original command, the result would not be positive.

In 1962, Ram Singh, a devotee, was approached by a political party to stand for elections against a very powerful candidate. Defeat was certain but Ram Singh was being compelled to contest the elections by his friends and he was looking for a way out. He approached the Paramhansa for permission, hoping that if the guru refused, he could use that as an excuse to back out. Surprisingly, the Paramhansa immediately gave him permission. In the ensuing elections, Ram Singh won a landslide victory!

Human nature is indeed strange. Ram Singh worked for five years in his constituency and became very popular among the masses. The time came again for elections and he approached his guru for permission to fight the elections. This time Ram Singh was sure to win, but the Paramhansa was not keen that he should contest and strongly discouraged him, as politics was a field where spiritually minded people can easily lose their way.

'You have served the masses honestly for five years. Now is the time for you to detach yourself from this materialism and devote time to spirituality.'

This time, however, Ram Singh was keen to contest, and he kept trying to convince the master until he reluctantly agreed. Against everyone's expectations, this time he lost badly. It was then that Ram Singh realised his mistake and decided to devote himself to spirituality, as his guru had advised.

Remote Materialisations

A lady whose son had run away from home some years ago was advised to approach the Paramhansa for help. He initially claimed inability to interfere in the ways of fate, but she persisted. He then gave her a mantra that had to be chanted sincerely for half an hour everyday. He assured her that if she did so, it would compel her child to return. The woman was so hopeful that she sat in a corner of the ashram and chanted it for eight hours at a stretch with complete concentration. She eventually collapsed and was carried to the Paramhansa, who asked a helper to revive her and give her sherbet made from honey.

When she awoke, he asked her to return to her home, assuring her that her child would certainly come back. Sure enough, a few days later, her son returned. She gratefully brought him to meet the Paramhansa in his ashram. However, he was terrified when he saw the yogi and refused to come close, saying, 'This sadhu is the one who was threatening to beat me up.'

The boy explained that he had run away with some sadhus and had been leading an aimless existence for a long time. A few days ago, they were in a village close to Calcutta, where he was warming himself in front of a bonfire, when he fell into a trance in which a tall, elderly sadhu, whom he had never met before, approached him. The yogi waved his stick menacingly at him, 'Here you are roaming around aimlessly, while your mother is in trouble and is desperately praying for your return!'

The boy claimed the sadhu had threatened to beat him up if he did not go back home. He had then made his way back to his overjoyed mother. She reassured him that the Paramhansa would not harm him, and the boy bowed before the saint, who affectionately advised him to never forsake his mother again.

Another remarkable incident of materialisation took place when some of the Paramhansa's disciples from Gujarat complained to him about a sorcerer in their hometown. The man had acquired magical skills, using certain tantric rituals, and employed these powers to trouble people. He also threatened and blackmailed them, warning them of dire consequences if they did not pay him money or give him some material benefit.

A few days later, the disciples found the sorcerer in the ashram, hundreds of miles away from his home. He claimed the Paramhansa had appeared before him in his hometown and had scolded him. The saint had ordered him to immediately reach Ayodhya. Once, he had reached the city, he was drawn magically to Gokul Bhawan. The Paramhansa convinced the man to give up his ways and to dedicate himself to genuine spiritual practices. After receiving initiation, the erstwhile sorcerer plunged into spiritual practices for a few weeks and then returned to his hometown a reformed individual.

Once, a disciple suffered a paralytic stroke and doctors told his wife that he would probably be bedridden for the rest of his life. The lady was so disturbed that she held the Paramhansa's photo to her head and cried throughout the night. In the early hours of the morning, before sunrise, the master appeared at the bed of the disciple, forced something into his mouth and disappeared. The man recovered shortly thereafter, and lived a healthy life for another twenty-seven years.

The Paramhansa looked upon all women with the same respect as he looked upon his mother. However, Ram Janaki, one of the closest devotees of the saint, felt unhappy that the master ignored his own mother, who was spending the last days of her life in the ashram. This was despite the fact that the Paramhansa acknowledged his mother to be spiritually a very advanced soul. Ram Janaki complained to the master, asking him to be more considerate.

'Why don't you ask her yourself?' he said, with a twinkle in his eyes. Ram Janaki approached the yogi's mother and asked her how she felt being ignored by her own son.

'A young boy of around five years appears in my room and spends a lot of time with me. He plays with me and sleeps with me,' was all the elderly lady said, not wishing to elaborate further. The devotee realised that the Paramhansa was giving his mother the gift of *bala leela*, or manifestation in the form of a child.

284

Disciples and Devotees

The Paramhansa was approached by thousands of devotees and he fulfilled their spiritual and material desires. Yet, he would often say that he could count his disciples on his fingertips. He never revealed the identity of these disciples. The fact that he did not nominate any successor probably indicated that the master did not find anyone of the calibre required to succeed the illustrious line of saints of which he was the last[10].

Some of the prominent disciples among the sannyasis included Ram Das, Ram Sewak Das, Gangaram Das and Paramananda Das. Of the householders, the key disciples included Dada Giridharilal, Ganesh Prasad Mathur, Jagat Narain, Vijay Kumar Bansal, Harnath Singh Mehrotra, Ram Janaki and Dr Ramesh Nigam. A few titbits from the lives of some of them are given here.

Ram Das

Ram Das was one of his earliest disciples and he was totally devoted to the Paramhansa, to the extent that some people called him Chhotey Maharaj (the little master). He meditated for many hours in deserted spots and ultimately began to live in a hut in Ayodhya, where he spent his time in meditation. Even during the master's lifetime, he had disciples of his own, though when he perceived the aspirant was at an advanced stage of spiritual quest, he would guide the person to the Paramhansa.

Ram Sewak Das

Ram Sewak Das was a member of the Criminal Investigation Department prior to becoming a disciple of the Paramhansa. He always had a spiritual temperament, but the nature of his work created a mood of permanent detachment within him, and he finally embraced the spiritual path. He became a disciple of the master. He served him with such dedication that people would liken his service to that of the Paramhansa's to his own guru. After the Paramhansa's *mahasamadhi*, several administrative problems cropped up in Gokul Bhawan.

Finally, Ram Sewak Das took up the responsibility of managing the affairs in the ashram. He not only managed the day-to-day activities in the hermitage, but also guided aspirants on behalf of the Paramhansa till he gave up his body in 2006. An aspirant sought initiation through Ram Sewak Das, while his wife remained in her home in Delhi. At the moment of initiation, the wife had a vision of the Paramhansa entering the body of Ram Sewak Das and giving initiation to the aspirant!

Gangaram Das

Gangaram Das was of a devotional temperament since childhood. He was initially a disciple of his uncle, Ram Lagan, also known as Falahari Baba. Gangaram, however, was not satisfied and kept searching for a true master until, at the age of fourteen, he met Paramhansa Ram Mangal Das, who completely captivated his heart and soul. The master asked Gangaram to leave other practices and gave him mantra initiation and also initiated him into Raja Yoga. Gangaram returned home but began his practices in a cave in a deserted spot by the River Ganga. In a short while, he experienced various awakenings. He had repeated visions of the Paramhansa in the cave and there would be a divine aura around him. However, Falahari Baba and his disciples were unhappy that Gangaram had switched his loyalties to the Paramhansa. They would trouble him and disturb his meditation; one day, he was mercilessly beaten up and asked to renounce the Paramhansa. Gangaram was unhappy, but he bore the injuries and moved to Bithoor (near Kanpur) and began meditating in a cave. One day, he heard that the master had come to Kanpur and met him there. The Paramhansa blessed him that, henceforth, nobody would disturb him (Gangaram) in his meditation. Thereafter, the devotee progressed rapidly on the spiritual path and eventually established his own ashram in Gazipur and dedicated his life to the service of humanity.

Dada Giridharilal

Dada Giridharilal was born in 1909, in Punjab. At a young age, he thirsted for a vision of the Lord. He studied Indian philosophy and decided to devote his life to sadhana. He vowed to remain a celibate throughout his life and to never acquire wealth in any form. He roamed for many days looking for a guru and reached Ayodhya in 1934. He was resting in Kanak Bhawan, a famous temple, when a tall saint entered the premises and began looking at the devotees. He seemed to be searching for someone. The saint's eyes stopped on Giridharilal. The yogi approached Giridharilal and asked him to come along to his ashram, Gokul Bhawan. The saint was Paramhansa Ram Mangal Das, and he had sought out the young aspirant on a direction from the Lord. The master initiated him into mantra and Raja Yoga. Giridharilal remained devoted to the Paramhansa and did not feel separation from him even after the master took *mahasamadhi* in 1984. After substantial research, he wrote the book *Paramhansa Ram Mangal Dasji – Memoirs and Homage,* a beautiful biography of his guru. He clearly felt the divine presence of the Paramhansa till the end of his life.

Ganesh Prasad Mathur

Ganesh Prasad Mathur grew up in an atmosphere of devotion and, as he grew older, he began his quest for a realised master who could guide him. Unfortunately, though he met many great saints, nobody could satisfy his spiritual curiosity, until at the age of nineteen, he met the Paramhansa. The master recognised Ganesh as a true seeker and called him for initiation. Ganesh Prasad was a rare embodiment of devotion and obedience to the word of the guru. He was instrumental in spreading the glories of the Paramhansa. His parents were worried that Ganesh would not marry and asked the yogi to intervene. The master knew through divine insight that Ganesh was destined to marry, but he played a *leela* with his disciple. He told the parents that he would only ask Ganesh to marry if they found a girl fitting the description he would give them. After listening to the words of the master, the anxious parents felt they would never find a girl matching the description in their community. Strangely, they found one in a short time and with the Paramhansa's blessings, Ganesha tied the knot.

In those days, finding suitable employment was considered a boon and people would seldom think of leaving a secure job. Ganesh was scrupulously honest in his work, and whenever he was compelled to be even slightly unethical, he would quit his job, but the Paramhansa's grace was always with him. Thus, in the worst of times, he always found a suitable job. Ganesh often appeared drunk in the love of God and progressed well in his sadhana. As a result of the master's grace and his own sadhana, Ganesh Prasad Mathur had a vision of the Lord in his lifetime. Ganesh was popularly known as Bhaktaraja (King of Devotees) among other devotees.

Jagat Narain

Jagat Narain was an employee of the department of revenue service in the imperial government. He was hard-working and honest to begin with, but the Second World War created financial difficulties. He, gradually, began to accept bribes and allowed himself to be wined and dined by those seeking illegitimate favours. One day, he was taken in a drunken state to a house of courtesans. When he was put in a room with a woman, he fell sick and had to be rushed home. After that, he began to see some disturbing visions, and he fell into prolonged depression; he began to look for succour. Someone introduced him to the Paramhansa, who seemed to recognise him, though they had never met before. He was initiated and gradually his life was transformed. Jagat Narain advanced spiritually and eventually, after completing his service, settled in Gokul Bhawan. One day, he received a divine command from the Lord to write the biography of the Paramhansa. The book written by Jagat Narain, *Sant Shiromani Paramhansa Ram Mangal Das Charitavali*, is a wonderful account of the life and *leelas* of the master.

Vijay Kumar Bansal

Vijay Kumar Bansal was a successful trader in Delhi but longed for a spiritual life. He met many saints in his search for a master, but when he read *Bhakta Bhagwant Charitavali*, a book written by the Paramhansa, he felt he could see his guru in the yogi. He sought initiation from the Paramhansa, who initiated him into both mantra and dhyana. Gradually, he converted one of his shops into a shrine dedicated to the Paramhansa and installed a life-sized statue of the master — he would also organise bhajans and kirtans here. The Paramhansa's grace was clearly on his entire family, and many family members had visions of the saint after he had left his body. He now spends all his time in spiritual activities and publishes a series of books called *Amrit Boond* (Drops of Divine Nectar), spreading the teachings of the master.

The Time to Leave

It was the latter half of 1984. The Paramhansa was unhappy with the state of morality in general, and in the holy city of Ayodhya, in particular. Previously, he would often comment that Ayodhya was the dwelling place of saints, and that many of them were doing yogic practices and austerities incognito in the holy city.

Now, he complained about the so-called sadhus who had gone astray. '*Bhagat nahi, hagat hain*' (they are not devotees; they are spreading dirt), or '*Sidhha nahi, gidhha hain*' (they are not perfect yogis; they are vultures, preying on unsuspecting devotees). The Paramhansa was close to ninety-two years, and his own guru had left his mortal coil at the age of ninety-three. It was time to leave.

The ashram of his guru's guru, Badi Chhavni in Ayodhya, witnessed murders and intrigue in a political battle for succession. India's Prime Minister, Mrs Indira Gandhi, was also assassinated by her own security guards in October. He was deeply disappointed by such tragic incidents. He also voiced his unhappiness at the fact that his disciples were ready to worship him but were not ready to follow his instructions.

The Paramhansa announced towards the middle of December that he was now going to give up his body. He stopped eating and lay wrapped up in a sheet in a constant meditative state. He asked his disciples to chant the *Kali Kavach*, a powerful incantation. Some of his disciples tried to coax him into eating or drinking something, but he refused.

Other disciples sought comfort in the fact that the master had even earlier planned to give up his body but had been coaxed to change his plan. They were hoping he would, once again, change his mind. Only this time, he remained determined.

Once, Rajeshwari, a dear disciple, came to him with a glass of fresh fruit juice, but he did not take it. Disappointed, she returned to her quarters where she picked up his photo and poured the juice onto it, imagining he was drinking it. The next time she met the Paramhansa, he nodded his head in mock disapproval saying, 'You are very stubborn. You eventually compelled me to drink the juice despite my refusal.'

He mentioned to some of his disciples that the Divine Mother had come to take him with Her, and that he would now soon give up his body.

Deep in the winter night of 30 December 1984, a storm engulfed the sleepy town of Ayodhya. Rains lashed the town and strong winds were blowing. Devotees remembered that the Paramhansa's guru had also left his body on such a stormy night. In the early hours of 31 December, the master steadied himself and sat upright in meditation. Somewhere around three o'clock in the morning, he merged his consciousness with the Absolute.

Some of the devotees could not believe this had happened and remained numb in shock, while others cried bitterly and still others mechanically bathed him and prepared the body for the last rites[11]. The next morning, the Paramhansa's body was placed in a palanquin bedecked with flowers and taken around the key places of worship in Ayodhya. A strange incident then perplexed his disciples. When he was taken to certain places of worship, the master's eyes would open and close. Some felt that he was not dead, despite the fact that his heartbeat and pulse were missing. His disciples approached the renowned saint Kartaliya Baba, enquiring whether the Paramhansa had truly left his body. Some others approached the great yogi Devraha Baba and asked him the same question. Both saints clearly said that the master had finally left his body.

On why the Paramhansa's eyes kept blinking after his death, Devraha Baba said, 'Whatever be said [in his glory] would be insufficient. He was truly an embodiment of the Lord Himself.'

An Eternal Saint

Many days after the passing away of the master, one of his disciples, Ram Lochan Verma, approached Swami Rama, 'The Himalayan Saint', and asked him, 'Does the Paramhansa still care for his disciples like he did when he was alive?' Swami Rama replied without hesitation, 'Yes, in the same way, nothing has changed[12].'

The day the master passed away, Vijay Singh, a devotee based in Mirzapur, was unaware of the event. Suddenly, he felt he was attending the last rites of the Paramhansa. Subsequently, he received news of his *mahasamadhi*, and he went into a state of depression for fifteen days and began to lose his health. The yogi appeared before him in his body and reassured him that he would always be with his disciples. He told Vijay that the great beings who incarnated in this world were never inactive after leaving their bodies. 'Where have I gone? What do you want?' After this incident, Vijay slowly recovered his health.

The Paramhansa still appears in bodily form to some of his disciples to guide them spiritually or assist them in their times of difficulty. He also guides others through some of his chosen disciples.

ॐ ॐ

Endnotes

1. The Ramanandi Sampradaya, or the spiritual sect owing its origin to Swami Ramananda, is a prominent Hindu school of worship within the fold of Vaishnava sects; adherents of this sect devote themselves to the worship of God in the form of Vishnu or his incarnations, prominently Rama. It is considered an offshoot of the Ramanuja Sampradaya. The founder of this sect, Jagadguru Ramananda, was a prominent medieval saint, and the guru of renowned saints such as Kabir, Anantananda and Raidas. The great saint Tulsidas, the author of the *Ramacharitamanasa*, also belonged to the Ramanandi Sampradaya. Ramanandis also broadly follow the Vishistadwaita philosophy of the Ramanuja Sampradaya, a philosophy of qualified monism.

2. The Udasina Sampradaya, literally, the 'sect based on the principle of indifference', is one of the well-known ancient spiritual houses of ascetics in India; the *sampradaya* was almost defunct when the medieval saint Srichand, the son of Guru Nanak and the disciple of Amaranatha Muni, revived the sect and made it famous. The Udasina Sampradaya also developed close linkages with the Sikhs in medieval times, and adopted their religious traditions. The monks of this order have supported Sikh soldiers in several battles.

3. Yogiraja Bhartrihari is popularly believed to have been the king of Ujjain in the sixth or seventh century and had renounced everything and adopted the path of yoga under the direction of the great Guru Gorakhnath. Bhartrihari was also a prolific writer, but his *Vairagya Shatak* (Hundred Verses on Worldly Detachment) is considered the most marvellous of his works. Legend has it that Bhartrihari had achieved victory over death due to his practice of Hatha Yoga, and he roams the Indian subcontinent incognito. The medieval saint, Guru Nanak, had also mentioned meeting Yogiraja Bhartrihari, centuries after the latter had achieved yoga siddhi. Shukadeva, the son of Veda Vyasa, was an *avadhuta* and a realised master from birth. According to Hindu mythology, he was born in Dwaparayuga, over a thousand years ago. He is believed to appear from time to time and guide spiritual aspirants, for example, the seventeenth-century saint Charandas considered Shukadeva as his guru.

4. This milk is called *dharoshna*, and is believed to have sattvic properties. The milk is warm since it has just been extracted, and it is said it should not be heated and consumed immediately.

5. In India, touching the feet of elders, learned people and saints is a symbol of reverence, and the person whose feet are touched normally blesses him or her. Traditionally, the disciple bows before the guru and not the other way round.

6. An appropriate translation would be *Heavenly Tales of Devotees and the Lord*. This book is based on the lives of many great and unknown and unsung devotees.

7. Advaitacharya was a disciple of the legendary saint (Palak Nidhi) Pathik Ji, and a grand-disciple of the *avadhuta* saint (Ramdas) Naga Maharaj.

8. According to the Hindu calendar, this is the full moon day in the month of Ashadh. This period corresponds roughly with the month of July in the English calendar. On this day, devotees worship their guru. This is the day Maharshi Veda Vyas, the famous saint, guru and the author of the *Mahabharata*, was born.

9. The Kaaba is a large masonry structure, roughly the shape of a cube (the name 'Kaaba' comes from the Arabic word meaning 'cube'). It is located inside a mosque in Mecca. The mosque was built around the original Kaaba. It is considered the holiest place in Islam.

10. In Ayodhya, the Paramhansa was treated as the Guru of Gurus. After his *mahasamadhi*, the question arose as to who would succeed him. The saints of Ayodhya held a meeting to ponder over the issue and felt that nobody they knew had the caliber as that of the Paramhansa's. They decided that whenever a saint in Ayodhya reached the spiritual level of the Paramhansa, irrespective of sectarian affiliation, that saint would be treated as the successor.
11. The Hindus believe in cremating their dead. On many occasions, they bury saints or immerse their bodies in a river.
12. Ram Lochan compiled the writings of the Paramhansa in many volumes, and also maintains a website dedicated to the saint.

Glossary

Adhyatma: The science of spirituality.

Aghori: *Aghoris* or *aughars* are people who do not follow norms of so-called civilised behaviour; the term *aghori* literally means 'not terrible', but their ways, sometimes, appear quite awful to observers. Though unpleasant in appearance, the techniques they use are born out of experimentation and revelation. *Aghoris* who strictly follow the path are able to transcend the self by these practices. Some *aghoris* who live and interact in society do not publicly follow the 'terrible' practices in general. Famous *aghori* saints of past include the medieval saint Kinaram and twentieth-century saints such as Bhagwan Ram (from Kashi) and Bhagwan Gopinath (from Kashmir).

Ajanabahu: One who has hands that reach down to the knees when he/she stands straight; this is considered a major sign of spiritual potential or accomplishment.

Alifnama: Sufi prayer based on the Arabic alphabet, which has couplets in praise of the Lord, with each couplet beginning with a successive letter of the alphabet.

Anahata Laya Yoga: A form of Laya Yoga, using the science of sound for meeting the objective of dissolution and leading to liberation.

Aarti: A ritual for worshipping in which lamps are lit and waved in front of deities, while songs are sung in their praise.

Ashtanga Yoga: The Eight-Fold path of Yoga as enunciated by Maharshi Patanjali in his *Yoga Sutras*. The *Yoga Sutras* primarily focus on Raja Yoga.

Ashtavadhani: These are people who can maintain perfect attention on eight focal points; for instance, they can pay perfect attention to eight people speaking at the same time and advanced aspirants can repeat what each of the eight had said to him; see also Shatavadhani.

Aulia: Plural for *wali*, which in Arabic means 'an ally', and in some Islamic traditions means 'an ally of Allah', roughly translating to a saint. In some Koranic Suras, the word *aulia* represents companion (of Allah or saints). In India, fakirs of the highest order, who were above 'human-hood', were given this appellation.

Avadhuta: One who is perfectly attained and free of bonds, attachments and obligations; it is the highest state of attainment for sannyasis and cannot be completely described in words.

Bahudaka: A stage of *sannyasa*, where the sannyasin has faith and confidence in the spiritual path, has experienced the inner world and is able to communicate with the guru at all levels; after some time, he leaves the ashram and becomes a mendicant or wanderer.

Bandhas: A yogic 'lock'. A *bandha* blocks the flow of spiritual energy in a psychic channel of the body by a particular yogic posture.

Bhairava: Bhairava is the fierce manifestation of Siva associated with annihilation.

Bhakti Yoga: The path of yoga through devotion to the guru or God.

Bhaktamala: Biographies of saints in verse, literally, 'A Garland of Saints'.

Bhava Samadhi: The state of *samadhi* created by ecstasy or emotion; those who experience this state stay in loving blissful identification with their object of devotion.

Bhikshu Rekha: Beggar's Line, according to Indian palmistry; a line on a person's palm denoting circumstances that will force him to beg.

Bhoga: The effect of accumulated *karma* that a person has to experience in this life.

Bija: Literally, the seed; *bija* is the mantra seed that causes vibrations and can influence the psychic environment.

Brahma or Brahman: The unchanging, infinite, immanent and transcendent reality, or in simple terms, the ultimate expression for God.

Brahmachari/Brahmacharin: One who practices *brahmacharya*, or those behaving as residing in God. This also refers to a category of spiritual aspirants who are unmarried and practice continence, follow spiritual practices and may also follow rules of some order.

Brahmacharya: Brahmacharya is the practice of residing in God. This is often confused with celibacy, which may be a result of Brahmacharya, but not necessarily a practice.

Brahma Muhurta: The pre-sunrise period — of roughly two hours — believed to be most suitable for meditation.

Chinnaswami: 'Small Swami' by combining *chinna* (small) in Tamil and *swami* in Sanskrit.

Diksha: Spiritual initiation of the aspirant by the guru. The ritual and content of the initiation varies widely across different sects. It may also constitute an exchange of karma between the guru and the disciple, or the opening of some psychic knots or the awakening of the latent spiritual potential of the disciple.

Dussehra: Also known as Vijaya Dashmi, falls on the tenth day of the bright half of the month of Ashwin by the Hindu calendar. It is the day when, mythologically, Lord Rama defeated the demon Ravana.

Dwaita: Duality; the philosophical position that there are two entities (the devotee and the Absolute or God).

Grahastha: Householder. It is also one of the stages of life as per Sanatan Dharma.

Granthis: Psychic knots. These knots include the Rudra Granthi, the Vishnu Granthi and the Brahma Granthi.

Guru Purnima: The day of the full moon in the month of Ashadh of the Hindu calendar. On this day, devotees worship their guru. This is the day Maharshi Veda Vyas, the famous saint, was born.

Gwalini: Milk maid.

Gyan Yoga: The path of yoga through discrimination and contemplation.

Hansa: A swan; a stage of *sannyasa*, reflecting purity of consciousness.

Hasta Diksha: Initiation by touch.

Hatha Yoga: The yoga that deals with harmonising the solar and lunar channels of the body and preparing it for higher yogic practices; practices involve *shatkarmas* (cleansing techniques), asana (physical postures), pranayama (techniques to stabilise, energise and awaken the prana), mudra (symbolic gesture) and *bandha* (locks).

Hathayogi: A practitioner of Hatha Yoga.

Isvarakoti: Belonging to the category of God.

Jal Samadhi: Usually refers to the immersion of the body of a saint into a water body (like a river).

Japam: Repetitive chanting of a mantra or the name of God, or a deity. *Japam* can be verbal (*vachik*), whispered (*upanshu*), mental (*manasik*) or written (*likhit*).

Kafni: A single garment that covers the entire body (like a loose, extended shirt reaching down to the ankles). Both Hindu and Muslim saints often donned it.

Kaivalya: The ultimate goal of yoga. Kaivalya refers to the transcendental state of absolute independence or final beatitude.

Kalpataru: Wish-fulfilling tree from Indian mythology.

Kaupeen: A frugal but tight underwear worn by monks and renunciates.

Khanda Yoga: An esoteric practice consisting of separating the various parts of the human body and, subsequently, bringing them together again.

Kheer: A type of rice pudding.

Kheyal: Thought or, as in Anandamayi Ma's case, spontaneous divine inspiration.

Kriya: Technique or practices.

Kriya Yoga: The path of yoga through techniques such as, pranayama, mudra and *bandhas* — that are intended to rapidly accelerate spiritual development and engender a profound state of tranquillity and communion with God.

Kutichaka: A stage in *sannyasa*, where the aspirant stays in one place — usually in an ashram or a hut — and performs sadhana.

Laya Yoga: The path of Yoga through dissolution. Laya Yoga refers to the dissolution of all the impressions that have accumulated throughout one's lives, thereby, liberating one's mind from all obstacles and limitations and freeing one from the hold of karma. Laya Yoga is also translated as the yoga of absorption, or absorbing the lower nature by the higher spiritual forces.

Leela: The play or sport of a satguru, a saint or an avatara (divine incarnation), in course of their lives. *Leela* also refers to their supernormal capabilities.

Mahabhava: A stage of continuous uncontrolled devotional absorption, where the complete physiological, neurological and chemical structure of the body undergoes a change.

Mahasamadhi: The 'final' *samadhi* in the life of a yogi/yogini, who merges his/her consciousness with the Absolute.

Mantra Diksha: Initiation by imparting a mantra to the spiritual aspirant.

Mantra Yoga: The path of Yoga through the science of sound (also considered the path through chanting of mantras).

Math/Mutt: Similar to an ashram, but usually with a more formal, rule-based framework.

Maya: This is the cosmic principle that hinders the process of liberation; Maya is treated as a form of the Divine Mother in Hinduism, the mythical Goddess of Temptation, who hinders aspirants in the path of liberation and tempts living beings and retards them on their quest for liberation. Paradoxically, she is also widely revered, as it is believed by some that her worshippers will never experience obstacles on the path of liberation and that She liberates those who worship Her.

Murshid: A guru or a guide as per Sufi terminology.

Naga sadhus: Naga sadhus do not wear clothes, and often carry weapons; they represent the protectors of Hinduism or Hindu monastic orders and are often aggressive in nature.

Nathayaga: The yogic path of yogis of the Natha sect.

Navaratri: The Navaratri—literally, nine nights—period is considered most appropriate for the worship of the Divine Mother. These nine days occur twice a year in the Chaitra and Ashwin months of the Hindu calendar.

Nirvikalpa Samadhi: The highest transcendental state of consciousness. In this state, there is no longer mind, duality, or subject-object relationship or experience. Upon entering Nirvikalpa Samadhi, the differences we might have perceived earlier fade and we can see everything as one. In this condition, nothing but pure awareness remains and nothing is missing to take away from wholeness and perfection.

Padmasana: The Lotus pose. One of the key meditative asanas.

Paramhansa: A stage of *sannyasa* when the sannyasin is completely attuned to the cosmic forces. The sannyasin is able to separate the essence of things from the surface appearance, the real from the unreal, the truth from the untruth.

Pasyanti Vak: Knowledge revealed by the Divine Mother in Her own words to one who is adept in the Kundalini yoga.

Purnima: Full moon night.

Raja Yoga: The path of yoga through meditative practices.

Saburi: Patience/forbearance.

Sadguru: A human guru who is also a realised master.

Sadhaka: A spiritual aspirant who follows a regular regimen of spiritual practices.

Sadhana: Spiritual practice.

Samadhi Sthal: The place where the mortal remains of a saint or his or her ashes are interred.

Sampradaya: Religious sect or groups of sects.

Samudrik Shastra: The science of divining facts relating to the past, present or future by looking at the body, or parts of the body like the face, the hands or the feet.

Sannyasa: Complete sannyasa; the fourth stage of life, in which, after fulfilling one's worldly obligations, one is free to pursue the goal of self-realisation.

Sanskara: Impressions created in the past, including past lives, part of the karma. Another meaning of *sanskaras* is sacraments. Hindu religious texts prescribe sixteen such Vedic ceremonies or sacraments to be carried out during a lifetime. The sacred thread ceremony is one of the most important of such ceremonies. These ceremonies or sacraments are called *sanskaras*. There is a relationship between the two meanings as the sacraments seek to infuse good karma into the participant of the sacrament, or reorient the structure of consciousness into one appropriate for the phase in life.

Satka: Short stick used by yogis and fakirs.

Sewa Yoga: The path of yoga through selfless service, or service to the guru.

Shabda Yoga: The path of yoga through the science of internal sound, the *anahata nada*.

Shakta: Worshipper of Shakti, the Mother Goddess.

Shaktipat: Transmission of energy by the guru to the disciple to stimulate spiritual awakening.

Shatavadhani: These are people who can maintain perfect attention on hundred focal points; for instance, they can pay perfect attention to a hundred people speaking at the same time and an advanced aspirant can repeat what each person said to him.

Shraddha: Faith.

Siddha Yogis or **Siddha Yogini:** Those who have attained perfection on the path of Yoga, in other words, those who have taken their sadhana to the point of siddhi or perfection in sadhana.

Siva: Lord Siva is the eternal yogi, one of the three principal aspects of the ultimate divinity as per Hindu mythology. Siva is also the original preceptor of Yoga. According to Hindu tradition, Siva is always immersed in a meditative state and moves in sparsely populated places, such as mountains and graveyards, and is easily pleased by devotion. Hindus consider him as one of the most important gods in their pantheon. Siva also signifies the absolute attainment possible when a soul (Jiva) completely transcends the attributes of humankind. The following quote from the Kularnava Tantra illustrates this:

Ghrina lajja bhayam shanka, jugupsa cheti panchami,
Kulam shilam tatha jatirashtau pashah prakirtitah;
Pashbaddhau bhavedjivah, pashamuktau sadashivah

One who is bound by the eight bonds—feelings of dislike, shame, fear, doubt, disgust, or pride in the family, in one's civilised behaviour, or in social status—is man, and one who is free of them is Siva.

Sivaratri or Mahasivaratri: Literally, the 'night of Siva' or 'The Great Night of Siva' is considered the 'night of wakefulness' in praise of Lord Siva. According to Hindu legend, this is the day that Siva wedded his consort, Parvati.

Swara Sadhana: Spiritual techniques relating to the psychic channels in the body.

Swara Yoga: The path of yoga utilising the awareness or observation and then control or manipulation of the flow of breath in the nostrils. It includes various spiritual techniques relating to the psychic channels in the body.

Tapasvi: One involved in tapas or tapasya.

Tapasya: Literally, the act of heating. In practice, it is used to denote spiritual practices involving suffering, mortification or austerity for the purification of the senses or the acquisition of supernatural powers.

Tapobhumi: Place of tapas or tapasya of a saint.

Turiyatita: A stage of *sannyasa* considered beyond the fetters of Nature.

Vairagya: Dispassion towards or detachment from the mundane.

Wada: A grand building (Marathi language).

Bibliography

Ramakrishna Paramhansa

1. *Sadguru Vandana, Siddha Prarthana*, (Hindi, Compilations of favourite Bhajans of Swami Satyananda Saraswati), Bihar School of Yoga, Munger, Bihar, twelfth revised, 2001.
2. Swami Chetanananda, *They Lived With God*, Advaita Ashram, First Indian Edition, Calcutta, 1991.
3. *The Life of Swami Vivekananda by His Eastern and Western Disciples* (Volume I), Advaita Ashram, Kolkata, 2007.
4. Swami Chetanananda , *God Lived With Them*, Advaita Ashram, First Indian Edition, Calcutta,1998.
5. Swami Saradananda, *Sri Ramakrishna Lila Prasanga*—Parts 1 & 2 (Hindi), Ramakrishna Math, Nagpur, (Eleventh edition) 2002.
6. *Life of Sri Ramakrishna*, Advaita Ashram, Mayawati, Champawat, Sixteenth Impression, 2005.
7. *Sri Sri Ramakrishna Kathamrita*, (four volumes), Vedanta Press (Sri Ma Trust) Chandigarh, 2001, 2002, 2005, 2009.
8. Swami Chetanananda, *Ramakrishna As We Saw Him*, Advaita Ashram, Second Reprint 1999.
9. Mukherji, Vishwanath, *Bharat ke Mahan Yogi*—Parts III-IV, Anurag Prakashan, Varanasi, 1997.
10. Ramlal, *Bharat ke Sant Mahatma* (Hindi), Vora and Company Publishers Pvt Ltd, Bombay, 1955.

Baba Lokenath Brahmachari

1. *Sivanamavalyastakam, Siddha Stotra Mala* (Hindi), Compiled by Swami Satyananda, Yoga Publications Trust, Munger, Bihar, (Second Revised) 2007.
2. Swami Shuddhananda Brahmachari, *In Danger Remember Me: Promises, Life and Teachings of Himalayan Master Baba Lokenath*, Lokenath Divine Life Mission, Calcutta,1991.
3. Sen, Bhudeb Chandra, *Mahayogi Shree Shree Lokenath Brahmachari — Life and Teachings*, Calcutta 1994.
4. Brahmachari, Kuladananda, *Shree Shree Sadguru Sangha* (Hindi translation by Ratna Mukherji), published by Shree Shankarnath Bandopadhyaya, Thakurbadi, Puri, Orissa, 2007.

5. Bhowmick, Haripada, *Mahavishwa Key Lokenath — Jiwani* (Hindi), Shree Shree Lokenath Mandir, Tegharia, Baguihati, Kolkatta, Third Edition, 2009.

Mahayogi Gambhirnath

1. Bandopadhyaya, Akshay Kumar and Shukla, Raghunath, *Shree Shree Gambhirnathashtakam, Adarsh Yogi — Shree Shree Yogiraj Gambhirnath* (Hindi), Digvijaynath Trust, Gorakhnath Mandir, Gorakhpur, 1987.
2. *Geetopanishad, Bhagavad Gita As It Is,* (The Song Celestial, verses 9–22) The Bhaktivedanta Book Trust, Bombay, eighth print, 1997.
3. Mukherji, Vishwanath, *Yogiraj Gambhirnath, Bharat ke Mahan Yogi*–Part VII–VIII (Hindi), Anurag Prakashan, Varanasi, 1993.
4. Ramlal, *Bharat ke Sant Mahatma* (Hindi), Vora and Company Publishers Pvt Ltd, Bombay, 1955.

Sai Baba of Shirdi

1. Upasani Maharaj, *Sai Nath Mahima Stotram,* Shri Sadguru Sainath Sagunopasana, Shri Sai Baba Sansthan, Shirdi, First Edition, 2003.
2. Rao, Ammula Sambasiva, *Life History of Shirdi Sai Baba,* Sterling Publishers Private Limited, New Delhi, 1998.
3. Dabholkar, Govind Raghunath (alias Hemadpant), *Shri Sai Satcharitra,* (English translation of original Marathi work by Nagesh Vasudev Gunaji), Shri Sai Baba Sansthan, Shirdi, twentieth edition, 2002.
4. Swami Sai Sharan Anand, *Shri Sai Baba,* Translated by V.B.Kher, Sterling Publishers Private Limited, New Delhi, 1997.
5. Warren, Marianne, *Unravelling the Enigma — Shirdi Sai Baba in the Light of Sufism,* Sterling Publishers Private Limited, New Delhi, First Edition 1999 (Reprint 2007).
6. Osborne, Arthur, *The Incredible Sai Baba,* Sangam Books, Delhi, 1997.
7. Kamath, M.V. and Kher, V.B. , *Sai Baba Of Shirdi — A Unique Saint,* Jaico Publishing House, Mumbai, Sixteenth Impression, 2005.
8. Kakariya, Dr Ravindra Nath, *Shri Sai Baba Ke Ananya Bhakta* (Hindi), Sterling Publishers Private Limited, New Delhi, 2004.
9. Ramlal, *Bharat ke Sant Mahatma* (Hindi), Vora and Company Publishers Pvt Ltd, Bombay, 1955.
10. Mukherji, Vishwanath, *Bharat ke Mahan Yogi*–Part VI (Hindi), Anurag Prakashan, Varanasi, 1989.
11. Bharti, Sushil, *Saishree Key Adbhut Devadoot* (Hindi), Diamond Books, New Delhi, 1998

Bhagwan Ramana Maharshi

1. Muni, Sri Kavyakantha Vasishtha Ganpati, *Sri Ramana Chatvarimshat* (Forty Verses in Adoration of Sri Ramana), Sri Ramanashram, Tiruvannamalai, 2004.
2. *Preceptors of Advaita,* Samata Books, Editor T.M.P. Mahadevan, Samata Edition, 2003.
3. Bhikshu, Sri Krishna, *Sri Ramana Leela* (*A Biography Of Bhagavan Sri Ramana Maharshi*) Telugu Original edited and translated into English by Pingali Surya Sundaram, Sri Ramanashram, Tiruvannamalai, 2003.
4. Osborne, Arthur, *Ramana Maharshi and the Path of Self-Knowledge,* Sri Ramanasramam, Tiruvannamalai, 2002.
5. Natarajan, A.R., *Timeless in Time, Sri Ramana Maharshi: A Biography,* Ramana Maharshi Centre of Learning, Fourth Edition, Bangalore, 2005.

302

Yogis of India

6. *At the Feet of Bhagavan, Leaves from the Diary of T.K.Sundaresa Iyer*, Edited by Duncan Greenlees, Sri Ramanashram, Tiruvannamalai, Fourth Edition, 2005.

7. Ramana, A.V., *Maha Tapasvi – Life Story of Kavyakantha Ganpati Muni*, Telugu edition translated into English by Sonti Anusuyamma, Sri Ramanashram, Tiruvannamalai, 2005.

8. *Ramana Maharshi's Miracles – They Happen Everyday*, Edited & Compiled by A.R. Natarajan, Ramana Maharshi Centre of Learning, Third Edition, Bangalore, 2000.

9. Ganesan, V., *Moments Remembered – Reminiscences of Bhagwan Ramana*, Sri Ramanashram, Tiruvannamalai, Second Edition, 1994.

10. Natrajan, A.R., *Ramana Maharshi, The Living Guru*, Ramana Maharshi Centre for Learning, Bangalore, 2000.

11. Ramlal, *Bharat ke Sant Mahatma* (Hindi), Vora and Company Publishers Pvt Ltd, Bombay, 1955.

12. Mukherji, Vishwanath, *Bharat ke Mahan Yogi*–Parts III–IV (Hindi), Anurag Prakashan, Varanasi, 1996.

Swami Sivananda Saraswati

1. *Sivananda Mangalam, Siddha Stotra Mala (Hindi)*, Compiled by Swami Satyananda, Yoga Publications Trust, Bihar, Second Revised, 2007.

2. *Early Teachings of Swami Satyananda*, Sharda Press, Bhagalpur, 1988.

3. *Miracles of Swami Sivananda*, The Divine Life Society, Shivanandanagar, Third Edition, 1992.

4. Ananthanarayanan, N., *From Man to God-Man: The Inspiring Life Story of Sri Swami Sivananda*, The Divine Life Society, Durban, 1998.

5. *Swami Sivananda, Biography of a Modern Sage*, The Divine Life Society, Shivanandanagar, First Edition, 2000.

6. Swami Sivananda, Article based on a talk by Swami Chidananda, *Yoga* magazine (English) , Sivananda Math, Munger, September 1993.

7. *His Holiness Sri Swami Sivananda Saraswati Maharaj*, The Divine Life Society, (www. dlshq.org).

8. *My Life–Autobiography of Swami Krishnananda*, The Divine Life Society, Rishikesh, 2001

9. *Teachings of Swami Satyananda*, Sharda Press, Bhagalpur, Vol I second Indian edition 1984, Vol II second edition 1984, Vol III first Indian Edition 1984, Vol IV second edition 1979, Vol V first edition 1986, Vol VI first edition 1988.

10. *Sivananda–Biography of a Modern Sage, Life and Works of Swami Sivananda*, The Divine Life Society, Shivanandanagar, 2006.

11. *Yoga Vidya* magazine (Hindi), Sivananda Math, Munger, Year 7/Issue 5/May 2008.

12. Swami Chidananda, *Light Fountain*, The Divine Life Society, Shivanandanagar, Fifth Edition, 1991.

13. Swami Chidananda, *Swami Sivananda–Saint, Sage and Godman*, the Divine Life Society, Shivanandanagar, Second Edition, 2005.

Anandamayi Ma

1. *Tantrokta Devisuktam, Siddha Stotra Mālā* (Hindi), Compiled by Swami Satyananda, Yoga Publications Trust, Munger, Bihar, 2007.

2. *Teachings of Swami Satyananda*, Part I, Sharda Press, Bhagalpur, Second Enlarged Indian Edition, 1984.

3. Swami Paramhansa Yogananda, *Autobiography of a Yogi*, Crystal Clarity Publishers, Nevada City, ÚSA, Reprint of Original 1946 Edition (1995).

4. Bhattacharya, Dr Buddhadev, *Anandamayee: The Universal Mother*, Translated from the original Bengali text by Shri Asim Chatterjee, Shree Shree Anandamayee Sangha, Kankhal, Haridwar, First Edition, 1995.
5. Dattagupta, Amulyakumar, *Sri Sri Ma Anandamayi Prasang (Part 1 and 2)*, Hindi, (translated by Vishwanath Mukherji), Shree Shree Anandamayee Sangh, Kankhal, Haridwar, Second Edition, 2007.
6. Mukerji, Bithika, *Bird on a Wing: Life and Teachings of Sri Ma Anandamayi*, Sri Satguru Publications, a division of Indian Books Centre, Delhi, Paperback Edition, 2005.
7. Chaudhuri, Narayana, *That Compassionate Touch of Ma Anandamayee*, Motilal Banarsidass, 1997, New Delhi.
8. Roy, Jyotish Chandra, *Mother As Revealed To Me*, Translated from Bengali by Sri Ganga Charan Dasgupta, Shree Shree Anandamayee Sangha, Kankhal, Haridwar; Revised edition, 2004.
9. Madhava , Prasanna, *Ma Anandamayee: The Divine Mother Showers Her Grace*, Sohan Printing Press, Meerut, 2004
10. Lannoy, Richard, *Anandamayi – Her Life And Wisdom*, Element Books Ltd, Shaftesbury, Dorset, 1996 .
11. Hallstrom, Lisa Lassell, *Mother of Bliss: Anandamayi Ma (1896-1982)*, Oxford University Press, US, 1999.
12. Mukherji,Vishwanath, *Bharat ki Mahan Sadhikayen* (Hindi), Anurag Prakashan, Varanasi, 1989

Paramhansa Ram Mangal Das

1. Sharan, Maithili, *Shri Maithili Sharan Bhaktamala*, Bhaktamala Chhappaya 125, Madhuri Kunj, Ayodhya.
2. Narayan, Jagat, *Sant Shiromani Paramhansa Ram Mangal Das Charitavali* (Hindi), Gokul Bhawan, Ayodhya, Third Edition, 1992.
3. Chauhan, Dr Pratap Singh, *Lokottar Mahapurush – Paramhans Ram Mangal Das Ji Maharaj* (Hindi), Paramhansa Prakashan, Faizabad, First Edition, 1988.
4. Shrivaishnav, Ramdas, *Shri Sadguru Jivan Darshan – Kripa Purushottam Paramhans Shri Ram Mangal Das Ji Maharaj* (Hindi), Gokul Bhawan, Ayodhya, 1988.
5. Das, Ram Sewak, *Kripa Purushottam Bhagwan Shri Ram Mangal Das Ji Maharaj* (Hindi), Gokul Bhawan, Ayodhya, 1995.
6. Lal, Giridhari, *Paramhansa Ram Mangal Dasji – Memoirs and Homage*, 'Guruchhaya', Gomti Nagar, Lucknow, 1994.
7. *Bhakta Bhagwant* (Hindi Periodical), Onkarnath Press, Faizabad, April, May, June, Consolidated Edition, 1990.

Websites and Ashrams

Ramakrishna Paramhansa

Websites
    www.belurmath.org
    www.ramakrishna.org
    www.sriramakrishnamath.org
    www.sriramakrishna.org
Ashram/Centre
    Ramakrishna Math & Ramakrishna Mission
    P.O. Belur Math - 711 202
    District Howrah, West Bengal
    India
    Phone :(91-33-) 2654-1144/1180/5391/8494/9581/9681

Baba Lokenath Brahmachari

Websites
    www.babalokenath.org
    www.babalokenathashrom.com
    www.loknathbaba.com
Ashrams/Centres
    Lokenath Divine Life Mission
    277 Shantipally,
    Kolkata - 700 042
    Phone: +91-98314-59958
    Mailing Address:
    24 Kali Temple Road
    Kolkata - 700 026
    India

Mahayogi Gambhirnath

Ashram/Centre
    Gorakhanath Mandir
    Gorakhpur (UP)
    India

Sai Baba of Shirdi

Websites

    www.saibaba.org
    www.saibabaofshirdi.net
    www.shrisaibabasansthan.org
    www.saibabaofshirdi.net
    www.shirdi-sai-baba.com
    www.baba.org
    www.shirdisaitemple.com

Ashram/Centre

    Shri Sai Baba Sansthan Trust
    PO: Shirdi Taluka
    Rahata District
    Ahmednagar
    Maharashtra, India
    Tel No:+ 91-2423-258500

Bhagwan Ramana Maharshi

Websites

    www.sriramanamaharshi.org
    www.arunachala-ramana.org
    www.arunachala.org
    http://www.energyenhancement.org/
    Ramana-Maharshi-Biography-Vichara-Meditation.htm

Ashram/Centre

    Sri Ramanasramam
    P.O. Sri Ramanasramam
    Tiruvannamalai
    Tamil Nadu - 606 603
    India
    Phone: +91-4175237200,+91-9244937292

Swami Sivananda Saraswati

Websites

    www.dlshq.org
    www.divinelifesociety.org
    ww.yogavision.net
    www.yogamag.net
    www.biharyoga.net
    www.rikhiapeeth.net
    www.sivananda.org

Ashram/Centre

    Divine Life Society:
    P.O. Sivanandanagar - 249 192,
    District Tehri-Garhwal, Uttaranchal,
    India.
    Tel: (91)-135-2430040
    Fax: (91)-135-2442046
    Sivanandashram/Sivananda Math/Bihar School of Yoga
    Munger Ashram:

Bihar School of Yoga
Ganga Darshan
Fort
Munger
Bihar - 811 201
India
Tel: +91 (0)6344 222430
Fax: +91 (0)6344 220169
Rikhia Peeth:
Bihar School of Yoga
P.O. Rikhia
Dist Deoghar
Jharkhand - 814 112
India
Tel: +91- 9304488889/ + 91 - 9304799449
Sivananda Yoga – Swami Vishnu Devananda
Sivananda Yoga Vedanta Centre
House No.18, TC 36/1238, Subhash Nagar
Vallakkadavu P.O., Perunthanni,
Thiruvananthapuram - 695 008, Kerala, India
Tel:+ 91-471-245-1398/245-1776

Anandamayi Ma

Website
www.anandamayi.org
Ashrams/Centres
Shree Shree Anandamayee Sangha
Daksh Mandir Road
P.O. Kankhal
Distt. Haridwar - 249 408
(Uttaranchal), India
Phone/Fax: +91-1334246345
Shree Shree Anandamayee Sangha
Shree Shree Ma Anandamayee Ashram, Bhadaini,
Varanasi - 221 001, India
Phone: +91-542 2310054/2311794

Paramhansa Ram Mangal Das

Website
www.rammangaldasji.org
Ashrams/Centres
Gokul Bhawan
Vashishta Kund
Ayodhya - 224 123
Uttar Pradesh, India
+91-5278-232484